LONDON BUS HANDBO

David Stewart & Colin Lloyd

Capital Transport

Twentieth edition 1999
ISBN 185414 203 8

Published by
Capital Transport Publishing, Harrow Weald

Printed by
CS Graphics, Singapore

Contents

Introduction

This book gives details at January 1999 of buses that operate London Transport Buses (LTB) contract services. We acknowledge the assistance given by some of the operating companies and the principal compiler of earlier editions of this series, Nicholas King. The fleet information is extracted principally from the records of the London Omnibus Traction Society (LOTS) and readers needing regular updated information are recommended to membership of LOTS or the PSV Circle.

The industry moved further toward consolidation in London in 1998, with two major fleets falling to the groups. MTL Holdings began the sale of London Northern to Metroline Holdings on 2nd July and the purchase was completed on 17th August. In the following months of 1998 about a third of their fleet was repainted to standard Metroline livery. Also after some months of rumour, Capital Citybus passed into FirstGroup ownership on 8th July. Within three months most of the London operations of Thamesway, also within the group, were taken on by Capital Citybus, by now trading as First Capital.

Arriva, having been re-launched as such in November 1997 from its earlier existence as the Cowie Group, unveiled a new livery, in turquoise outside London and red within, with a cream (officially called 'stone') frontal area. Three London versions resulted, as will be seen in our photo selection in this book. Eleven Arriva companies provide services into London, and the group

Top: The purchase of Capital Citybus by FirstGroup during 1998 soon caused a very close liaison with fellow group member Thamesway, and most of its routes and vehicles were taken over. This bus already has First titles, is still in Thamesway livery, but has Capital fleet number 569 applied. It is one of the Reeve Burgess bodied Mercedes-Benz minibuses that had been with Thamesway on LT services ever since the company was created out of part of Eastern National in 1990, and is seen in winter sunshine near Canary Wharf. *Colin Lloyd*

Bottom: Thamesway bought large numbers of Mercedes-Benz minibuses, for both their London and Essex services. An unusual purchase was of nine Varios with narrow Marshall bodywork specifically for routes 362 and 462. However a long-winded dispute with the local authority and local residents over a width restriction has caused them to be used also on other routes. Nevertheless No.415 (now 575 with Capital) was pictured on the 362 at King George Hospital, Goodmayes, in full First Thamesway regalia. *Colin Brown*

has about one quarter of the total LT bus market. A reorganisation of Arriva management from 1st August 1998 saw the Greater London, northern and southern 'country areas' of Arriva put into three groups. Then on 3rd October the former County Bus depot at Edmonton transferred to be under the wing of Arriva London North.

London Transport require that buses operating in the Central Zone 1 should be in at least 80% red livery, although existing buses did not have to be treated until contract renewal. First Capital, having already introduced an 80%-red version of its livery specifically for its buses on route 91 from January 1997, added further such buses when four more routes were gained through LT tendering in 1998. They then decided to adopt the livery universally as repaints became due. Meanwhile, changes to route and vehicle allocations within the Arriva group resulted in buses in the former Kentish Bus and Londonlinks liveries going into red, to be compatible with their new allocated bases. Not only that, but Arriva London North East (more familiarly known as Grey-Green) embarked on a red repaint programme. All this resulted in almost every bus operating in Zone 1 being in a mainly red livery (including the orange-red of Sovereign) by the end of 1998. By this time only a handful of buses in Grey-Green colours were to be seen in the centre, mostly on route 188. Ironically it was Grey-Green that was the first to run non-red buses on a central London route, the 24 back in November 1988.

The activities of the groups meant that the amount of competition for LT Buses contracts was gradually reduced. Not only that, but an increasingly serious driver shortage meant that some operators had to surrender routes in an attempt to concentrate resources. London General (who had already given up the 413, C3 and S1 in late 1997) and the former Kentish Bus seemed to be worst affected, though they were not the only ones. Selkent was to come to the rescue several times, first of all in conjunction with Metrobus on the C1 for about three months, and then – in order – on routes 127, 60, 225, X72, 272. Both Selkent and Metrobus were among those who helped out Limebourne in

November 1998 when that company suffered operational problems. Limebourne's local management achieved a buy-out of their company, but had to hire vehicles and buy new and second-hand ones to replace those re-possessed.

Operational problems beset Capital Logistics, who were successful in gaining LT routes U3, 726 and 60 during 1998, but appeared to be over-optimistic

London Traveller is one of three companies which in the main do school contract work (including some for LT Buses) and rail replacement services (including for London Underground) over many parts of London. Many of the buses so used are somewhat elderly, but the exception is this East Lancs bodied Dennis Arrow, launched with great ceremony in spring 1998 but never used to its full potential. It is normally based at the Potters Bar depot, from where one LTB school route (626) and several services in Hertfordshire are operated. These latter now trade under the 'Bus Link' name mainly with buses in a white and blue livery.   R1LTB was pictured at Wembley Park on rail replacement work in June 1998. *Russell Young*

5

about the 60. They never obtained buses, a base or staff in time for the take-up of the contract, and Selkent and Blue Triangle were to run the route for the last four months of 1998. The LT contract was then re-assigned to a new operator, Omnibus London, from January 1999 and they were to take up Capital Logistics' order of sixteen new low floor double deck buses which, once delivered, would make them the first UK operator of the new Plaxton President bodied DAF DB250. Another problem route in south London, the 127, was relet to Mitcham Belle Coaches, an old established operator though new to bus work, and this was also due to be taken up early in 1999.

There had been two new operators to LT bus work in 1998, both being part of the National Express Group. Travel London, in reality part of the much larger Travel West Midlands, took routes C1 and 211 in the summer, while Speedlink, familiar as a major coach and contract operator at the airports, took new route H30 from 1st November.

During 1998 approximately 750 new buses were delivered to companies listed herein, with about 80% of the chassis total being split roughly equally between the double deck Volvo Olympian and the single deck Dennis Dart SLF. The other 20% were evenly spread between eight other double deck, minibus and single deck types. The low floor revolution which, just a couple of years ago, was only just starting, is well and truly established – at least it is in the single deck market, with all single deck buses and some of the minibuses being low floor. However, after the anticipation in early 1998 of large numbers of low floor double deckers being delivered, only a mere trickle actually appeared during the year. Nevertheless over 450 were in the order books at the year's end, plus options on many more.

At the turn of 1998/99 there were no standard floor double deckers outstanding for any of the companies, the last to be delivered in autumn 1998 being examples for Metrobus, First Capital and Metroline, culminating in eight for Sovereign's route 292. Unless existing vehicles continued to be used, or there was a specific problem on a route, London Transport specified low floor buses for all its future double deck contract awards from autumn 1998. However, it is recognised by LT that vehicle delivery times are now often greatly extended and recently several route contracts have been awarded with open-ended comments such as 'a proportion of new buses will be introduced later in 1999'. The Disability Discrimination Act insists that all new buses must be fully accessible within three years, with new standard single deck buses all so equipped by 1st January 2000, new double decks by 2002, new minibuses and coaches by 2005. Even then, there is a fifteen-year overlap period (ten years for minibuses) by which time all buses, new or otherwise, must be accessible.

The fleet intake has not been matched by disposals, as it is increasingly the case that LT contracts require higher frequencies, and thus more buses. Routine vehicle disposals were concentrated mostly on Titans and Metrobuses, with a few early Darts and quite a lot of MetroRiders and StarRiders. Group ownership has been quite beneficial, with many surplus London vehicles able to be cascaded to provincial subsidiaries.

The Dennis Dart is still the dominant single deck type, and over the years has developed from the original 8.5 metre version into very many versions up to 11.3 metre. However, the wheel is turning full circle with the introduction of an 8.8 metre low floor model in late 1998 and, with the new Optare Solo of similar length, these are obviously major competitors for the MetroRider and Mercedes-Benz Vario. The first examples of both the short Dart and Solo in the London area entered service at the beginning of 1999, the former with Epsom Buses (soon followed by CentreWest) and the latter with Travel London.

Route branding is becoming increasingly common, and often serves to make a particular route or vehicle type stand out from the crowd. Harris Bus and London United have some of the most striking examples, while about half of London's Routemaster services have an amount of branding. A different base livery, such as that for Stagecoach East London's London City Airport service, or an individual fleetname such as those used by CentreWest for each garage, can also have an impact. The use of a route strip on the bus sides, detailing places served, attracts attention to where the bus goes, examples including First Capital's Darts on the S2 and the new Sovereign Olympians on route 292. Advertisement buses have been a rarity in London for many years, although they can be seen on buses used only on contract or training duties. However, a recent phenomenon is the 'Super Rear' advert, covering the entire rear of double deck vehicles, and this continues to escalate with about 500 in the London area.

Not everything in London's bus world can possibly be contained in this one volume, and we have covered just the companies on regular local bus work on LT services. There are three smaller companies who concentrate on school services (including some for LT Buses), contracts and rail replacement work in various parts of London. These are Blue Triangle of Rainham, Nostalgiabus of Mitcham, and London Traveller of Neasden and Potters Bar. By and large, rather elderly second-hand buses are operated, although London Traveller has one new Dennis Arrow and may obtain more new buses in 1999. Blue Triangle were helping out on LT route 60 in late 1998, and is due to take up a new LT route (474) in east London during summer 1999, for which new buses will be sought.

We hope that you will enjoy the full colour photographic selection which follows and that you will find the fleet lists of the operators useful. The book represents the situation as it applied at the beginning of 1999, but is obviously subject to change as LT route tendering and route changes take effect, and as new buses are delivered. In particular, the Jubilee Line Extension will prompt large scale changes to bus services in east and south-east London.

January 1999   DAVID STEWART

Front Cover: Dennis Arrows with the striking East Lancs Pyoneer bodywork are the standard fare on First Capital routes 76 and 259, which were won from Arriva during 1998, and thirty-eight of the type are now in stock, this second batch coming over the period when Capital passed into First ownership. No.452 claimed its place in history as the first new S-registered bus to enter service in London at the stroke of midnight on 1st August. It pauses on Waterloo Bridge in full daylight a few days later. *Stephen Madden*

Rear Cover: The Volvo Olympians delivered to London General over the turn of 1997/98 for route 74 were to the Northern Counties Palatine II design, and were the first batch of new buses to introduce high-backed seating as routine on an ordinary central London bus service. NV 167 turns out of Orchard Street into Oxford Street in the summer of 1998. *Capital Transport*

Title page: In Edgware and Harrow one can still see the remnants of a long-gone livery, a new company livery and now a national corporate livery – all on the same batch of buses with the same operator. Arriva the Shires run LTB routes 142 and 340 with Olympians dating from the 1985–92 period, and throughout 1998 ten of them had persisted in carrying the old green and grey London Country North West colours. In December 1998, itself having by-passed the Shires own blue and yellow colours, the first of these buses was at last treated to the Arriva national brand and 5111 (alias LR 81) is seen in Harrow Weald. *Capital Transport*

Page two: It has long been a tradition in London for garages to put out their newest classes of buses on Sundays on routes with otherwise older types during the week. Sunday driver-only operation is now universal on routes such as the 12 with crew Routemasters on weekdays. London Central use as many spare NVs as possible on routes 3, 12 and 196 on Sundays, and Olympian NV 71 typifies these practices in the Walworth Road, Camberwell. *Colin Stannard*

This is the shape of one of the things to come. The first production Plaxton President visited London briefly on 3rd September 1998, in this case S201JUA on a DAF DB250 chassis. This particular bus is the first one to be ordered by Arriva for evaluation, and is expected to come to London during 1999 for service. In the meantime, Omnibus London (route 60), First CentreWest (route 18, also 23 on Sundays), First Capital (route W8) and Metroline London Northern (routes 17,43,134) should be putting the body type into service during 1999, those on the 60 on DAF chassis, the rest on Dennis Trident.

ARMCHAIR

Armchair Passenger Transport Co Ltd, Armchair House, Commerce Way, Brentford, TW8 8LZ

Armchair's fortunes have fluctuated, with routes that once worked in Surrey and Berkshire no longer operated. They have been quite successful with LT tendering, although their first route, the 260, has since been lost. The bus fleet is now concentrated on LT work, routes operated being all local to their base; indeed two of them (E2 and E8) actually terminate there. The three batches of Olympians are mixed on routes 65 and 237, standard Darts on the 117 and 190 and Dart SLFs on routes E2 and E8. The SLFs carry a revised livery with a white roof and black window surrounds and skirts. LT routes operated are 65, 117, 190, 237, 371 (school bus only), E2, E8. The fleet carries orange and white livery, and is housed at Commerce Way, Brentford. There is also a large coach fleet, details of which are in the London Coach Handbook.

Armchair's double-deck fleet is composed entirely of Olympians, bought in three batches. The Alexander bodied G-reg and Leyland-bodied H-reg examples are the mainstay on route 65, and H562GKX, an example of the latter, nears its destination in Kingston in September 1998. *Stephen Madden*

Seven Palatine II bodied Olympians were added to the fleet over the winter of 1997/98, nominally to upgrade route 65. However, they are most often to be found on route 237 which was added to the company's increasing portfolio in June 1998. R780SOY pauses outside Hounslow bus station in August 1998.
Colin Brown

Thirteen standard floor Pointer-bodied Darts came in 1996 for newly-won routes 117 and 190, followed by twenty-five low-floor versions for routes E2 and E8 in 1997. The winning of these services was most convenient for the company's base at Brentford. David Beckham sees P31MLE away to Staines in the World Cup month of June 1998.
Stephen Madden

ARRIVA

This large group has eleven of its subsidiaries running local bus routes within Greater London and, as far as London is concerned, is organised into three groups of operating companies for management purposes. *Arriva serving London* is controlled from Wood Green, and comprises London North (formerly Leaside), Leaside Travel, London North-East (Grey-Green) and London South (South London Transport). Apart from Leaside Travel, it is progressing toward a London red livery with cream relief, although some former County Bus and Grey-Green liveries will be evident during 1999. Garages are at Battersea, Barking, Brixton, Clapton, Croydon, Edmonton, Enfield, Norwood, Palmers Green, Stamford Hill, Thornton Heath, Tottenham and Wood Green.

The 'country' operators mostly run buses in their former liveries although a fairly small proportion has been repainted to the national version of Arriva livery of turquoise and cream (officially called aquamarine and light stone), with appropriate fleetnames (officially known as strap-lines). *Arriva serving the Shires* is controlled from Luton and the former County Bus fleets (with Townlink, Lea Valley and Thameside names) now trading as *Arriva serving East Herts and Essex*, operate from bases at Debden, Grays, Harlow and Ware. *Arriva Southern Counties* at Maidstone controls the fleets of Kent Thameside (the former Kentish Bus), Kent & Sussex (M&D) and the former London & Country and Londonlinks fleets which are divided into three operations: Arriva Croydon & North Surrey, Guildford & West Surrey, West Sussex. All three are gradually adopting the trading name *Arriva serving Surrey & West Sussex*. Garages of this group running buses into London are at Crawley, Croydon, Dartford, Guildford, Hounslow, Leatherhead, Merstham, Northfleet, Tunbridge Wells and Woking.

Arriva London North operate two very frequent Routemaster services (38 and 73) with RMLs. However five standard RMs were added recently to increase the 38's frequency a little more. Route branding is quite common in London, but the unusual style of the 38 is quite striking. No evidence whatsoever is given of Arriva, Cowie or even Leaside ownership in this view of RM 2185 at Victoria in September 1998.
Colin Brown

In contrast to the RM on the 38, the Olympians which are used on the route on Sundays as well as the 253 daily, mostly sport Cowie yellow stripes, Leaside fleetname and the original Arriva logo, although from late 1998 some examples have started to be treated to Arriva's corporate style. The white 'swirls' logo was applied in October 1997 to those buses normally used on routes serving the City of London, the idea being to impress the square-mile financiers. L 352 leaves Victoria Bus Station in July 1998 on its busy journey back to Clapton Pond. *Colin Brown*

Thirteen DAF DB250s came to Leaside in 1995 when they won route 263, and at the time of writing many retained Cowie-style yellow-stripe livery. However, at the time of transition from Cowie to Arriva late in 1997, all reference to Cowie in fleetnames was summarily obliterated. Representing route 263, from which they rarely stray and nowadays covering much of the old trunk 609 trolleybus route, DBS 9 powers up into hill-top Chipping Barnet in July 1998. *Stephen Madden*

In 1994 the low-floor revolution began in a small way, with batches of Dennis Lance and Scania vehicles introduced on five routes (101,120,144,186,222) in different parts of London. All had Wright Pathfinder bodywork. Leaside was the recipient of fourteen of the Scanias, and SLW 11 was to be found four years later on its original route, at the 'Cambridge' in Edmonton. *Geoff Rixon*

As has often been found to be the case, introduction of new buses – especially fully accessible ones – has boosted passenger loadings. Route 144 was no exception and in early 1998 three DAF SB220s with the new Plaxton Prestige bodywork were added to the allocation on the service. DLP 2, decked in Arriva London's livery but looking much more stylish without the 'cow horns', leaves Turnpike Lane in July 1998. *Stephen Madden*

The first low-floor double-deck buses to go into service in London did so with Arriva London North. DLA 1 was briefly operated on routes 29 & 144 in June, with the first production batch entering service in November 1998 on route 242. During that first month, DLA 3 is seen at Holborn. *David Heath*

Now a very rare type in London is the little MCW Metrorider. However, three survive at Arriva London North's Clapton garage for use on a contract service for the Department of Health. They can be found in the Waterloo and Lambeth area during the Monday to Friday daytime, like MR 105 pictured in August 1998.
Stephen Madden

A large batch of Northern Counties Paladin bodied Darts was delivered to Kentish Bus in 1994 for their mass of LT work newly obtained. Within a few years most of those routes had been either lost or surrendered. One of those routes, the 225, was passed to Grey-Green with five of the Darts (115-119), but they soon gave it up themselves and the buses moved to fellow Arriva London North, who have made good use of them on route 192. London North have adopted the red and full cream-front livery for its buses running in the outer areas, as shown on DRN 116 at Edmonton Green. *Colin Lloyd*

In October 1998 the *Leaside Travel* fleet of buses and coaches, for a couple of years under the stewardship of County Bus, was restored to what is now Arriva London North. The unit had adopted this unusual livery and its buses can often be found working school contract services (including several for LT Buses) and rail replacement services. However, they also provide Arriva's private hire and special service fleet, and one of these is T 83, calling at Picketts Lock, Edmonton on the summer only 333 service which connects points along the Lea (or Lee) Valley through north London and into Essex and Hertfordshire. *Colin Lloyd*

The former County Bus services at Edmonton depot came to Arriva London North ownership in October 1998. That depot had won LT Buses route 34 (Walthamstow and Barnet) a year earlier – ironically from Leaside – and had bought sixteen Darts to run it. These were delivered in County Bus cream and dark green livery, and to date all continue to wear these colours, complete with their 'Lea Valley' fleetnames, while in true 'County Bus' style no fleet numbers are displayed. Confounding its outward appearance, here is DPP 430 of Arriva London North arriving in Barnet. *Stephen Madden*

The Grey-Green name and identity is being rapidly eliminated with an intensive repaint programme under way at the turn of 1998/99. The most numerous double-deck type is the Volvo B10M/ Alexander combination, and the black fleet number application on No.119 is the only clue to its former heritage. Route 168 is due to receive some of Arriva's large order for DLA low-floor buses during 1999. *Stephen Madden*

The nine Scanias in the Arriva London North East fleet are now all in red livery, although if you look closely at the buses on the route you will see some minor differences to the livery application. For example this one has a yellow fleet number. Former Grey-Green No.179 shows the present order on route 24 which, in November 1988, had been the first route in central London to pass to an operator of non-red buses – the wheel has come full circle. *Colin Lloyd*

Not all buses in the Arriva London NE fleet have gone into red, and the batch of seventeen Dart SLFs delivered in 1997 for routes 20 and 167 in the Loughton area are likely to be the last to retain Grey-Green colours. Since the last edition of this book, all buses in this livery had their large fleet-names above the cab (offside) or entrance door (nearside) replaced by smaller ones on the orange side relief band. This one is seen in Leyton in May 1998. *Gerald Mead*

A rapid progression of liveries on route 78 has seen Londonlinks greens, Kentish Bus and Grey-Green colours replaced by red. From 14th November 1998 the LT route contract was retained by Arriva London NE, and a second batch of fifteen Alexander ALX200 bodied Dart SLFs came into the fleet for the service, shown here by No.977 approaching Tower Bridge. Note the application of orange for the Arriva strap-line, legal lettering and the easy access branding. *Dave Stewart*

A batch of eleven standard Darts came to County Bus in 1996 to provide larger buses on LTB routes 256 and 346 in the Hornchurch and Upminster area. Routes 370 and 373 plying between Grays and Romford gained new Dart SLFs at the same time to replace the elderly Atlanteans thereon, and the routes were adopted into the LTB network on their long section within Greater London. However here one of the former batch, 3409, has strayed to the latter route 373 at Upminster Station in August 1998. *Philip Wallis*

The former Luton & District and London Country North West fleets were re-launched as 'The Shires' in April 1995, and a blue, yellow and mushroom livery was adopted. However the Shires never used its own name, preferring to adopt local identities for each garage. Even after Arriva took over, 'Network Watford' and indeed even the 'Watford Bus' branding of LCNW still survive on buses used on the two LTB routes 142 and 340 in north west London. Olympian 5113 (once more familiarly LR 83) heads for Harrow. *Capital Transport*

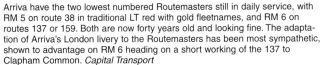

Arriva have the two lowest numbered Routemasters still in daily service, with RM 5 on route 38 in traditional LT red with gold fleetnames, and RM 6 on routes 137 or 159. Both are now forty years old and looking fine. The adaptation of Arriva's London livery to the Routemasters has been most sympathetic, shown to advantage on RM 6 heading on a short working of the 137 to Clapham Common. *Capital Transport*

South London Transport took over Kentish Bus route 19 and its RMLs in one of many switch-arounds of work between Cowie and Arriva operating companies in recent times. This batch of buses never had a repaint in their years with Kentish Bus and were swiftly transformed into red by spring 1998. After several experiments with livery styling, this Arriva London style has been adopted for Routemasters, as with RML 2715 seen here near Tottenham Court Road in August 1998. *Geoff Rixon*

This is a representative of the Cowie-style livery still to be seen on the majority of Metrobuses and Olympians with Arriva London South. The 'South London' fleetname is non-existent except on about four Ms. Over a hundred buses in London currently run under registrations formerly on Routemasters, and L 16 is one of these. It is seen at Marble Arch on route 2, the sole London bus route to terminate at Marylebone Station. *Stephen Madden*

Opposite Page: Virtually all Kentish Bus London operations have gradually been transferred to more appropriate garages, and their forty-three Northern Counties bodied Olympians are now all red and split between London North and South, those in the south being allocated to Norwood garage for routes 2, 68, 176 and 188 alongside more traditional Ls. This move, together with the repaint of Grey-Green's buses into red, has been instrumental in restoring red buses to all services in zone 1. Route 188 has had more than its fair share of operators and even now it is worked by 'Grey-Green' on weekdays and by 'South London' on Sundays. L 528 represents the latter on Waterloo Bridge in May 1998, and still devoid of adverts it displays Arriva's London livery to the full. *Geoff Rixon*

Something of a surprise in the spring of 1998 was the repainting of many South London midibuses into a red and cream version of the national livery, and opinions will be divided over whether the full cream front or the 'cow horns' variation is more attractive. Defying London Transport's 80%-red rule, DRL 151 is at Vauxhall in May 1998 just a mile from LT's headquarters. Route 322 runs its last stretch from Vauxhall to the Elephant along the boundary of zones 1 and 2.
Geoff Rixon

Route 319 does go into Zone 1 to Sloane Square, and so it must have more red paint on its buses than those on the 322. Arriva London South's first low-floor buses were eighteen Dart SLF/ Pointers, exemplified by DDL 6 carrying a fair load to points south of the River. On this journey it will terminate at its operational garage of Brixton (BN), though this location has never been thus described, to avoid confusion with the town centre some distance away. *Geoff Rixon*

After the decimation of Arriva Kent Thameside's LT Buses work in January 1999, relatively few routes now run in Greater London. One that remains unscathed is the 126, plying between Eltham and Bromley, and most of the buses used thereon have been treated to Arriva corporate colours. Northern Counties Darts come all the way from Northfleet and Dartford garages to work the route, shown here by No.3112, numerically the first of the batch, at Bromley North in October 1998. *Colin Lloyd*

London's first Darts were 8.5-metre Carlyle-bodied versions with 168 examples coming in 1990/91. Although some have been sold on, most survive in daily service, and Thornton Heath garage mix them with DRs and DRLs on routes 249,255,450 and they are the main type on the G1. DT 69 leaves the Croydon Tramlink works behind in August 1998. Note the orange Arriva name on the full cream front. *Stephen Madden*

A limited-stop bus route dubbed 'TL 1' covers the former rail service between West Croydon and Wimbledon via Mitcham, until the Croydon Tramlink opens later in 1999. Five DAF-Ikarus buses once in the stock of Arriva's dealership are used, and DIB 3 crosses a piece of road which would soon see tram-lines. It seems that the trams will carry a similar red and cream livery to the bus. *Stephen Madden*

The former London & Country and Londonlinks fleets are now under the Arriva banner, trading as 'Arriva serving Surrey and West Sussex' although buses operate under three separate Operator's Licences, depending on which garage works the route. The vast majority of buses in this 'group' to be seen within Greater London are from Arriva Croydon & North Surrey, and it is this arm that has the most buses in Arriva national turquoise and stone livery. Thus, displaying a fleetname totally inappropriate to LTB route 85 between Kingston and Putney is one of thirteen DAF DB250s. Some also incorrectly carry '00' as part of the fleet number, as shown on DFD 4 at Putney Heath in July 1998. *Geoff Rixon*

Showing how members of the 'L&C group' fleet have been switched frequently between garages, Dennis Lance LS 18 displays its 'Guildford & West Surrey' fleet-name in the heart of Croydon on LTB route 289. This batch of handsome East Lancs bodied buses is now the principal type on this route, following the sale of all the Lynxes formerly to be seen thereon. *Stephen Madden*

There are seven different fleet numbering systems concurrent in the 'L&C group' fleets, and Mercedes-Benz 811D No.437 represents one of the former L&C single-deck systems, later passing via the Kentish Bus system and back again, all the time with Londonlinks names. Although this separate operation passed into oblivion in June 1998, a number of buses – like those on route 367 – continued to carry its fleetname into 1999. They retain the two-tone green colours, running with a company transforming into turquoise in an area that should perhaps rather see red buses. Are you confused yet? *Stephen Madden*

Probably one of the more unlikely locations for a bus on an LTB route is Dorking, yet the 465 is an LTB contract service. However, its transition from a 'country bus' route to LTB control was not smooth, with several problems over fares and ticket availability between London and Surrey. Even now, LT travelcards are only valid as far south as Leatherhead. DSL 92 displays the traditional London & Country name and livery at Dorking Station.
Dave Stewart

After a period of massive expansion when, not that long ago, Kentish Bus was the largest LTB contractor outside of the former London Buses companies, LT tender losses have reduced it to around thirty buses on a handful of routes in the south-east outskirts of London. Nevertheless, Arriva national livery is quite common hereabouts, with the former Kentish Bus green & yellow and maroon & primrose liveries very rare on services entering Greater London. A batch of Dart SLFs maintain LTB route 286 between Greenwich and Sidcup and No.3265 nears its terminus in September 1998.
Laurie Rufus

CAPITAL CITYBUS

(First Capital) Capital Citybus Ltd, Chequers Lane, Dagenham, Essex, RM9 6QD

The origin of this large fleet came when Ensignbus of Purfleet gained LT route 145 (Dagenham to Redbridge Station) from 21st June 1986, and a blue and silver livery was used. Many more routes and vehicles followed until the business was sold to the CNT group of Hong Kong on 29th December 1990. A new yellow livery was introduced, featuring Chinese characters in the fleetname. The company was bought back by a management-led team on 21st December 1995, and a revised fleetname started appearing on vehicles following the breaking of ties with its former owner. More and more LT routes were won, and by 1997 three depots were being used, at Dagenham (Chequers Lane), Northumberland Park (Marsh Lane) and Hackney (Waterden Road).

After some months of speculation, the company was sold to the FirstGroup on 8th July 1998, and buses gradually acquired the group's logo and the 'First Capital' trading name started to be used. Most of the fleet carries a livery of yellow with red relief, though about a third now have 80% red livery with yellow relief, and this is being adopted on new and repainted vehicles. During the late summer of 1998, the Thamesway buses and routes were assimilated and a programme of repaints into Capital's red and yellow livery soon began.

Capital Citybus now trades under the First Capital name, and the livery is gradually changing from yellow to mainly red. At the turn of 1998/99, about 30% of the fleet was red, and the First logos were still to be applied to most of the fleet. The first buses delivered under the new regime did of course arrive correctly dressed, and Olympian No.221 proudly performs on yet another LTB route won at the expense of another operator, in this case Arriva. It is seen departing from the Northumberland Park terminus of route 341 in October 1998.
Colin Stannard

Opposite page: The 80% red livery was at first developed by Capital Citybus for use on routes that ran into the central London fare zone 1, after many years of only working routes outside the zone. Their first zone 1 route was the 91, won in January 1997 from London Northern, and the buses bought to service it were Alexander (Belfast) bodied Olympians like No.226 seen here in Trafalgar Square in June 1998. *Stephen Madden*

Showing how the red livery was also adopted for routes newly-won outside the central area, when the local route W8 in the Enfield area was gained in July 1998 its stock was former London General Metrobuses. More came later in the year for route 1, but this time the first choice was from its newly-found colleague CentreWest within the FirstGroup. No.316 departs from Edmonton Green in July 1998. *Colin Brown*

Left: There is a considerable number of variations within the Capital double deck fleet, including Olympians, Metrobuses and Dominators and with differing bodywork, many of which have been illustrated in earlier editions of this book. Although not the first of such oddities, in a batch of one is No.250, a former Leyland demonstrator, performing here on route 91 in Caledonian Road. *Colin Stannard*

Right: These long Dennis Arrows with East Lancs Pyoneer bodywork are the main fare on route 369, and were the first of their body style to appear on the company's routes in 1997. Here No.424 traverses one of the many twists and turns of Ilford town centre. *Colin Stannard*

Though not quite the first such example in the fleet, one Dennis Arrow was fitted with a full rear blind display. This unusual feature has not been perpetuated, but it provides a rare opportunity to make the back-end of a bus an interesting picture. No.426 nears the end of its D6 course from the Isle of Dogs to Hackney in this January 1998 view. *Colin Lloyd*

The first sixteen Dennis Arrows carried Northern Counties Palatine II bodies, and some are now on their third livery in three years as some had first been used in orange colours on an East London Line rail replacement service. No.415 is in Westbury Avenue on route 123, although this bus – with several sisters – has since moved to another service, and Arrows are now rare on this one. *Colin Stannard*

Representing the older fleet is Dominator No.203, once part of the London Buses experimental fleet introduced in 1984 and one of the first three Dominators to operate in London. It is in traditional Citybus livery, which is still worn by the majority of the fleet, and working route D6 in South Hackney in September 1998.
Gerald Mead

Usually to be found spread over routes 299, W6 and W10, the ten MetroRiders were among the first minibuses in the Capital Citybus fleet, though dating only from 1992. No.623 scoots along on its back-road route W6 in July 1998 – like many such routes it has seen an upsurge in passengers and frequency. *Geoff Rixon*

A unique vehicle in the fleet, and indeed carrying a very rare body in its Wadham Stringer Portsdown design, provides the first and thus far only example of such a body to run on bus routes in Greater London. Dating from 1991 and bought from Wealden of Kent in 1996, No.669 is rather elusive but can sometimes be found on the commercial routes outward from Romford. *Clydemaster Preservation Group*

Opposite page: Four short 10.0 metre Optare Excels were bought in 1996 to operate LTB route 396, the first direct bus service from Ilford and Gants Hill to the King George Hospital, and upon which their easy access capability could be made so useful. No.702 is seen between Harris Buses in Ilford in September 1998. This class of bus was earmarked to have wheelchair ramps fitted in 1999. *Capital Transport*

On 28th February 1998 the East Lancs Spryte body made its first appearance on London Transport service, with the introduction of thirteen Dart SLFs in this style. Route S2 was yet another LT tender success by Capital, and an innovation in the company was the addition of a line diagram style of route branding applied to the vehicle sides. No.706 passes Bow Church in July 1998. *Russell Young*

Alexander Dash bodied Volvo B6 No.676 departs from Finsbury Park on route 236, with the low railway bridge behind that has claimed more than a few double deck roofs over the years. Most of the B6s in the fleet are now in red livery, having been the first single-deck class in the fleet to start this process. *Philip Wallis*

In summer 1998 seven former DW-class Darts were obtained from fellow First company CentreWest, and were soon painted red. It had been intended that they should replace hired Thamesway minibuses, but in the event they took their place mostly on routes W6 and W10, with Sunday appearances on the 97A and 212. No.645 is at Crews Hill on the W10 on its first day in service. *Russell Young*

The third 'batch-of-one' to be featured in this sequence is No.796. It is a former Dennis Lance demonstrator with Alexander PS body and in spite of dating from 1992, it had never been registered by Dennis. It was only first registered for passenger service in October 1998. It does still remain quite elusive and is often used on private hire and railway services. Its first outing was to Showbus at Duxford, where it is seen in this view. *Malcolm King*

The majority of Thamesway's London Transport operations came under the control of First Capital in stages, culminating on 26th September 1998 when the depot at Ponders End and its routes were assumed. Plenty of vehicles still display Thamesway livery and names, though a start has been made on repainting into First Capital's 80%-red livery and this example – now numbered 776 – was the very first to be so treated. Almost matching the Arriva bus behind, it is seen here at Edmonton Green in October 1998. *Colin Lloyd*

CAPITAL LOGISTICS

Capital Logistics Ltd, Heathrow Coach Centre, Sipson Road, West Drayton, UB7 0HN

Capital Logistics operate a large fleet of coaches at both Heathrow and Gatwick Airports, mainly for car park, aircrew and hotel contracts. The fleetname was altered from Capital Coaches in October 1997 following the purchase of Whyte's Coaches. The firm entered tendered bus work in a small way in August 1993 with LT route H26, buses being kept at an outstation at the Eastern Perimeter Road at Heathrow and operate in a mainly white livery. During 1998 LT routes U3, 726 and 60 were gained, although they were never to take up the 60 in their own right, with the contract and the buses ordered for it transferred to Omnibus London from early in 1999. Optare Excels run the U3 in a white, red and dark blue adaptation of the coach livery, while the 726 uses the vehicles in white and red 'Expresslink' livery acquired from their former owner with the route. These buses and the coach fleet are based at Sipson Road, West Drayton.

Capital Logistics was enthusiastic in going for LT contracts and won the U3 and 726 in early 1998. A later enterprise with route 60 at Croydon resulted in failure to get buses, staff or a base in time and the route was sub-contracted to other companies. Eventually the new vehicles ordered for the 60 were diverted to a new company, Omnibus London. However, back to the U3 and this service was significantly upgraded in May 1998 with double-glazed, air-conditioned Optare Excels. R992EWU sets down in Wise Lane, West Drayton in August 1998. *Geoff Rixon*

CENTREWEST

CentreWest London Buses Ltd, Macmillan House, Paddington Station, London W2 1TY

CentreWest was purchased from London Buses by a management-led team on 2nd September 1994, taking 507 vehicles. A large proportion were midibuses, CentreWest having made the greatest strides of the LBL subsidiaries in converting routes to this format. In December 1995 CentreWest branched out across London when they took over a number of LT contract routes in the Orpington area. In March 1996, the holding company of CentreWest purchased the Bee Line and London Buslines companies, and some interchange of vehicles has since taken place between the fleets, particularly to improve the age profile of the acquired operations.

On 26th March 1997 the CentreWest group was sold to FirstBus (renamed to FirstGroup in November 1997). The group's *f* logo and First names now precede the local marketing names which are used by buses based at Acton Tram Depot and Uxbridge (Uxbridge Buses), Alperton (Challenger), Greenford (Ealing Buses), Orpington (Orpington Buses) and Westbourne Park (Gold Arrow). Traditional London red livery continued to be carried by most of the fleet, although most have now been adapted with yellow relief and fleetnames, and have lost the grey skirt. Driver training vehicles are allocated to various garages as required and are painted mostly in yellow with a red rear area.

The stock of RMLs used on busy central London routes 7 and 23 is presently being smartened up with the addition of First logos and route branding. RML 2428 passes through the City in September 1998. Note the large driver's duty number in the cab window – these have replaced the traditional London bus running numbers, though CentreWest is the only major London company to have done this. *Stephen Madden*

Opposite page: Leaving one in no doubt as to its First ownership, open-top RMC 1510 frequently appears on route 23 on fine, and often not-so-fine, days. Although few people seem to be taking advantage of one of the former days, 24th June 1998 to be precise, the bus rounds Marble Arch. *Stephen Madden*

Metrobuses are now getting fairly thin on the ground in CentreWest territory, with the 83 and 92 having lost them and the 18 due to do so in summer 1999. The trunk route 207 is, however, still their main home, but a slight variation in Hayes End shows the now rare sight of a suffix letter on a London bus route. M 360 on the 207A is in a part of Uxbridge High Street still available to buses. *Colin Brown*

Fifteen Volvo Olympians with coach seating are dedicated to express route 607 between Uxbridge and Shepherd's Bush. However it is common to find the spare bus on route 222, and one such appearance depicts V 49 on the Bath Road near Heathrow Airport. Luckily, the original posters that advertised route 607 have been replaced. *Colin Brown*

Opposite page: Once the company was bought by CentreWest, the double deck fleet of London Buslines was soon taken over. The Buslines routes either went over to Dennis Darts, were lost on re-tender or switched with the parent company. One such bus to transfer to CentreWest is LA 52, arriving at Ealing Broadway on the busy route E1 – the other routes in the E-network are all midibus-operated. *Colin Brown*

The Palatine II bodywork is quite a popular choice, complete with its nearside tree-branch deflectors. CentreWest, though based in west London, also have quite a large network in the far south-east at Orpington, and V 6 prepares to depart from Bromley North on the circuitous 61 service to Chislehurst; it will take 50 minutes to get there, the direct 269 route taking only 15. *Colin Lloyd*

Several former Red Arrow Nationals were used on route 607 until passenger loadings forced the change to double deckers. These Volvo engined machines then went onto driver training work, and eventually into this yellow and red livery. Two similar buses (LSs 470 & 497) retain a similar livery, even though they now work with the associated Beeline at Slough. If you want to be a driver, take a look at LS 444. *Stephen Madden*

Opposite page: Another special livery is one designed by Best Impressions and supported by the British Airports Authority and Stockley Park. The A10 route is a fast and frequent link between Uxbridge and Heathrow, but Uxbridge garage is renowned for mixing up its bus allocation on the wrong routes. L 3 was found on a more mundane route, the 222, turning into West Drayton Station. *Colin Brown*

A fairly sudden development was the commencement on 23rd June 1998 of a 'Hotel Express' link from Paddington Station to take passengers from the Heathrow Express railway to hotels in the Marble Arch area. Four of CentreWest's DML order were hastily diverted to this contract, and another four added to the eventual intake. DML 251, newly re-registered like its fellows, passes Marble Arch in September. *Laurie Rufus*

A class due to depart by spring 1999 is the Mercedes-Benz Marshall MM class, with replacement by yet more Marshall Dart SLFs. However MM 5 on route R4 bursts onto the War Memorial roundabout at Orpington in August 1998 on what was one of the original 'Roundabout' routes in an earlier regime. *Stephen Madden*

Opposite page: The Marshall integral Minibus has never found much favour among operators, but CentreWest did order sixteen for routes E5,E6,E10 in the Greenford scheme of May 1997. It took until the end of August 1998 for all to be delivered, and they never came in fleet number sequence. One of the first few was ML 114, here travelling through the turns of the Golf Links Estate on route E5 on one of the many fine sunny days of February 1998. *Colin Brown*

Above: A total of 156 buses with essentially similar Marshall Capital bodywork have been supplied to CentreWest in a short space of time, some short some long, some single- some dual-doored. One of the 34 short (9.4 metre) dual door versions on Dart SLF chassis supplied for route 31 is seen here, heading a convoy of 31s on this very busy route. Yet more are due in spring 1999 to complete the 77-bus allocation on routes 28/31 and their new variants. *Colin Brown*

The longer versions of the Dart SLF/Marshall combination are based at Greenford (route 282), Alperton (92) and Uxbridge (U1 and U4), some being route branded for the U1. One such, DML 196, sets down in Uxbridge High Street in July 1998. *Colin Brown*

Quite a few CentreWest buses have had only a superficial addition of new identity. However some have gained the full treatment, now with yellow relief replacing the former LBL white, and with the grey skirt over-painted. Buses on route 28, having gone from RMs down to little Mercedes, got bigger with the DWs, but larger DMLs and a night service are to be introduced during 1999. A jam-packed DW 169 heads for Wandsworth on this busy route. *Capital Transport*

CRYSTALS

C J Springham, 127 Dartford Road, Dartford, Kent, DA1 3EN

Starting life as a taxi firm in 1970, Crystals bought their first minibus in 1972. The company was one of the first operators of LT tendered routes when route 146 was taken over in August 1985, although the contract was lost in 1993. The company has since gained two minibus routes at Orpington and a range of LT Mobility Bus routes right across south London from Putney to Bexleyheath and Southwark to Croydon. Vehicles on the bus routes carry a livery of turquoise, whilst those on Mobility Bus routes are in red with yellow relief. Vehicles are kept at the 127 Dartford Road address.

Crystals are principally an operator of accessible minibuses, but they also have two midibus routes running in the Orpington area. Three shorter MB709Ds operate on the R2, three longer MB811Ds on the R7. One of the former, N602JGP, leaves Orpington for the narrow country lanes which will bring it to Biggin Hill, on the very fringe of the Greater London county.
Stephen Madden

EPSOM BUSES

H R Richmond Ltd, Blenheim Road, Longmead Estate, Epsom, Surrey, KT19 9AF

Epsom Buses is the trading name for the local bus work undertaken by Epsom Coaches, founded in 1920 by Mr H R Richmond. Bus work started in 1986 with one minibus route, but blossomed with several former London Country routes assumed at deregulation in October 1986. Subsequently there have been several adjustments to the network, with a mix of commercial and Surrey county council routes operated. LT work began when routes 413 and S1 were taken over from London General during the autumn of 1997, and routes 166, 404, 463, S4 and S5 have followed. Other routes in the Epsom and Kingston area are E3, E5, K9, K10, 518 and 562. The fleet livery for buses is cream with maroon relief, applied in different proportions, and they are based at the Blenheim Road address. The large coach fleet is listed in the London Coach Handbook.

Epsom Buses had run their own route 498 into Croydon for some years but, with a large LT network change from 29th August 1998, the route was adopted as part of the overall frequency on LT route 166 between Croydon and Chipstead Valley. Although the other operator, Arriva London South, continue to work on the aforementioned main section, Epsom Buses still run right through to Epsom but now under the 166 rather than the 498 number. One of seven standard Darts in the fleet, N401SPA, departs from Croydon in September 1998. *Geoff Rixon*

Routes K9 & K10 between Epsom and Kingston were the subject of a financial crisis in July 1998 and were threatened with withdrawal. In the event, Surrey County Council supported them 'over the border' and LT tickets are accepted on the London side, while in November 1998 brand new Mercedes-Benz Varios were introduced. One such vehicle, S452LGN, passes Kingston Hospital. *Geoff Rixon*

Epsom Buses have invested heavily in new buses to upgrade several routes. Eleven short 8.5 metre Dart SLFs with Plaxton Pointer 2 bodywork entered service at the beginning of 1999 on LT Buses routes 404,413,S1 and S5 to replace the MetroRiders that had been hastily acquired from London General in October 1997, but which had never been popular. These new buses were the first examples of the 'MPD' (Mini Pointer Dart) to enter service in the London area. *Geoff Rixon*

HARRIS BUS

Harris Bus Company Ltd, Parker House, Manor Road, West Thurrock, Essex, RM16 1EH

Harris Bus was set up as a separate company from the associated Frank Harris (Coaches) in September 1986 in preparation for bus work following deregulation, and developed a network centred on the Lakeside shopping centre. The company decided to branch into LT tendered work, and gained LT route 108 from 19th April 1997, following this with 128, 129, 150 later in 1997 and 132 and 180 in 1998. Vehicles carry a livery of blue and green and carry appropriate branding for the various routes. Buses for routes 128,129,150 are based at West Thurrock, and for routes 108,132,180 at Crabtree Manor Way North, Belvedere, south of the River.

Harris Bus have two batches of Optare Excels, servicing routes 108 and 132. Both batches carry prominent route branding but often escape onto the wrong route. One such example shows 'Eltham Link' R379DJN for route 132, advertising travel to Eltham and Bexley whilst loading in Stratford in east London on the 108. From 21st November 1998 the 108 became the first bus route to be diverted to serve the Millennium Dome site, even though one could not alight there without a permit. *Colin Lloyd*

Eight DAF DB250s with Palatine II bodies help out the more numerous Olympians with East Lancs Pyoneer bodies on the 'Ilford Link' routes 128, 129 and 150. P318KTW departs from Ilford on the 150 to Chigwell Row, showing the unusual colours and application of the livery, prior to gaining the usual side adverts. *Tony Wilson*

Thirteen Volvo Olympians (360-372) formed a follow-on batch after those for Ilford, once Harris Bus had added route 180 to their portfolio on London bus routes. R366DJN represents these dramatic looking vehicles, at the well-known bus stand behind the Lewisham Centre. *Mark Lyons*

INTERNATIONAL COACH LINES

19 Nursery Road, Thornton Heath, Surrey, CR7 8RE

Formerly known as Time Travel, this company specialises in the hire of vintage London buses in red liveries. They also run a Tuesday and Friday cross-London commercial service between Caterham and Waltham Cross. This is the only bus service in Greater London offering local bus travel outside the formal LT fares system; the only other examples are those routes with just one or two stops on the periphery of the county, or are special routes of some sort such as Summer Leisure routes 70D and 333.

Probably the strangest service to begin in London for years was the 709 on 5th June 1998. It is run with one bus, one of two RMA-class Routemasters, between Caterham and Waltham Cross with a through journey time of about three hours. Initially it ran on Fridays only, but a Tuesday service was later added. RMA 57, liberally decorated with posters which are almost illegible except at close quarters, travels north on the third Friday of operation – in later months a proper blind-box had been retro-fitted.
Stephen Madden

LIMEBOURNE

Independent Way Ltd, t/a Limebourne, Silverthorne Road, Battersea, London, SW8 3HE

After London Buslines and Berks Bucks Bus Company were sold to CentreWest on 20th March 1996, Q Drive retained its London coach business. One LT route (C10) had been won and thus a bus operation was set up at the Battersea base from May 1996. The mainly red livery used was the first by a contract operator to utilise an 80% red livery as was then laid down by LT for buses operating contracts within Central London Fare Zone 1. The company later assumed routes 42 and 156 with Dennis Dart SLFs, and route C3 followed in October 1997, using hired London General Marshall Minibuses. However, the Q Drive group was put into receivership in October 1998, and on 20th November the local management staged a buy-out of the bus business in the name of Independent Way Ltd. All the existing buses were re-possessed by finance companies, and the new managers had to hire and buy replacements. Initially these were Grey-Green single deck Volvos and Metroline Darts, while the London General Marshalls remained.

Independent Way Ltd was the name for the management buy-out of the former Limebourne bus operation in November 1998. All of Limebourne's Darts and MetroRiders were taken away by finance companies, and a temporary fleet of hired buses came in. The only constant was the ongoing hire of six of London General's Marshall Minibuses. They are usually to be found on route C3, and showing its LG fleet number of ML 3 and Limebourne name, this example prepares to depart from Earl's Court. *Colin Brown*

LONDON BUSLINES

Berks Bucks Bus Co Ltd, Middlesex Business Centre, Bridge Road, Southall, Middlesex, UB2 4AB

In the very first round of LT tendering, Len Wright gained LT route 81 (Hounslow and Slough) from July 1985, and a yellow and brown livery was adopted with London Buslines names. Various routes and vehicles came and went under Mr Wright's Q Drive group ownership. On 20th March 1996 the Q Drive bus operations, which included Berks Bucks Bus and its Beeline and London Buslines fleets, was purchased by CentreWest. In 1997 a swap of some routes took place with CentreWest, resulting in the fleet becoming all Dart except for three Renault minibuses used on Mobility Bus routes 981-994. LT routes are 105, 203, 258, 285, 490, and the Darts also appear on Sundays on Surrey County Council services 441, 446, 456, 461, 481 and K3. The fleet now bears a livery of yellow with red relief, and is kept at the Bridge Road, Southall base.

Apart from three Renault minibuses on Mobility Bus work, the entire fleet of London Buslines consists of Darts, 32 standard-floor and 25 low-floor examples. The former all have Plaxton Pointer bodywork and are used on routes 203,258 and 285, and on six Sunday routes in north-west Surrey for the county council. Carrying First branding and the latest red-skirted livery which has become universal, is L 237 pausing at Hounslow on route 203 in August 1998.
Colin Brown

The SLFs can be found on routes 105 and 490 and most of them are branded for these. The 'Freeflow Heathrow' symbol and the side flash, tracking 'into the wild blue yonder' is prominent on buses used on the 105. Buslines do not display fleet numbers, even though they are allocated by parent CentreWest. DML 643 travels along the Bath Road, Cranford in August 1998.
Geoff Rixon

LONDON CENTRAL

London Central Bus Co Ltd, One Warner Road, Camberwell, London, SE5 9LU

London Central was purchased by the Go Ahead Group on 18th October 1994, taking 498 vehicles. The basic bus livery has remained traditional London red with white relief, accompanied by a stylised fleet logo based on a Thames clipper ship. The purchase by the Go Ahead group of London General has resulted in most administrative functions moving to the Mitcham base of London General during 1997, though some offices remained based at Camberwell, but were also due to move in 1999. The livery has also been modified with a thin yellow band above the grey skirt, this being a London General influence. The fleet operates from garages at Bexleyheath, Camberwell, New Cross and Peckham.

The Go-Ahead Group's standard double decker in London has become the Northern Counties bodied Volvo Olympian. In London Central they are the main type on routes 21, 35, 40, 45, 51, 171 and D1, those on the D1 carrying special branding for the 'Docklands Express' – at least until the Jubilee Line Extension opens, that is. Here NV 86 pauses on Waterloo Bridge on the 171, having just passed over the Kingsway Subway through which its antecedent tram services passed 46 years earlier.
Stephen Madden

London Central briefly dabbled with the Alexander Royale bodywork on Olympians, with nine taken into stock in May 1995 to allow an upgrade from midibuses on route P11. This route serves the Rotherhithe peninsula, which has been greatly developed for housing since the days of the old Surrey Commercial Docks, and some of this can be seen behind AV 4 in this view. The P11 itself has needed even more buses and Titans now provide part of the service. *Russell Young*

In London Buses days over the winter of 1992/93, a batch of Optare Spectras provided the first sight of what was then a revolutionary style of bodywork to the streets of London. The main batch has always worked route 3, and SP 12 duly depicts this operation in Regent Street. Their lack of a rear window provides a perfect platform for the so-called 'super-rear' advert, a feature that has been adopted on many other classes since. *Capital Transport*

The Titan still forms a substantial proportion of the fleet, although a great many have been sold in recent years. They are prominent at Bexleyheath garage, and are still the only type on trunk route 63 from Peckham garage. They are also a well-used top-up type on many routes from Camberwell and New Cross garages, but not all are so well turned-out as T 892 here seen fully dressed in current company livery on route 45. Both routes 45 and 63 reach King's Cross, the most northerly point reached by London Central buses, and both routes will receive new low floor double deckers in due course. *Stephen Madden*

London Central's two Routemaster services continue unabated, with very high frequencies. RML 883, unusual in its class (along with two others) in having non-opening upper-deck front windows, is decked with the yellow ribbon branding for the service on route 12, still plying over the course of one of the oldest routes in London. It is passing Horse Guards in Whitehall in September 1998. *Colin Brown*

Route 36 is one of just two London routes still with a large principal allocation of standard RMs, although about one-third of the service is now covered with RMLs. Most vehicles have similar branding to that on route 12. Most operators of Routemasters have had them re-engined in recent years to extend their lives, and London Central has chosen Scania engines – those so converted carry a Scania badge by the rear platform. *Colin Lloyd*

A small private hire and special events fleet is maintained by London Central and General, and the buses are occasionally switched between the companies. LC's contingent also includes RM 9, VC 3, T 1129 and T 803, all in non-standard liveries of some kind. Our view of this selection shows OM 420, a General bus with Central fleetnames, here on the 'Greenwich Clipper', a service which ran during summer 1998 but was very poorly used. *Colin Lloyd*

Eleven East Lancs bodied Darts were an unusual purchase in 1994, and have remained unique in the former LBL fleets. Used principally on route 484, they also turn out on the P5 as well, as depicted here by DEL 5 with the familiar pink architecture at the Elephant & Castle shopping centre in the background.
Stephen Madden

As the MRL MetroRiders gradually fell by the wayside, and London General suffered some route losses, about two-dozen DW class Wright bodied Darts transferred from General to Central, in turn allowing a cascade of DRLs within both companies. London Central's two main DW routes are the P5 and P13, and DW 51 is seen on the former service, at the Elephant in June 1998. *Stephen Madden*

After delivery of 44 low-floor Pointer bodied Darts to London General for a major scheme at Sutton and Merton in December 1996, two more batches totalling 43 came to London Central for new routes 345 and 321, in both cases increasing the frequency over the services they replaced. The blue band over the top of LDP 59 in Sidcup extends to the nearside where the 'low floor easy access' branding will be found. *Laurie Rufus*

LONDON GENERAL

London General Transport Services Ltd, 25 Raleigh Gardens, Mitcham, Surrey, CR4 3NS

London General was purchased by a management-led team on 2nd November 1994, taking 636 vehicles, the largest fleet of any of the privatised London Buses companies. In May 1996 the company was in turn purchased by the Go-Ahead Group, and rationalisation with London Central has since taken place at the management level. Traditional London livery of red with white relief has been retained, accompanied by a white and orange fleetname incorporating a vertical orange stripe and a thin yellow band. A few buses retain "Streetline" branding though this is being discontinued. Although the privatisation logo, a B-type bus from the General of the First World War era, has now been largely abandoned, a small handful of buses carries a traditional pre-war style of livery and retains this emblem. The fleet operates from garages at Merton, Putney, Stockwell, Sutton and Waterloo.

There is little to distinguish London General's NV-class Olympians from those of London Central save for the fleetname. The grey skirt was an unchanged inheritance from LBL days, but the thin yellow stripe above it was on London General buses long before it spread more recently to those of London Central. NV 152 works the 213 route in Kingston, a service which has linked the town with Sutton for many decades. *Colin Brown*

Often regarded as London's unofficial bus tour, passing such tourist traps as Westminster and St Paul's Cathedral, route 11 has been treated to route branding and the RML buses were put through a repaint programme during 1998. However, although no crew buses are scheduled anywhere in London on Sundays, unusually the RMLs on the 11 also do not operate on Saturdays. Cutting a fine figure in May 1998 is RML 2725 at Victoria. *Stephen Madden*

Sometimes used as a 'special events' bus, RML 2732 has gained a huge General fleet-name to the pre-war LGOC style, and other gold trim. However, on most weekdays it is usually to be found on route 11, as seen here performing a short-working to St Paul's, calling at Terminus Place, Victoria in July 1998. *Laurie Rufus*

Opposite page: Some of General's NVs were ordered with the Palatine II rather than the Mark I design, and these were introduced onto route 74 at the end of 1997. They even have coach-style high-backed seats, which are an unexpected luxury on a central London route. On Sundays spare buses from the 74 are also used on route 14, and the side branding only shows the three points that can be regarded as common between the two routes. NV 165 travels along Piccadilly in May 1998. *Mark Lyons*

Above: The comfortable coach seating on the NVs on route 74. *Capital Transport*

Opposite page: A casual visitor to Clapham Junction or Tooting could be forgiven for believing that London General Metrobuses were the main type in town, though few of them penetrate the West End. Stockwell's Ms have a higher profile at weekends when they work route 11, as seen here by M 1302 in the City. *Capital Transport*

Above: VCs, the very high floored Volvo B10Ms, are the principal type on route 133, and can provide a spirited ride. Almost half of the class of 39 have been re-registered, most with former Routemaster marks, VC 4 being no exception in this view in Brixton. The RMs in the background have since lost their yellow bands, these being a short-lived pre-Arriva exercise. *Capital Transport*

The Leyland National 2s were given the 'Greenway' treatment in 1992/3/4 for further service on the Red Arrow network in central London. The routes are designed mainly for commuters from and to main-line railway stations, and thirty-seven are needed for service on Monday to Friday, though none are scheduled at weekends. Therefore they are often used on rail replacement work at such times. The forward standee area on GLS 480 can be seen here. *Stephen Madden*

A whole succession of Pointer-bodied Darts of the DR,DRL classes in 1991/2/3 and DPLs in 1995 were eventually followed by 44 low-floor LDP versions in 1996 to inaugurate the low-floor revolution on a whole series of routes at Sutton, Morden, Merton and Wimbledon, and more followed in the same area at the turn of 1998/99. Typifying these is LDP 10 at New Malden on route 152, heading for Pollards Hill, one of many areas opened up to buses in recent years. *Colin Brown*

Fifteen Marshall Minibuses were bought by London General in late 1996, but never seemed to find too much favour with the engineers. Putney garage was the home of LG's examples at the turn of 1998/9 and ML 14 looks smart on this bright spring day in Roehampton on route 265. Some of them were due to be transferred to London Central at Bexleyheath in January 1999. *Colin Brown*

LONDON UNITED and WESTLINK

London United Busways Ltd, Wellington Road, Fulwell, Middlesex, TW2 5NX   Stanwell Bus Co Ltd, 6 Pulborough Way, Hounslow, Middlesex, TW4 6DE

London United was purchased by a management-led team on 5th November 1994, taking 464 vehicles. Eventually, the traditional London red livery was adapted to a new style and Routemasters have received grey (instead of white) relief. The new standard livery for other buses is red with silver grey roof, grey upper-deck window-surrounds, and a thin white band above the grey skirt. Yellow is used for external transfers such as fleet numbers and garage codes.

In September 1995 the holding company of London United purchased Stanwell Bus, trading as Westlink. This company had been bought by a management team on 20th January 1994, but passed on to West Midlands Travel on 24th March 1994; they, in turn, were purchased by the National Express group early in April 1995. In the summer of 1997, Transdev, a French-based holding company who are also involved with the Connex railways in southern England, purchased the London United group. Westlink's own livery of red with white and turquoise relief has been largely eliminated, with most buses now in London United style, albeit with Westlink fleetnames.

London United's "Harrier" branding was used on its Dart routes, but this has been abandoned (though some buses still carry the name). A strong brand that is kept is Airbus, for the various services between Heathrow Airport and central London. The Airbus fleet operates from an open site at the West Ramp on the north side of Heathrow, Westlink from Kingston and Hounslow Heath, while the main LU fleet is kept at garages at Fulwell, Hounslow and Shepherd's Bush. Buses and route allocations have been switched from time to time between LU and Westlink bases as required.

Fifty-four VAs, of the Volvo Olympian and Alexander combination have transformed routes 131, 57 and 281, all of which serve Kingston. Those for the 281 are the newest, and different slogans adorn the sides, exhorting students, shoppers and commuters to use the 281 for their differing purposes. Only a couple of unlikely-looking commuters seem to be aboard VA 52 in this August 1998 view. *Geoff Rixon*

Opposite page: The VAs used on route 57 carry a huge orange 57 logo at their rear, and display the Westlink fleetname, befitting their allocation to the old Kingston (K) garage. In recent times there has been much blurring of the distinction between London United and Westlink, the latter name now covering buses that happen to be worked from the bases at Kingston and Hounslow Heath. Routes have been switched several times between the two arms. VA 30 is in Kingston in November 1998. *Geoff Rixon*

Opposite page: The Airbus services A1 & A2 between central London and Heathrow Airport were significantly upgraded in 1995/96 with these Alexander Royales on Volvo Olympian chassis. Though they carry no fleet numbers, they are known in the records as A 112-130. At Victoria Station A 125 carries the latest version of the branding, with Toshiba having a most prominent exposure. *Colin Brown*

The light grey relief seems almost white in this July 1998 view at Hyde Park Corner of RML 2464, as it sets off with a good load down the old Number Nine Road. The route now reaches only as far west as Hammersmith since a weight restriction on the suspension bridge left the traditional section onward to Mortlake to smaller and lighter Darts.
Stephen Madden

Still a major Metrobus operator, London United is now disposing of a number, and this process should accelerate during 1999 with the delivery of large numbers of new buses. The old coat-of-arms of the pre-war tramway company is proudly displayed on M 183 in this June 1998 scene on the H32, a route recently double-decked again and which is soon to receive low-floor double deckers.
Stephen Madden

Opposite page: London United may have lots of standard Ms and Darts, but they also have a fair number of small classes of buses only to be found in south-west London. Eight CDs, Dart SLFs but with Wright Crusader bodies, are in stock for Feltham and Hampton local route H25. However, Hounslow garage is well known for its propensity to put buses out on the 'wrong' routes, and CD 8 gives such variety to route H98 out to Hayes. *Colin Brown*

Above: Nine DAF-Optare Deltas are at the Westlink base at Hounslow Heath for route 81, although most are now painted into LU company livery styling. With the Westlink titling and underlining, this is arguably one of the most attractive yet simple liveries to be seen. DA 2 pauses on the Bath Road at Harlington Corner on what was the only sunny day in rainy April 1998. *Colin Brown*

The six Lynxes are mostly to be found on route H98 plying between Hounslow and Hayes End, as depicted on LX 3 leaving Hounslow in June 1998. As may be seen, London United uses small yellow characters for its fleet numbers and these appear in different places on different types.
Stephen Madden

A last stronghold of the Leyland National is in London United, though very few now remain. The majority were given a major engineering upgrade to provide extra capacity on route H37. As is often the case at Hounslow, not all will always be on the right route, and LS 335 belies its years when crossing the railway at Hampton Station on route 111. However, most single-deck routes from Hounslow garage were to gain new low-floor buses in 1999, so their days are likely to be numbered. *David Heath*

There are eight Optare Vectas and six Optare Excels in use on route 371 between Kingston and Richmond via Ham, and all carry slogans about things to do or see along the route. Some of the slogans are a bit contrived but often amusing, and are even different on each side of each bus. Still, at least they only had to devise 28 captions for their buses! MV 7 and XL 4 were both photographed in September 1998. *Stephen Madden*

Opposite page: In spite of the spread of the new London United livery, most of the older Pointer Darts which came in the early 1990s in LBL days show little difference from when they were new, except that some now display Westlink names and fewer carry the 'Harrier' branding which had characterised the DR and DRL buses when new. The H22 route and its Hounslow West destination, are destined to be the subject of change in spring 1999. *Stephen Madden*

Left: The little Carlyle-bodied 8.5 metre Darts from 1989 had a new lease of life breathed into them when some were treated to coach seating and air conditioning for a variation of the Airbus services. Rather a lot were done and some have since reverted to bus use, but numerically the first London Dart is still at work here at Marble Arch in June 1998.
Stephen Madden

Just over half of the ordinary non-Airbus DTs are in London United colours, the rest still in an earlier condition. One of the former is Fulwell-based DT 146 working local Kingston route K2 in its home town in September 1998. *Stephen Madden*

Decidedly in a minority in London bus operation is the all-over advert bus, and those that are around are almost exclusively only used on private contract or driver training duties. One that does carry passengers on a regular basis is DT 12, running a series of services for the Marks & Spencer store at Kew Retail Park, which is remote from any other bus services. However, the empty bus and the remoteness of the complex indicates that 99% of the customers no doubt come by car. *Colin Brown*

The earlier livery of Westlink, before it was absorbed by London United, was red with turquoise and white vinyl stripes. Only one or two buses still survived in this livery as at late 1998, and DWL 11 shows this style when seen in June 1998 heading out to Heathrow's south side.
Stephen Madden

Just five Metroriders remain from a once substantial fleet, and three are adapted for disabled access on route H20. Two standard examples provide support, like MRL 81 or 185, depending on whether you take the original LBL fleet number of 81 or the adopted one of 185. Westlink never used fleet numbers when independent, buses being known only by registrations. When they adopted London United practice, no-one seemed to know that this bus had a number already allocated!
Laurie Rufus

Low floor Dart SLFs to 10.6 metre length with Plaxton Pointer 2 bodywork form the DP class, and were introduced onto route R70 between Richmond and Hanworth in August 1998. The company has developed route branding into something of an art form, as can be seen in the photographs in this book. Many more SLFs are due to appear in 1999 in the Hounslow area, so many that the Mobility Bus network in the area is to be largely withdrawn. *Geoff Rixon*

London United's proximity to Heathrow Airport provides an opportunity to carry route branding for services to that important objective. The group of routes 555/6/7 between Heathrow and the Sunbury and Walton areas are serviced by both DRs and DRLs in this special livery. The 'London' shade of red at the front end subtly changes to a darker hue just aft of the front wheels. The small marker lights at the top corners of the bodywork are a feature of many modern buses, but appear in slightly different positions on different models of apparently similar buses.
Clydemaster Preservation Group

METROBUS

Metrobus Ltd, Oak Farm, Farnborough Hill, Green Street Green, Orpington, Kent, BR6 6DA

Following the collapse of the Orpington & District Bus Company in February 1981, operations were taken over by the Tillingbourne Bus Company from 2nd March 1981 and a local company was formed, Tillingbourne (Metropolitan) Ltd. Public confidence was soon restored and new routes were developed in the area between Orpington and Croydon on roads never before served by London Transport services. However, the routes were adopted into the LT network in 1985. Following a management-led buy out on 24th September 1983, Metrobus Ltd was born and has since gone from strength to strength. Further commercial routes were developed in the Bromley and Beckenham areas, and more LT contracts were won; other routes have been taken on when other operators surrendered them. During 1997, the buses and routes of East Surrey Buses of South Godstone were acquired, and further expansion took the company to Brighton and the south coast with another base at Lewes.

Bus routes operated on LT contract or with LT agreement are 64, 119, 138, 146, 161, 181, 233, 246, 261, 284, 320, 351, 352, 353, 354, 358, 359, 361, 464, 630, 654, 693. The fleet is in blue and yellow livery, and those for LT work are kept at Green Street Green, although those on routes 146, 246, 464 come from the South Godstone base. The fleet list in this book covers only the buses normally used on these services.

Metrobus has 62 Olympians based at Orpington, of three body styles, and they are fairly strictly allocated to certain routes. Nineteen of the Northern Counties Palatine I model operate on routes 261 and 320, whilst 28 East Lancs Pyoneers run on the 64 and 119, and 15 Leyland examples on the 161 and 353. Typifying the latter is No.803 pausing at Eltham Well Hall Station, which was re-sited a few years back and incorporates a new bus station after the A2 trunk road was rebuilt across its original site. *Colin Brown*

Opposite page: Similarly to First Capital in north London, Metrobus's success with LT tendering has caused a route and fleet expansion that shows no sign of abating. In the autumn of 1998 two routes (119 and 320) were gained from Selkent, and one of the new buses purchased for the 119 is seen here in Denning Avenue, Croydon. No.850 is one of the latest batch of East Lancs Pyoneers. *Geoff Rixon*

The Leyland Lynx is a rare type in the London area, with fewer than fifty even taking into account the country as well as the metropolitan areas of London. Metrobus has seven, only one of which was bought new, and they can usually be found on routes 354 and 359 on the very edges of south London. No.165 meanders through the leafy suburb of Selsdon on the local 359 introduced in 1998. *Colin Stannard*

Ten Optare Excels provide the main service on route 358, with No.507 pictured in the familiar surroundings of Bromley High Street. In recent years Metrobus has built up quite a network of services outside the formal LT contract system in the Bromley area, and every one has seen an expansion of traffic. Route 358 is no exception, with a limited operation building up to a 20-minute frequency between Orpington and Crystal Palace with low-floor modern buses. *Stephen Madden*

Formerly one of Kentish Bus's many LT routes in south-east London, route 181 was one of those services taken on by Metrobus when KB fell into difficulties on some of them. Recently, it has been upgraded to new low-floor Dart operation, evidenced here in the gloomy summer of 1998 by No.745 in Lewisham High Street. *Clydemaster Preservation Group*

Buses in Biggin Hill, once all green, have progressed through yellow and red to blue, with Metrobus now very much the major presence there. The service from Bromley to Westerham has firmly reverted to its 'country bus' form, and has been projected to Edenbridge. This is a town where Metrobus now has 90% of the bus market, typifying the company's expansion. Route 246 provides an LT service for half its length, and Dart No.759 wearing the East Surrey name, heads south through Biggin Hill with a good load aboard. *Colin Stannard*

METROLINE

Metroline Holdings plc (Metroline Travel and Metroline London Northern), 118–122 College Road, Harrow, Middlesex, HA1 1DB

Metroline Travel was purchased by a management-led team on 7th October 1994, taking 386 vehicles. Very soon afterwards, on 28th November 1994, Atlas Bus was acquired from the Pullmans Group, together with 26 Leyland Titans and route 52, these later moving to nearby Willesden garage. Metroline also purchased the coach fleet of Brent's of Watford, and these vehicles have subsequently moved to the re-opened former Atlas Bus base at Harlesden, which has also been used as a storage point for surplus buses. In June 1997, Metroline Holdings plc was floated on the Stock Exchange.

London Northern had been purchased by MTL Trust Holdings on 26th October 1994, taking 341 vehicles. The operations of London Suburban Bus, already owned by MTL, were absorbed on a staged basis up to June 1996. R&I Tours were taken over in October 1995, and absorbed into the MTL London fleet in June 1996. In August 1997 coaching operations in London were discontinued. In early 1998 MTL Trust Holdings intimated that all or part of its enterprise was to be sold, and eventually the London Northern business was sold to Metroline Holdings in summer 1998. Within a couple of months, the Highgate offices were closed and the whole combined operation was run from Harrow.

The bus livery is red with a blue skirt and the all-red MTL London fleet is being swiftly repainted to match. The fleet operates from garages at Cricklewood, Edgware, Harrow Weald, Holloway, North Acton, North Wembley, Potters Bar and Willesden. Vehicles of the Contract Services fleet are based at Cricklewood.

'To and from the West End' it says on the side, and so it plies. Metroline has also used its fleetname style to include slogans such as 'low floor bus' or 'contract services'. As with all London Routemaster operators, the livery has been adapted and on RML 2728 heading down the Edgware Road one can see the very thin blue skirt, compared with the usual much deeper version on other types. *Colin Brown*

Looking for all the world like an ordinary Metroline machine, Scania S 16 is one of the London Northern fleet newly repainted from all-over red to standard blue-skirt style. About one third of the ex-London Northern fleet had been so treated by the end of 1998, though a few classes had still to have any examples, and the Ms had been hardly touched. Metroline inherited several commercial services into or within Hertfordshire with the London Northern purchase, including the 84 at its southern terminus of New Barnet Station. *Colin Brown*

Other than a few in contract liveries, repaints to all-over red with MTL London names had progressed to within five of completing the entire stock, when Metroline took over in July 1998. The last major class to be treated under the former ownership was the DNL, several of which were in a special style for route C2. During the autumn of 1998 the MTL names were removed, pending new Metroline names; however so far these are not being applied until the blue skirts are added. At the end of 1998 over 200 buses were still running in plain all-over red. *Colin Brown*

New Dart SLFs were in the process of delivery to London Northern over the takeover period. DML 33-47 came in all-red and had the blue skirts added at Holloway garage, but DMS 13-29 were delivered already with blue skirts, albeit without fleetnames at the delivery stage. Very soon, all were decked in Metroline's corporate style, and earlier DMS and DML deliveries were retrospectively and speedily dealt with. Brent Cross is now a major meeting point of the two arms of Metroline, with seven of the eight garages sending buses there. DMS 19 departs on route 326 on 1st October 1998. *Colin Brown*

There are a large number of Metrobuses within Metroline's two arms, although many are now getting very old. It may be recalled that it was in this area, at Cricklewood garage, that Metrobus operation began twenty years earlier. M 109 in August 1998, then one of the garage's oldest and finest, departs from Brent Cross while substituting for a low-floor Dart which would normally be expected to be seen on route 189. *Colin Brown*

Below left: Metroline have a very large number of buses with 'super rear' adverts, in vinyl which covers the paintwork, and which can be easily removed or replaced. The somewhat alarming design on the rear of M 85 shows that it is difficult for following motorists to ignore. *Capital Transport*

Below right: Metroline's Contract Services, having inherited a number of Titans from an earlier purchase of Atlas Bus when route 52 was assumed, rather suprisingly continue to hang on to nine of them. Eight are in the Contract Services fleet which, apart from doing private hire and special work, operate a number of school services in the Watford area. On its way to perform such a duty, T 432 passes through Harrow. *Capital Transport*

Opposite page: Billed as the last standard-floor Volvo Olympians to be delivered to London – in fact, they were not, as First Capital and Sovereign had examples later in 1998 for LT services – they were indeed the last new ones to come to a former LBL company. Metroline took sixteen for route 16 and AV 33 traverses the Marble Arch roundabout in late September 1998, when brand new. *Colin Brown*

Route 186 was one of the first five low-floor routes in London in 1994, and the batch of Dennis Lances continue to operate their original service, as evidenced by LLW 31 in Edgware. The much larger expanse of blue on these vehicles is perhaps a little overpowering, and would provide a good platform for special branding. *Capital Transport*

Newly repainted into Metroline fleet colours, DRL 27 has had its appearance greatly enhanced from its former all-red MTL condition, a livery which tended to present a rather drab sight. Taken on Remembrance Day 11th November 1998, it was a sunny autumn day, and shows the vehicle to its sparkling best at Marble Arch. *Geoff Rixon*

Pointer-bodied Darts are a major type in the combined Metroline fleets, with over one hundred each of standard-floor or low-floor versions. Not only that, a fair number of the modified Pointer 2 design have recently been included. This view at Edgware shows, on the left, DL 83 – a low floor Pointer 2 and, on the right, EDR 32 – a standard floor ordinary Pointer, a picture rather like one of those 'spot the difference' puzzles in magazines. *Capital Transport*

SOVEREIGN

London Sovereign Ltd, Station Road, Borehamwood, Herts, WD6 1HB   Sovereign Buses (Harrow) Ltd, Babbage Road, Stevenage, Herts, SG1 2EQ

Sovereign Bus & Coach was established in January 1989, but now forms part of the Blazefield Group, set out into several small divisions. Sovereign Harrow was set up in December 1990 for locally-based LT contracts, and currently runs five minibus routes (H10, H11, H13, H17, 398) from the Venture garage at 331 Pinner Road, Harrow. The Harrow minibuses share the blue and cream livery with the main Sovereign operation in Hertfordshire.

Borehamwood Travel Services was formed from the fleet of C J Franklin of Borehamwood in August 1984. BTS ran LT route 292 from 1988 until November 1993, losing it to Metroline. They also gained the contract to operate crew route 13 (Golders Green to Aldwych) using RMLs leased from London Buses, and later the 114 using Olympians. Blazefield Holdings, the owners of Sovereign, acquired BTS in August 1994 and the trading name was changed from BTS to London Sovereign in September 1996. Buses on the 13 and 114 are in poppy red livery with yellow relief. Then route 292 was won back from 5th December 1998, and a fleet of Olympians in a new version of Sovereign blue and cream was bought for the route. The fleet is housed at Station Road, Borehamwood, but it is likely that it will move to Edgware during 1999 due to the sale of the site for housing.

Now carrying Sovereign fleet-names, the RMLs on route 13 still display their original operator's poppy-red and yellow livery. The BT garage code also gives this away as a bus from the former BTS of Borehamwood. Sovereign does not have enough opo double-deckers to work the evening and Sunday service and so Metroline London Northern cover the service at those times. RML 2598 passes through Trafalgar Square in April 1998. *Colin Lloyd*

Opposite page: Three Titans act as support to the main batch of Olympians that work route 114, although they are principally in the London Sovereign fleet for school routes in the Borehamwood area. Originally the former London fleet numbers were used, but T 620 became 720 in a numbering exercise by Sovereign in 1996, and it is seen at Ruislip Station in August 1998. *Colin Brown*

BTS of Borehamwood have operated the 292 route once before, but it was lost to Metroline. In a further round of tendering BTS's successor Sovereign won the route back, and introduced eight fine new Olympians on 5th December 1998. Due to the multiplicity of speed humps and tables along the route in Borehamwood, standard – rather than low-floor – buses were specified. The basic livery as applied to other parts of the Blazefield Group's empire at Huntingdon and for Yorkshire Coastliner is on these vehicles, coupled with bold route branding. No.63 is seen at Edgware. *Geoff Rixon*

Sovereign operate five minibus routes in the Harrow area, although the H17 was not one of their original operations, it having been first worked by R&I Buses. Mercedes-Benz No.413 is pictured in central Harrow. *Capital Transport*

SPEEDLINK

Speedlink Airport Services Ltd, Crawley and Heathrow.

A large operator of coach and contract services at all the London airports, there is just a brief mention here of the operation of six buses on an LT and British Airways joint contract route H30 at Heathrow Airport. Through the joint ownership within the National Express Group, initial vehicles are loaned from Travel West Midlands, although six dedicated buses should be on the route by spring 1999. The buses operate from the Armadale Road, North Feltham coach base.

Speedlink Airport Services are a large National Express Group subsidiary operating many coach, car park and hotel services centred on the various London airports. However, their first and so far only local bus service began on 1st November 1998 and is unusual in being free of charge. This is because it runs entirely within the Heathrow free-fare area as can hardly be missed if one looks along the side of the bus. The initial stock were six Volvo B6LEs from the large order presently going to fellow NEG company Travel West Midlands, hence the appearance of the TWM livery at Heathrow on No.644 on route H30, technically an LT contract service. *Colin Brown*

STAGECOACH EAST LONDON and SELKENT

East London Bus & Coach Co Ltd, 2-4 Clements Road, Ilford, Essex, IG1 1BA   South East London & Kent Bus Co Ltd, 180 Bromley Road, London, SE26 2XA

East London was purchased by Stagecoach Holdings on 6th September 1994, taking 595 vehicles, and Selkent on the same date, with 414 vehicles. Major fleet updating has continued since acquisition, with around 500 new and acquired buses replacing older types. Stagecoach has actively cascaded these older vehicles to other UK subsidiaries. In July 1997 East London took over control of Docklands Transit following its purchase by Stagecoach Holdings, and full integration took place in October 1997. The fleet shares a common fleet numbering system and operates from East London garages at Barking, Bow, Leyton, Romford, Stratford and Upton Park, and Selkent garages at Bromley, Catford and Plumstead.

The two Stagecoach fleets in London are combined for our photographic coverage, as the all-red livery is the same. There is a combined fleet numbering, several classes are common to both fleets, and buses are often transferred as route requirements dictate. Our first picture however immediately confounds all those statements, as East London maintains RMC 1461 restored to its original 1962 Green Line condition. It is part of the operational fleet and turns out most days on route 15, seen here at Charing Cross in June 1998.
Stephen Madden

Even Stagecoach, with its predilection for standard liveries throughout the country, is sympathetic to the Routemaster, with cream relief and gold fleetnames and numbers. Four standard RMs were added recently to support the fleet of RMLs, which are to be found on trunk routes 8 and 15. One such, RM 1289, was found in Regent Street in September 1998. *Laurie Rufus*

All of Stagecoach's Scania double deckers are with East London, the majority of them at Upton Park garage, and all except eight Alexander-bodied examples carry Northern Counties bodywork. A few did operate from Leyton garage for a while and S 63 was caught in Walthamstow on that garage's 69 route, otherwise a Titan stronghold. *Colin Stannard*

The standard Titan is still very numerous with both East London and Selkent, but is diminishing fairly rapidly. Many buses that had been earmarked for transfer onward to other UK Stagecoach subsidiaries were converted from dual-door to single door configuration. T 1099 is one such, converted in February 1998 but still in London stock at the end of the year. It performs on route 160 in Sidcup, a route which during 1998 seemed to be regarded as a 'buffer zone' for type changes. *Laurie Rufus*

Opposite page: The recent enormous intake of Volvo Olympians was split between Alexander (VA) or Northern Counties (VN) bodywork. The largest contingent of VAs is at Bow garage, used with a smaller number of VNs on routes 25, 26, 277 and D7, as well as the 8 on Sundays. VA 70 heads toward Bank junction in the City on the 26 – this section was once the eastern end of the traditional Number Six service, one of those cross-London services split some years ago.
Capital Transport

Above: VN 32 at Old Ford has just come round three-and-a-half sides of a square to avoid the low bridge (the sign says 13ft 6in, still too low for these low-height Olympians) between this point and its base at Bow garage. This is not the only London company that has Northern Counties blind-boxes that are just too small for the standard London bus blind display, although in this example someone has taken great care to get the display as close as possible to the edges.
Colin Stannard

Selkent has a large contingent of the former LBL ECW-bodied Olympians, at both Plumstead and Catford garages and used indiscriminately on all double deck routes from those garages. Although principally meant to be in the hands of the later N-registered Olympians shown in the picture on the right, route 53 still sees the occasional older example, as evidenced by L 42 in June 1998.
Stephen Madden

The principal fare on route 53 are the 301-352 batch of Olympians, introduced in 1995. Unusually, this introduction was not a product of LT tendering, but was a Stagecoach initiative to upgrade the profile of this major trunk route. However, proposals now exist to split what is currently one of London's longest bus routes. No.351 passes the National Gallery in June 1998.
Stephen Madden

The early 1990s saw the development of several new single deck bus types, but none of them ever really caught on in the London market, being eclipsed by the all-conquering Dennis Dart. East London had a batch of DAF SB220/ Optare Deltas and these have always been employed on routes in the Ilford area, nowadays mainly on the 145 and 169. The blinds on these buses tend to be set back a little, sometimes making the number blind unclear from the offside – so here is a nearside view of DA 32 in Ilford town centre.
Capital Transport

The Dennis Lance was also tried out, Selkent receiving twelve with Plaxton Verde bodywork in 1994. Although switched around between several routes, they have now found a good home on the busy but short route 227, which passes under a low bridge at Shortlands station. This home was found after Kentish Bus gave up the route in November 1997.
Philip Wallis

The Alexander Dash bodied Dart is rapidly leaving the Stagecoach London fleets for pastures new in the provinces. Those with East London had DAL class letters, those with Selkent had none, being in the 6xx series. Selkent has helped out London Transport on seven routes in the latter half of 1998, as other operators were unable to provide a service. One such example gives the bizarre sight of 'DAL' number 628 from Plumstead garage, in far-away territory on route 127 between Purley and Tooting. This service was due to pass to the more local Mitcham Belle early in 1999, and this bus to Oxford. *Colin Stannard*

There are DRLs and PDs in both fleets, but they are basically the same – standard Pointer bodied Darts. Some of those classified PD came from Docklands Minibus and from Stagecoach Oxford, while others were bought new. The batch of eighteen (PD 1-18) delivered in October 1997 for route 106 were the last standard-floor Darts delivered new to London companies, and PD 14 is seen in Stoke Newington six months later. *Colin Lloyd*

The SLD class of Alexander ALX200 bodied Dart SLFs has expanded rapidly since the first examples came in September 1996, with short and long, single- and dual-doored versions. Both East London and Selkent have adopted the design as their standard single deck bus. The first batch within Selkent was used to upgrade route 314 from MetroRiders, although they are also to be found on routes 160, 162 and P4. SLD 27 is at Bromley North in October 1998. *Colin Lloyd*

East London run a daily express service between Liverpool Street Station and the City Airport via Canary Wharf, now using these blue liveried Dart SLFs, which are essentially similar to the SLDs other than the livery. The route had been pioneered by D&J International of Barking, who folded early in 1997, Stagecoach taking over at very short notice. The class code of LCY is derived from the international air industry code for London City Airport, and the allocation on the route has gradually been increased from three to ten buses. *Capital Transport*

Relatively few minibuses exist nowadays in any of the London bus fleets, so the delivery of eighteen Mercedes-Benz Varios to Selkent in the last months of 1997 was a relative surprise. They were needed to replace older MetroRiders which were then swiftly sold onward after only about seven years service. These buses can normally be found on routes 273,380 and 386 in south east London, like MB 12 here turning at Blackheath village. *Colin Stannard*

A batch of 98 Dennis Trident low floor double deckers with Alexander ALX400 bodywork started to be delivered in the early part of 1999. The first examples were for Leyton garage (routes 48,55,56), and others were to follow for Barking (5) and Upton Park (115 formerly 15B), causing a cascading of older (Titan) and not-so-older (VN) buses to other garages. *Colin Lloyd*

TELLINGS-GOLDEN MILLER

Tellings-Golden Miller Ltd, 20A Wintersells Road, Byfleet, Surrey, KT14 7LF

In June 1985, Tellings Coaches of Byfleet took control of the stage carriage operations of Golden Miller of Feltham, and their bus routes continued to be worked for a few years. Eventually, the two businesses were merged, and the LT contracts for bus routes 116 and 117 were won, but after a difficult period, the routes were soon re-assigned to London & Country who ran them for a few more years. The Company returned to LT tendered work with new midibus route S3 in the Sutton area from April 1995. Further successes astride or just over the border in Surrey have seen several more routes gained, and routes 471, 511, 512, 513, 561, 564 are currently worked for Surrey county council, together with services for students at the various Kingston University campuses. LT route 235 was assumed from January 1998. Fleet livery is blue and white with yellow relief, and vehicles are garaged at Wintersells Road, Byfleet.

Tellings-Golden Miller present a most professional image on their smartly turned-out vehicles, and have been successful during the last year in gaining contracts from both LT and Surrey county council. Services 511/512/513 run between Kingston and points in Surrey on contract to Surrey but with LT agreement and ticket availability within London. Varios are the normal type on these routes and suitably branded P701LCF leaves Kingston in September 1998. *Stephen Madden*

Opposite page: The first fourteen Dart SLFs were introduced in January 1998 onto former London United service 235, won on LT tender by Tellings-Golden Miller. As with so many similar alterations, these buses significantly improved the lot of the passengers over the old Metrobuses they replaced. More similar Dart SLFs have been added to cover contract services for Kingston University and Surrey county council, these later examples being to the revised Pointer 2 frontal design. *Stephen Madden*

THAMESWAY

Essex Buses Ltd, Stapleford Close, New Writtle Street, Chelmsford, Essex, CM2 0SD

In July 1990 the LT routes and other western operations of Eastern National passed to the new Thamesway company, and subsequently the LT operations were expanded. This resulted in the arrival of many new Mercedes-Benz minibuses and Dennis Darts. From 1st December 1995 the Company was re-united with Eastern National to become Essex Buses Ltd, but both retained their individual names, and both are part of FirstGroup. Once Capital Citybus had passed to FirstGroup in July 1998, Capital almost immediately took on the operational control of Thamesway's LT routes and, within three months also took over most of the vehicles. The only ordinary LT contract route now operated by Thamesway in its own right is the 193 from the new Romford depot at Bryant Avenue, Harold Wood, while Basildon depot continue to run Mobility Bus routes 951-959,961.

Thamesway passed over the majority of its LT contracted work to First Capital during 1998, largely retracting to the more traditional territory of Essex. However just one LT route (193) was retained in Romford, together with a set of Mobility Bus services in the same area. The only fully contracted LT bus service that goes all the way out to the Lakeside shopping centre in Thurrock is the Friday only 957, and Thamesway's Marshall-bodied Dart No.853 parks up there while its customers, some of whom will be disabled, enjoy the shopping facilities. *Malcolm King*

THORPE'S

F E Thorpe & Sons Ltd, 272 Latimer Road, North Kensington, London, W10 6QY

Frank E Thorpe & Sons Ltd started as a small private coach company back in 1968, with a fleet of coaches and minibuses on private hire, school and local authority contracts. The company moved into LT work in October 1992 with the winning of the central London inter-station route, marketed as Stationlink. The route was originally run with three Optare City Pacers, but when the circular route was retained upon re-tender, new low floor wheelchair-accessible vehicles were specified and new Optare Excels were bought, the first of the type to appear on the streets of London. LT minibus route C4 (Putney Pier to Hurlingham) was gained from April 1995, and in August 1997 Thorpe took over the LT contracts of Javelin Coaches, Wandsworth with a large group of Mobility Bus routes in west and south west London. Something of a coup was the assumption of route 210 in September 1998 for which new Dart SLFs have been obtained. Vehicles carry red and yellow livery, and a new larger operating base at Unit 5, Fourth Way on the Wembley Stadium trading estate houses the LT bus fleet.

A most useful service for anyone with any disability needing to cross London is the Stationlink service. It connects all the main line stations, running hourly in each direction around a wide loop, and avoids having to use the Underground, which can be totally inaccessible to some people. Optare Excel N100FET on the clockwise SL1 is en route from Victoria to Paddington in this view at Marble Arch in September 1998. *Colin Brown*

Above and Opposite page: Thorpe's have been well known for their expertise in fully accessible services, and were successful in winning their first important London bus service, taking over the 210 (Brent Cross & Finsbury Park) from 26th September 1998. The buses used are dual-doored Dart SLFs, also fully accessible; they have introduced a striking new colour scheme, working from a new base near Wembley Stadium. They are also the first buses in the fleet to have fleet numbers, this feature and a variation of the livery being extended to some Mercedes-Benz minibuses in the fleet. Two first day views here depict DLF 29 at Brent Cross and DLF 40 leaving the photographer behind on Hampstead Heath. *Colin Brown, Geoff Rixon*

TRAVEL LONDON

Travel London, Stewarts Lane rail depot, off Dickens Lane, London SW8 3EP.

Travel London is the trading name of Travel West Midlands in London, part of the National Express Group. They won two LT contract routes, C1 and 211, which were taken up in June 1998. New Optare Excels ran the 211 from the start, but new Optare Solos for the C1 were not delivered until the very end of the year, with Volvo B6LEs from TWM helping out in the meantime.

Central London routes C1 and 211 were offered for tender and won by Travel London in June 1998. Both had been London General services, although the C1 had been temporarily worked by Metrobus and Selkent for a few months due to staff shortages at General. Travel London is the London name for the parent Travel West Midlands, and the similarity of livery can be seen, albeit with the colours reversed to make the red the prominent colour. An unusual feature is the garage location, at the Gatwick Express railway depot – both GE and TWM are part of the same National Express Group. Short-length Optare Excel 415 works the frequent 211 in August 1998. *Stephen Madden*

The first user in the London area of the Optare Solo, the first truly low-floor midibus, is Travel London. Ten had been ordered early in 1998 for route C1 (Victoria & Kensington) but it was December before they had been delivered. In the meantime Travel London had used ten Volvo B6LEs from the West Midlands, similar to the example pictured earlier in this book with Speedlink. S240EWU is seen at Sloane Square in January 1999. *Philip Wallis*

FLEET LISTS

Standard body codes are used in the following fleet lists, showing the body type, seating capacity and entrance position in that order.

Body Type

Single-deck bus	B
Single-deck coach	C
Convertible open-top double-deck bus	CO
Dual-purpose vehicle	DP
Dual-purpose double-deck vehicle	DPH
Highbridge double-deck bus	H
Open-top double-deck bus	O
Partial open-top double-deck bus	PO

The further prefix 'F' is used for full-fronted vehicles where this is not normal for the type.

Seating capacity

For double-deckers the upper-deck capacity is shown first, followed by that for the lower deck. Standee capacities have not been shown as there are sometimes local variations between the licensed capacity of a vehicle and the operational capacity agreed with road staff.

Entrance position

Separate entrance and exit (front and centre) with doors	D
Front entrance with platform doors	F
Rear entrance without doors	R
Rear entrance with platform doors	RD

The further suffix 'L' indicates a vehicle fitted with a wheelchair tail-lift. 'T' indicates a vehicle which contains a toilet compartment. '+' indicates a vehicle fitted with an offside door.

Fleet number suffixes

Vehicle restricted to staff bus duties	s
Vehicle restricted to training work	t
Vehicle unlicensed long-term	u
Withdrawn	w

ARMCHAIR (Bus Fleet)

MUH289Xt	Leyland Olympian ONLXB/1R			Eastern Coach Works		H45/32F	1982	Ex Rhondda, 1995	
G361-372YUR	Leyland Olympian ONCL10/1RZ			Alexander RL		H47/30F	1990		
G361YUR	G363YUR	G365YUR		G368YUR	G370YUR			G372YUR	
G362YUR	G364YUR	G366YUR		G369YUR	G371YUR				
H546-563GKX	Leyland Olympian ON2R50C13Z4			Leyland		H47/31F	1991		
H546GKX	H549GKX	H552GKX		H556GKX	H559GKX			H563GKX	
H547GKX	H550GKX	H553GKX		H557GKX	H561GKX			H564GKX	
H548GKX	H551GKX	H554GKX		H558GKX	H562GKX				
P27-35MLE	Dennis Dart SFD412BR5TGD1			Plaxton Pointer 9.8m		B37F	1996		
P27MLE	P28MLE	P29MLE		P31MLE	P32MLE			P34MLE	P35MLE
P154-160 MLE	Dennis Dart SFD412BR5TGD1			Plaxton Pointer 9.8m		B37F	1996		
P154MLE	P156MLE	P157MLE		P158MLE	P159MLE			P160MLE	
P675-699RWU	Dennis Dart SLF SFD212BR1			Plaxton Pointer 10.0m		B35F	1997		
P675RWU	P679RWU	P683RWU		P687RWU	P691RWU			P695RWU	P699RWU
P676RWU	P680RWU	P684RWU		P688RWU	P692RWU			P696RWU	
P677RWU	P681RWU	P685RWU		P689RWU	P693RWU			P697RWU	
P678RWU	P682RWU	P686RWU		P690RWU	P694RWU			P698RWU	
R417-782SOY	Volvo Olympian OLY-4953			Northern Counties Palatine II		H47/29F	1997/8		
R417SOY	R418SOY	R419SOY		R420SOY	R780SOY			R781SOY	R782SOY

Vehicles listed below are those most likely to appear on LT supported services. Additional vehicles of similar types will be seen on peripheral routes in the Waltham Cross, Loughton and Romford areas.

2287-2318			Mercedes-Benz 709D			Reeve Burgess Beaver*		B23F	1989-92		*2313-8 are Plaxton Beaver
2287	G927WGS	2290	G930WGS	2299	G919UPP	2311	G926WGS	2314	J934WHJ	2317	J937WHJ
2288	G928WGS	2291	G931WGS	2309	G924WGS	2312	G932WGS	2315	J935WHJ	2318	J938WHJ
2289	G929WGS	2298	G918UPP	2310	G925WGS	2313	J933WHJ	2316	J936WHJ		

3404-14			Dennis Dart SFD212			Plaxton Pointer 9m		B34F	1996		
3404	P324HVX	3406	P326HVX	3408	P328HVX	3410	P330HVX	3412	P332HVX	3414	P334HVX
3405	P325HVX	3407	P327HVX	3409	P329HVX	3411	P331HVX	3413	P833HVX		

3419-31			Dennis Dart SLF SFD322BR1			Plaxton Pointer 10.8m		B43F	1996		* on loan to Arriva Colchester
3419*	P419HVX	3421	P421HVX	3423	P423HVX	3425	P425HVX	3427	P427HVX	3429	P429HVX	3431	P431HVX
3420*	P420HVX	3422*	P422HVX	3424	P424HVX	3426	P426HVX	3428	P428HVX	3430*	P430HVX		

4335-39			DAF SB220LC550			Ikarus Citibus		B48F	1992		Ex Grey-Green, 1997
4335	J56GCX	4336	J926CYL	4337	J927CYL	4339	K124TCP				

5349	GYE419W	MCW Metrobus DR101/12	MCW	H43/28D	1980	Ex Arriva London, 1998
5351	GBU1V	MCW Metrobus DR101/6	MCW	H43/30F	1979	Ex Leaside, 1997
5353	GYE493W	MCW Metrobus DR101/12	MCW	H43/28D	1980	Ex Arriva London, 1998
5354	GBU4V	MCW Metrobus DR101/6	MCW	H43/30F	1979	Ex Leaside, 1997
5355	GBU5V	MCW Metrobus DR101/6	MCW	H43/30F	1979	Ex Leaside, 1997
5358	GBU8V	MCW Metrobus DR101/6	MCW	H43/30F	1979	Ex Leaside, 1997
5359	GBU9V	MCW Metrobus DR101/6	MCW	H43/30F	1979	Ex Leaside, 1997
5362	BYX232V	MCW Metrobus DR101/12	MCW	H43/28D	1980	Ex Arriva London, 1998
53xx	BYX233V	MCW Metrobus DR101/12	MCW	H43/28D	1980	Ex Arriva London, 1998
5368	BYX208V	MCW Metrobus DR101/12	MCW	H43/28D	1980	Ex Arriva London, 1998

5374-83			Leyland Olympian ONTL11/1R			Roe		H43/29F	1982		Ex LCNE, 1989
5374	TPD104X	5377	TPD107X	5380	TPD110X	5382	TPD115X	5383	TPD123X		

M 233	BYX233V	MCW Metrobus DR101/12	MCW	H43/28D	1980	Ex Arriva London, 1998

On order:

4 Dennis Dart SLF/ Plaxton Pointer

ARRIVA SERVING THE SHIRES

Vehicles listed below are those normally used on routes 142, 340 and 350.

2171-2198		Mercedes-Benz O814 Vario			Plaxton Beaver 2			B27F*	1997/8	*2196-98 are B31F
2171	R171VBM	**2173**	R173VBM	**2175**	R175VBM	**2197**	R197DNM			
2172	R172VBM	**2174**	R174VBM	**2196**	R196DNM	**2198**	R198DNM			

5077-82		Leyland Olympian ONTL11/1R		Eastern Coach Works		H43/29F	1985	Ex LCNW, 1990
5077	B273LPH	**5080**	B270LPH	**5082**	B272LPH			

5111-25		Leyland Olympian ONCL10/1RZ		Leyland				H47/31F	1989/90	Ex LCNW, 1990
5111	G281UMJ	**5114**	G284UMJ	**5117**	G287UMJ	**5120**	G290UMJ	**5123**	G293UMJ	
5112	G282UMJ	**5115**	G285UMJ	**5118**	G288UMJ	**5121**	G291UMJ	**5124**	G294UMJ	
5113	G283UMJ	**5116**	G286UMJ	**5119**	G289UMJ	**5122**	G292UMJ	**5125**	G295UMJ	

5126-33		Leyland Olympian ON2R50C13Z4		Leyland				H47/29F	1991	
5126	H196GRO	**5127**	H197GRO	**5128**	H198GRO	**5129**	H199GRO	**5132**	H202GRO	**5133** H203GRO

ARRIVA SERVING LONDON (Arriva London North [including Leaside Travel], London North East and London South)

BOV 595†	G545JOG	Bova FHD12-280		Bova Futura		C46FT	1990	Ex Arriva EH & E, 1998
BOV 596†	JIW3696	Bova FHD12-290		Bova Futura		C47FT	1988	Ex Arriva EH & E, 1998

DBS 1-13		DAF DB250RS505*		Northern Counties Palatine II		H47/30F	1995	*(DBS12 & 13 are DE02RSDB250)	
DBS 1	N601DWY	**DBS 3**	N603DWY	**DBS 5**	N605DWY	**DBS 7**	N607DWY	**DBS 9** N609DWY	**DBS 11** N611DWY	**DBS 13** N613DWY
DBS 2	N602DWY	**DBS 4**	N604DWY	**DBS 6**	N606DWY	**DBS 8**	N608DWY	**DBS 10** N610DWY	**DBS 12** N612DWY	

DDL 1-18		Dennis Dart SLF SFD212		Plaxton Pointer 2 10m		B26D	1998	
DDL 1	S301JUA	**DDL 4**	S304JUA	**DDL 7**	S307JUA	**DDL 10** S310JUA	**DDL 13** S313JUA	**DDL 16** S316JUA
DDL 2	S302JUA	**DDL 5**	S305JUA	**DDL 8**	S308JUA	**DDL 11** S311JUA	**DDL 14** S314JUA	**DDL 17** S317JUA
DDL 3	S303JUA	**DDL 6**	S306JUA	**DDL 9**	S309JUA	**DDL 12** S312JUA	**DDL 15** S315JUA	**DDL 18** S318JUA

† Leaside Travel vehicle

DI 4†	P754RWU	DAF DE33WSSB3000	Ikarus 396	C53F	1997	Ex Arriva EH & E, 1998
DIB 1	J929CYL	DAF SB220LC550	Ikarus Citibus	B48F	1992	Ex County Bus, 1997
DIB 2	J930CYL	DAF SB220LC550	Ikarus Citibus	B48F	1992	Ex Grey-Green, 1997
DIB 3	J931CYL	DAF SB220LC550	Ikarus Citibus	B48F	1992	Ex Grey-Green, 1997
DIB 4	J413NCP	DAF SB220LC550	Ikarus Citibus	B48F	1992	Ex Birmingham Omnibus, Tividale, 1997
DIB 5	J414NCP	DAF SB220LC550	Ikarus Citibus	B48F	1992	Ex Birmingham Omnibus, Tividale, 1997

DLA 1-89		DAF DB02RSSB250LF	Alexander ALX 400	H45/19D	1998/9

This class of vehicles will be allocated to all three London fleets during 1999 and will be numbered in the same sequence irrespective of operator.

DLA 1	R101GNW	DLA 14	S214JUA	DLA 27	S227JUA	DLA 40 S240JUA
DLA 2	S202JUA	DLA 15	S215JUA	DLA 28	S228JUA	DLA 41 S241JUA
DLA 3	S203JUA	DLA 16	S216JUA	DLA 29	S229JUA	DLA 42 S242JUA
DLA 4	S204JUA	DLA 17	S217JUA	DLA 30	S230JUA	DLA 43 S243JUA
DLA 5	S205JUA	DLA 18	S218JUA	DLA 31	S231JUA	DLA 44 S244JUA
DLA 6	S206JUA	DLA 19	S219JUA	DLA 32	S232JUA	DLA 45 S245JUA
DLA 7	S207JUA	DLA 20	S220JUA	DLA 33	S233JUA	DLA 46 S246JUA
DLA 8	S208JUA	DLA 21	S221JUA	DLA 34	S234JUA	DLA 47 S247JUA
DLA 9	S209JUA	DLA 22	S322JUA	DLA 35	S235JUA	DLA 48 S248JUA
DLA 10	S210JUA	DLA 23	S223JUA	DLA 36	S236JUA	DLA 49 S249JUA
DLA 11	S211JUA	DLA 24	S224JUA	DLA 37	S237JUA	DLA 50 S250JUA
DLA 12	S212JUA	DLA 25	S225JUA	DLA 38	S238JUA	DLA 51
DLA 13	S213JUA	DLA 26	S226JUA	DLA 39	S239JUA	DLA 52

DLA 53, DLA 54, DLA 55, DLA 56, DLA 57, DLA 58, DLA 59, DLA 60, DLA 61, DLA 62, DLA 63, DLA 64, DLA 65
DLA 66, DLA 67, DLA 68, DLA 69, DLA 70, DLA 71, DLA 72, DLA 73, DLA 74, DLA 75, DLA 76, DLA 77, DLA 78
DLA 79, DLA 80, DLA 81, DLA 82, DLA 83, DLA 84, DLA 85, DLA 86, DLA 87, DLA 88, DLA 89

DLP 1	R151GNW	DAF DE02GSSB220	Plaxton Prestige 12m	B32DL	1998	
DLP 2	R152GNW	DAF DE02GSSB220	Plaxton Prestige 12m	B32DL	1998	
DLP 3	R153GNW	DAF DE02GSSB220	Plaxton Prestige 12m	B32DL	1998	
DP 3†	P753RWU	DAF DE33WSSB3000	Plaxton Premiere 350	C53F	1997	Ex Arriva EH & E, 1998

DP 301-313		Dennis Dart 9SDL3002/3011	Plaxton Pointer 9.0m	B35F	1991	Ex Arriva EH & E, 1998

DP 301	J301WHJ	DP 303	J303WHJ	DP 305	J305WHJ	DP 307	J307WHJ
DP 302	J302WHJ	DP 304	J304WHJ	DP 306	J306WHJ	DP 308	J308WHJ

DP 309 J309WHJ, DP 311 J311WHJ, DP 313 J313WHJ
DP 310 J310WHJ, DP 312 J312WHJ

DPL 1†	N551LUA	DAF DE33WSSB3000	Plaxton Premiere 350	C49FT	1996	Ex Arriva EH & E, 1998
DPL 2†	N552LUA	DAF DE33WSSB3000	Plaxton Premiere 350	C49FT	1996	Ex Arriva EH & E, 1998

DPP 416-431		Dennis Dart SLF SFD212BR1VGW1	Plaxton Pointer 10.0m	B36F	1997	Ex Arriva EH & E, 1998

DPP 416	R416COO	DPP 419	R419COO	DPP 422	R422COO	DPP 425 R425COO
DPP 417	R417COO	DPP 420	R420COO	DPP 423	R423COO	DPP 426 R426COO
DPP 418	R418COO	DPP 421	R421COO	DPP 424	R424COO	DPP 427 R427COO

DPP 428 R428COO, DPP 431 R431COO
DPP 429 R429COO
DPP 430 R430COO

† Leaside Travel vehicle

DR 20-31 Dennis Dart 8.5SDL3003 Plaxton Pointer 8.5m B28F 1991

DR 20	H120THE	DR 22	H122THE	DR 24	H124THE	DR 26	H126THE	DR 28	H128THE	DR 30	H130THE
DR 21	H621TKU	DR 23	H123THE	DR 25	H125THE	DR 27	H127THE	DR 29	H129THE	DR 31	H131THE

DRL 38-52 Dennis Dart 9SDL3016 Plaxton Pointer 9m B34F 1992

DRL 38	K538ORH	DRL 41	K541ORH	DRL 44	K544ORH	DRL 47	K547ORH	DRL 50	K550ORH
DRL 39	K539ORH	DRL 42	K542ORH	DRL 45	K545ORH	DRL 48	K548ORH	DRL 51	K551ORH
DRL 40	K540ORH	DRL 43	K543ORH	DRL 46	K546ORH'	DRL 49	K549ORH	DRL 52	K552ORH

DRL 147-158 Dennis Dart 9SDL3024 Plaxton Pointer 9m B34F 1993

DRL 147	L247WAG	DRL 149	L149WAG	DRL 151	L151WAG	DRL 153	L153WAG	DRL 155	L155WAG	DRL 157	L157WAG
DRL 148	L148WAG	DRL 150	L150WAG	DRL 152	L152WAG	DRL 154	L154WAG	DRL 156	L156WAG	DRL 158	L158WAG

DRL 210-212 Dennis Dart 9SDL3053 Plaxton Pointer 9m B34F 1995

DRL 210	N710GUM	DRL 211	N711GUM	DRL 212	N712GUM

DRL 213-218 Dennis Dart SLF SFD212BR5TGD1 Plaxton Pointer 9.2m B34F 1996

DRL 213	P913PWW	DRL 214	P914PWW	DRL 215	P915PWW	DRL 216	P916PWW	DRL 217	P917PWW	DRL 218	P918PWW

DRN 115-119 Dennis Dart 9SDL3034 Northern Counties Paladin 9m B35F 1994

DRN 115	L115YVK	DRN 116	L116YVK	DRN 117	L117YVK	DRN 118	L118YVK	DRN 119	L119YVK

DT 58-143 Dennis Dart 8.5SDL3003 Carlyle Dartline 8.5m B28F 1990 (132 & 143 ex Metroline, 1997)

DT 58	H458UGO	DT 61	H461UGO	DT 64	H464UGO	DT 67	H467UGO	DT 70	H470UGO
DT 59	H459UGO	DT 62	H462UGO	DT 65	H465UGO	DT 68	H468UGO	DT 132	H132MOB
DT 60	H460UGO	DT 63	H463UGO	DT 66	H466UGO	DT 69	H469UGO	DT 143	H143MOB

DVH 5†	G905TYR	DAF MB230LB615	Van Hool Alizee H	C53F	1990	Ex Arriva London North East, 1998
DVH 6†	G906TYR	DAF MB230LB615	Van Hool Alizee H	C53F	1990	Ex Arriva London North East, 1998
DVH 7†	G907TYR	DAF MB230LB615	Van Hool Alizee H	C49FT	1990	Ex Arriva London North East, 1998
DVH 8†	G908TYR	DAF MB230LB615	Van Hool Alizee H	C49FT	1990	Ex Arriva London North East, 1998
DW 314	J314XVX	Dennis Dart 9SDL3011	Wright Handybus 9m	B35F	1992	Ex Arriva EH & E, 1998
DW 315	J315XVX	Dennis Dart 9SDL3011	Wright Handybus 9m	B35F	1992	Ex Arriva EH & E, 1998
L 1	A101SYE	Leyland Olympian ONTL11/1R	Eastern Coach Works	H47/28D	1984	Ex London Buses, 1994
L 2	A102SYE	Leyland Olympian ONLXB/1R	Eastern Coach Works	H47/28D	1984	Ex London Buses, 1994
L 3	A103SYE	Leyland Olympian ONLXB/1R	Eastern Coach Works	H47/28D	1984	Ex London Buses, 1994

† Leaside Travel vehicle

L 4-259 — Leyland Olympian ONLXB/1RH — Eastern Coach Works — *H42/26D — 1986-7 — Ex London Buses, 1994 *166-171 DPH42/26D

L 4	C804BYY	L 45	C45CHM	L 148	D148FYM	L 171	D171FYM	L 194	D194FYM	L 217	217CLT	L 240	D240FYM
L 5	C805BYY	L 46	C46CHM	L 149	D149FYM	L 172	WLT372	L 195	D195FYM	L 218	D218FYM	L 241	D241FYM
L 6	C806BYY	L 47	VLT47	L 150	D150FYM	L 173	VLT173	L 196	D196FYM	L 219	519CLT	L 242	D242FYM
L 8	WLT807	L 49	C49CHM	L 151	WLT751	L 174	D174FYM	L 197	D197FYM	L 220	D220FYM	L 243	D243FYM
L 13	VLT13	L 50	C50CHM	L 152	D152FYM	L 175	D175FYM	L 198	D198FYM	L 221	D221FYM	L 244	VLT244
L 14	C814BYY	L 52	C52CHM	L 153	D153FYM	L 176	D176FYM	L 199	D199FYM	L 222	D222FYM	L 245	D245FYM
L 16	WLT916	L 56	C56CHM	L 154	WLT554	L 177	D177FYM	L 200	D200FYM	L 223	D223FYM	L 246	D246FYM
L 17	C817BYY	L 58	C58CHM	L 155	D155FYM	L 178	D178FYM	L 201	D201FYM	L 224	D224FYM	L 247	D247FYM
L 20	C820BYY	L 59	C59CHM	L 156	656DYE	L 179	D179FYM	L 202	D202FYM	L 225	D225FYM	L 248	D248FYM
L 21	C21CHM	L 63	C63CHM	L 157	D157FYM	L 180	480CLT	L 203	D203FYM	L 226	D226FYM	L 249	D249FYM
L 22	C22CHM	L 65	C65CHM	L 158	D158FYM	L 181	D181FYM	L 204	D204FYM	L 227	D227FYM	L 250	D250FYM
L 24	C24CHM	L 66	C66CHM	L 159	D159FYM	L 182	D182FYM	L 205	D205FYM	L 228	D228FYM	L 251	D251FYM
L 25	C25CHM	L 78	C78CHM	L 160	D160FYM	L 183	D183FYM	L 206	D206FYM	L 229	D229FYM	L 252	D252FYM
L 26	C26CHM	L 79	C79CHM	L 161	D161FYM	L 184	D184FYM	L 207	D207FYM	L 230	D230FYM	L 253	D253FYM
L 27	VLT27	L 99	C99CHM	L 162	D162FYM	L 185	D185FYM	L 208	D208FYM	L 231	D231FYM	L 254	D254FYM
L 31	C31CHM	L 102	C102CHM	L 163	D163FYM	L 186	D186FYM	L 209	D209FYM	L 232	D232FYM	L 255	D255FYM
L 32	C32CHM	L 113	C113CHM	L 164	D164FYM	L 187	D187FYM	L 210	D210FYM	L 233	D233FYM	L 256	D256FYM
L 33	330CLT	L 135	D135FYM	L 165	D165FYM	L 188	D188FYM	L 211	D211FYM	L 234	D234FYM	L 257	D257FYM
L 35	C35CHM	L 139	D139FYM	L 166	D166FYM	L 189	D189FYM	L 212	D212FYM	L 235	D235FYM	L 258	D258FYM
L 36	C36CHM	L 140	D140FYM	L 167	D167FYM	L 190	319CLT	L 213	D213FYM	L 236	D236FYM	L 259	D259FYM
L 37	C37CHM	L 143	D143FYM	L 168	D168FYM	L 191	D191FYM	L 214	D214FYM	L 237	D237FYM		
L 38	C38CHM	L 146	D146FYM	L 169	D169FYM	L 192	D192FYM	L 215	815DYE	L 238	D238FYM		
L 41	C41CHM	L 147	D147FYM	L 170	7CLT	L 193	D193FYM	L 216	D216FYM	L 239	D239FYM		

L 315-354 — Leyland Olympian ON2R50C13Z4 — Alexander RH — H43/25D — 1992 — Ex London Buses, 1994

L 315	J315BSH	L 321	J321BSH	L 327	J327BSH	L 333	J433BSH	L 339	J339BSH	L 345	J345BSH	L 351	J351BSH
L 316	J316BSH	L 322	J322BSH	L 328	J328BSH	L 334	J334BSH	L 340	J340BSH	L 346	J346BSH	L 352	J352BSH
L 317	J317BSH	L 323	J323BSH	L 329	J329BSH	L 335	J335BSH	L 341	J341BSH	L 347	J347BSH	L 353	J353BSH
L 318	J318BSH	L 324	J324BSH	L 330	J330BSH	L 336	J336BSH	L 342	J342BSH	L 348	J348BSH	L 354	VLT32
L 319	J319BSH	L 325	J325BSH	L 331	J331BSH	L 337	J337BSH	L 343	J343BSH	L 349	J349BSH		
L 320	J320BSH	L 326	J326BSH	L 332	J332BSH	L 338	J338BSH	L 344	J344BSH	L 350	J350BSH		

L 514-556 — Leyland Olympian ON2R50C13Z* — Northern Counties — H47/27D — 1990 — Ex Arriva Kent, 1997

L 514	G514VBB	L 521	G521VBB	L 528	G528VBB	L 535	G535VBB	L 542	G542VBB	L 549	G549VBB	L 556	G556VBB
L 515	G515VBB	L 522	G522VBB	L 529	G529VBB	L 536	G536VBB	L 543	G543VBB	L 550	G550VBB		
L 516	G516VBB	L 523	G523VBB	L 530	G530VBB	L 537	G537VBB	L 544	G544VBB	L 551	G551VBB		
L 517	G517VBB	L 524	G524VBB	L 531	G531VBB	L 538	G538VBB	L 545	G545VBB	L 552	G552VBB		
L 518	G518VBB	L 525	G525VBB	L 532	G532VBB	L 539	G539VBB	L 546	G546VBB	L 553	G553VBB		
L 519	G519VBB	L 526	G526VBB	L 533	G533VBB	L 540	G540VBB	L 547	G547VBB	L 554	G554VBB		
L 520	G520VBB	L 527	G527VBB	L 534	G534VBB	L 541	G541VBB	L 548	G548VBB	L 555	G555VBB		

LDR 1-21 Dennis Dart 9.8SDL3054 Plaxton Pointer 9.8m B40F 1995

LDR 1	N671GUM	LDR 4	N674GUM	LDR 7	N677GUM	LDR 10	N680GUM	LDR 13	N683GUM	LDR 16	N686GUM	LDR 19	N689GUM
LDR 2	N672GUM	LDR 5	N675GUM	LDR 8	N678GUM	LDR 11	N681GUM	LDR 14	N684GUM	LDR 17	N687GUM	LDR 20	N690GUM
LDR 3	N673GUM	LDR 6	N676GUM	LDR 9	N679GUM	LDR 12	N682GUM	LDR 15	N685GUM	LDR 18	N688GUM	LDR 21	N691GUM

LDR 22-55 Dennis Dart SFD412BR5TGD1 Plaxton Pointer 9.8m B40F 1998

LDR 22	P822RWU	LDR 27	P827RWU	LDR 32	P832RWU	LDR 37	P837RWU	LDR 42	P842PWW	LDR 47	P847PWW	LDR 52	P852PWW
LDR 23	P823RWU	LDR 28	P828RWU	LDR 33	P833RWU	LDR 38	P838RWU	LDR 43	P843PWW	LDR 48	P848PWW	LDR 53	P853PWW
LDR 24	P824RWU	LDR 29	P829RWU	LDR 34	P834RWU	LDR 39	P839RWU	LDR 44	P844PWW	LDR 49	P849PWW	LDR 54	P854PWW
LDR 25	P825RWU	LDR 30	P830RWU	LDR 35	P835RWU	LDR 40	P840PWW	LDR 45	P845PWW	LDR 50	P850PWW	LDR 55	P855PWW
LDR 26	P826RWU	LDR 31	P831RWU	LDR 36	P836RWU	LDR 41	P841PWW	LDR 46	P846PWW	LDR 51	P851PWW		

M 6-51 MCW Metrobus DR101/8 MCW H43/28D 1978/9 Ex London Buses, 1994

M 6t	WYW6T	M 7t	WYW7T	M 14t‡	WYW14T	M 38t	WYW38T	M 40t	WYW40T	M 49t	WYW49T	M 51	WYW51T

M 60-205 MCW Metrobus DR101/9 MCW H43/28D 1979 Ex London Buses, 1994

M 60t	WYW60T	M 65t	WYW65T	M 69t	WYW69T	M 149t	BYX149V	M 170†	BYX170V	M 175†	BYX175V	M 205t	BYX205V
M 63u	WYW63T	M 66t	WYW66T	M 132t	BYX132V	M 168u	BYX168V	M 173	BYX173V	M 200	BYX200V		

M 210-503 MCW Metrobus DR101/12 MCW H43/28D 1980 Ex London Buses, 1994

M 230	BYX230V	M 283u	BYX283V	M 372	GYE372W	M 396	GYE396W	M 441	GYE441W	M 464u	GYE464W	M 492	GYE492W
M 251u	BYX251V	M 290	BYX290V	M 378	GYE378W	M 398	398CLT	M 445t‡	GYE445W	M 469t	GYE469W	M 496	GYE496W
M 263u	BYX263V	M 298	BYX298V	M 382t‡	GYE382W	M 399	GYE399W	M 450t‡	GYE450W	M 474	GYE474W	M 500	GYE500W
M 266†	BYX266V	M 317‡	EYE317V	M 384	GYE384W	M 417u	GYE417W	M 454	GYE454W	M 478t	GYE478W	M 503	GYE503W
M 280	BYX280V	M 346u	GYE346W	M 388u	GYE388W	M 422t‡	GYE422W	M 456	GYE456W	M 485t	GYE485W		
M 282t‡	BYX282V	M 365	GYE365W	M 395	GYE395W	M 426t	GYE426W	M 458	GYE458W	M 491†	GYE491W		

M 507-805 MCW Metrobus DR101/14 MCW H43/28D 1981/2 Ex London Buses, 1994

M 507	GYE507W	M 531	GYE531W	M 557	GYE557W	M 586	GYE586W	M 612	KYO612X	M 632	KYV632X	M 650	KYV650X
M 508	GYE508W	M 534	GYE534W	M 559	GYE559W	M 587	GYE587W	M 613	KYO613X	M 633	KYV633X	M 651	KYV651X
M 510	GYE510W	M 535	GYE535W	M 562	GYE562W	M 590	GYE590W	M 614	KYO614X	M 634	KYV634X	M 652	KYV652X
M 511	GYE511W	M 536	GYE536W	M 567	GYE567W	M 591	GYE591W	M 615	KYO615X	M 635	KYV635X	M 653	KYV653X
M 515	GYE515W	M 537†	GYE537W	M 568	GYE568W	M 593	GYE593W	M 617	KYO617X	M 636	KYV636X	M 654	KYV654X
M 517	GYE517W	M 538	GYE538W	M 569	GYE569W	M 596	GYE596W	M 619	KYO619X	M 637	KYV637X	M 657	KYV657X
M 518	GYE518W	M 540	GYE540W	M 573†	GYE573W	M 600	GYE600W	M 622	KYO622X	M 638	KYV638X	M 658	KYV658X
M 519	GYE519W	M 541	GYE541W	M 575	GYE575W	M 601	GYE601W	M 625†	KYO625X	M 641	KYV641X	M 659	KYV659X
M 520	GYE520W	M 544†	GYE544W	M 577	GYE577W	M 602	GYE602W	M 626	KYO626X	M 642	KYV642X	M 660	KYV660X
M 521	GYE521W	M 547	GYE547W	M 580	GYE580W	M 603	GYE603W	M 627	KYO627X	M 644	KYV644X	M 661	KYV661X
M 522	GYE522W	M 548	GYE548W	M 581	GYE581W	M 605	GYE605W	M 628	KYO628X	M 645	KYV645X	M 663	KYV663X
M 528	GYE528W	M 549	GYE549W	M 582	GYE582W	M 609	KYO609X	M 629	KYO629X	M 647	KYV647X	M 664	KYV664X
M 529	GYE529W	M 551	GYE551W	M 584	GYE584W	M 610	KYO610X	M 630	KYO630X	M 648	KYV648X	M 665	KYV665X
M 530	GYE530W	M 555	GYE555W	M 585	GYE585W	M 611	KYO611X	M 631	KYO631X	M 649†	KYV649X	M 666	KYV666X

† Leaside Travel livery (maroon and blue) ‡ All-over advertisement

M 669	KYV669X	M 699	KYV699X	M 716	KYV716X	M 733	KYV733X	M 751	KYV751X	M 773	KYV773X	M 789	KYV789X
M 671	KYV671X	M 700	KYV700X	M 717	KYV717X	M 734	KYV734X	M 752	KYV752X	M 774	KYV774X	M 790	KYV790X
M 673	KYV673X	M 701	KYV701X	M 718	KYV718X	M 736	KYV736X	M 753	KYV753X	M 775	KYV775X	M 791	KYV791X
M 675	KYV675X	M 702	KYV702X	M 719	KYV719X	M 737	KYV737X	M 756	KYV756X	M 776	KYV776X	M 792	KYV792X
M 676	KYV676X	M 703	KYV703X	M 720	KYV720X	M 738	KYV738X	M 757	KYV757X	M 777	KYV777X	M 793	KYV793X
M 679	KYV679X	M 704	KYV704X	M 721	KYV721X	M 740	KYV740X	M 758	KYV758X	M 778	KYV778X	M 795	KYV795X
M 680	KYV680X	M 705	KYV705X	M 722	KYV722X	M 741	KYV741X	M 761	KYV761X	M 780	KYV780X	M 796	KYV796X
M 681	KYV681X	M 708	KYV708X	M 723	KYV723X	M 742	KYV742X	M 762	KYV762X	M 781	KYV781X	M 798	KYV798X
M 682	KYV682X	M 709	KYV709X	M 724	KYV724X	M 743	KYV743X	M 765	KYV765X	M 782	KYV782X	M 799	KYV799X
M 684	KYV684X	M 710	KYV710X	M 726	KYV726X	M 744	KYV744X	M 766	KYV766X	M 783	KYV783X	M 803	KYV803X
M 686	KYV686X	M 711	KYV711X	M 727	KYV727X	M 745	KYV745X	M 767	KYV767X	M 784	KYV784X	M 805	KYV805X
M 688	KYV688X	M 712	KYV712X	M 728	KYV728X	M 746	KYV746X	M 768	KYV768X	M 785	KYV785X		
M 691	KYV691X	M 713	KYV713X	M 729	KYV729X	M 747	KYV747X	M 770	KYV770X	M 786	KYV786X		
M 692	KYV692X	M 714	KYV714X	M 731	KYV731X	M 749	KYV749X	M 771	KYV771X	M 787	KYV787X		
M 694	KYV694X	M 715	KYV715X	M 732	KYV732X	M 750	KYV750X	M 772	KYV772X	M 788t	KYV788X		

M 809-954 MCW Metrobus DR101/16 MCW H43/28D 1983 Ex London Buses, 1994

M 809	OJD809Y	M 850	OJD850Y	M 865	OJD865Y	M 894	A894SUL	M 919	A919SUL	M 936	A936SUL	M 954	WLT954
M 825	OJD825Y	M 858	OJD858Y	M 869	OJD869Y	M 895	A895SUL	M 929	A929SUL	M 939	A939SUL		
M 827	OJD827Y	M 863	OJD863Y	M 891	OJD891Y	M 903	A903SUL	M 930	A930SUL	M 948	A948SUL		

M 959-1036 MCW Metrobus DR101/17 MCW H43/28D 1984 Ex London Buses, 1984

M 959	A959SYF	M 984	A984SYF	M 996	A996SYF	M 1000	A700THV
M 973	A973SYF	M 988	A988SYF	M 998	A998SUL	M 1036	A736THV

M 1044	A744THV	MCW Metrobus DR101/19	MCW	H43/28D	1984	Ex London Buses, 1994
M 1062	B62WUL	MCW Metrobus DR101/17	MCW	H43/28D	1985	Ex London Buses, 1994
M 1070	B70WUL	MCW Metrobus DR101/17	MCW	H43/28D	1985	Ex London Buses, 1994
M 1074	B74WUL	MCW Metrobus DR101/17	MCW	H43/28D	1985	Ex London Buses, 1994
M 1075t	B75WUL	MCW Metrobus DR101/17	MCW	H43/28D	1985	Ex London Buses, 1994

M 1084-1105 MCW Metrobus DR134/1 MCW H43/28D 1985 Ex London Buses, 1994

M 1084	B84WUL	M 1088	B88WUL	M 1092	B92WUL	M 1096	B96WUL	M 1100	B100WUL	M 1104	B104WUL
M 1085	B85WUL	M 1089	B89WUL	M 1093	B93WUL	M 1097	B97WUL	M 1101	B101WUL	M 1105	B105WUL
M 1086	B86WUL	M 1090	B90WUL	M 1094	B94WUL	M 1098	B98WUL	M 1102	B102WUL		
M 1087	B87WUL	M 1091	B91WUL	M 1095	B95WUL	M 1099	B99WUL	M 1103	B103WUL		

M 1109-1437 MCW Metrobus DR101/17 MCW H43/28D* 1985/6 Ex London Buses, 1994
*(M 1359, 1367 & 1398 are DPH43/28D, 1379 is DPH43/28F, M1437 is DPH43/24F)

M 1109	B109WUL	M 1137	B137WUL	M 1209	B209WUL	M 1253	B253WUL	M 1290	B290WUL	M 1314	C314BUV	M 1379†	VLT88
M 1112	B112WUL	M 1138	B138WUL	M 1210	B210WUL	M 1254	B254WUL	M 1291	B291WUL	M 1316	C316BUV	M 1398†	C398BUV
M 1116	B116WUL	M 1139	B139WUL	M 1213	B213WUL	M 1255	B255WUL	M 1293	B293WUL	M 1317	C317BUV	M 1399	C399BUV
M 1121	B121WUL	M 1140	B140WUL	M 1214	B214WUL	M 1263	B263WUL	M 1294	B294WUL	M 1318	C318BUV	M 1401	C401BUV
M 1123	B123WUL	M 1152	B152WUL	M 1216	B216WUL	M 1265	B265WUL	M 1295	B295WUL	M 1319	C319BUV	M 1402	C402BUV
M 1124	B124WUL	M 1154	B154WUL	M 1217	B217WUL	M 1275	B275WUL	M 1296	B296WUL	M 1320	C320BUV	M 1404	C404BUV
M 1126	B126WUL	M 1155	B155WUL	M 1219	B219WUL	M 1276	B276WUL	M 1297	B297WUL	M 1321	C321BUV	M 1405	C405BUV
M 1127	B127WUL	M 1162	B162WUL	M 1221	B221WUL	M 1278	B278WUL	M 1298	B298WUL	M 1322	C322BUV	M 1406	C406BUV
M 1128	B128WUL	M 1164	B164WUL	M 1227	B227WUL	M 1279	B279WUL	M 1299	B299WUL	M 1323	C323BUV	M 1407	C407BUV
M 1129	B129WUL	M 1165	B165WUL	M 1228	B228WUL	M 1280	B280WUL	M 1300	B300WUL	M 1324	C324BUV	M 1413	C413BUV
M 1130	B130WUL	M 1169	B169WUL	M 1229	B229WUL	M 1281	B281WUL	M 1303	B303WUL	M 1326	C326BUV	M 1417	C417BUV
M 1131	B131WUL	M 1170	B170WUL	M 1231	B231WUL	M 1282	B282WUL	M 1307	C307BUV	M 1327	C327BUV	M 1424	C424BUV
M 1132	B132WUL	M 1173	B173WUL	M 1233	B233WUL	M 1283	B283WUL	M 1308	C308BUV	M 1332	C332BUV	M 1437†	VLT12
M 1133	B133WUL	M 1175	B175WUL	M 1239	B239WUL	M 1285	B285WUL	M 1309	C309BUV	M 1354	C354BUV		
M 1134	B134WUL	M 1176	B176WUL	M 1248†	B248WUL	M 1286	B286WUL	M 1310	C310BUV	M 1359	C359BUV		
M 1135	B135WUL	M 1179	B179WUL	M 1249	B249WUL	M 1288	B288WUL	M 1312	C312BUV	M 1362	C362BUV		
M 1136	B136WUL	M 1182	B182WUL	M 1252	B252WUL	M 1289	B289WUL	M 1313	C313BUV	M 1367†	C367BUV		

M 1441	A441UUV	MCW Metrobus DR102/45	MCW	H43/28D	1984	Ex London Buses, 1994
M 1442	A442UUV	MCW Metrobus DR132/5	MCW	H43/28D	1984	Ex London Buses, 1994
MBT 713	L713OVX	Iveco Turbo Daily 59.12	Marshall C31	B18FL	1994	Ex Arriva EH & E, 1998
MBT 714	L714OVX	Iveco Turbo Daily 59.12	Marshall C31	B18FL	1994	Ex Arriva EH & E, 1998
MBT 715	L715OVX	Iveco Turbo Daily 59.12	Marshall C31	B18FL	1994	Ex Arriva EH & E, 1998
MBT 716	L716OVX	Iveco Turbo Daily 59.12	Marshall C31	B18FL	1994	Ex Arriva EH & E, 1998
MBV 951	R951VPU	Mercedes-Benz O814 Vario	Plaxton Beaver 2	B27F	1998	Ex Arriva EH & E, 1998

MD 601-612 Mercedes-Benz 811D Plaxton Beaver B28F 1991 Ex Arriva EH & E, 1998

MD 601	J601WHJ	MD 604	J604WHJ	MD 606	J606WHJ	MD 608	J608WHJ	MD 610	J610WHJ	MD 612	J612WHJ
MD 603	J603WHJ	MD 605	J605WHJ	MD 607	J607WHJ	MD 609	J609WHJ	MD 611	J611WHJ		

MR 102	F102YVP	MCW Metrorider MF150/115	MCW	B23F	1988	Ex London Buses, 1994
MR 104	F104YVP	MCW Metrorider MF150/116	MCW	DP23F	1988	Ex London Buses, 1994
MR 105	F105YVP	MCW Metrorider MF150/116	MCW	DP23F	1988	Ex London Buses, 1994
MRL 129	F129YVP	MCW Metrorider MF158/16	MCW	B28F	1988	Ex London Buses, 1994

RM 5-2217 AEC Routemaster R2RH Park Royal H36/28R 1959-65 Ex London Buses, 1994, 1997

RM 5	VLT5	RM 311	KGJ142A	RM 531	WLT531	RM 970	WLT970	RM 1324	324CLT	RM 1725	725DYE	RM 1872	ALD872B
RM 6	VLT6	RM 348	WLT348	RM 664	WLT664	RM 997	WLT997	RM 1330u	KGH975A	RM 1734	734DYE	RM 1978	ALD978B
RM 25	VLT25	RM 385	WLT385	RM 676	WLT676	RM 1003	3CLT	RM 1361	VYJ808	RM 1801	801DYE	RM 2179	CUV179C
RM 275	VLT275	RM 432	SVS617	RM 719	WLT719	RM 1124	VYJ806	RM 1398	KGJ118A	RM 1811	EGF220B	RM 2185	CUV185C
RM 295u	VLT295	RM 467	XVS651	RM 736u	XYJ418	RM 1125	KGH858A	RM 1593	593CLT	RM 1822	822DYE	RM 2217	CUV217C

† Leaside Travel livery (maroon and blue)

Fleet	Reg	Chassis	Body		Layout	Year	Notes
RMC 1453x	453CLT	AEC Routemaster R2RH	Park Royal		H32/25RD	1962	Ex Arriva EH & E, 1998
RMC 1464x	464CLT	AEC Routemaster R2RH	Park Royal		O36/25RD	1962	Ex Arriva EH & E, 1998

RML 882-901		AEC Routemaster R2RH	Park Royal	H40/32R	1961	Ex London Buses, 1994

RML 882	WLT882	RML 888	WLT888	RML 895	WLT895	RML 897	WLT897
RML 884	WLT884	RML 892	WLT892	RML 896	WLT896	RML 901	WLT901

RML 2261-2759		AEC Routemaster R2RH/1	Park Royal	H40/32R	1965-68	Ex London Buses, 1994

RML 2261	CUV261C	RML 2333	CUV333C	RML 2383	JJD383D	RML 2491	JJD491D	RML 2544	JJD544D	RML 2611	NML611E	RML 2688	SMK688F
RML 2264	CUV264C	RML 2334	CUV334C	RML 2386	JJD386D	RML 2492	JJD492D	RML 2545	JJD545D	RML 2617	NML617E	RML 2692	SMK692F
RML 2266	CUV266C	RML 2340	CUV340C	RML 2387	JJD387D	RML 2494	JJD494D	RML 2546	JJD546D	RML 2619	NML619E	RML 2708	SMK708F
RML 2267	CUV267C	RML 2343	CUV343C	RML 2391	JJD391D	RML 2503	JJD503D	RML 2548	JJD548D	RML 2625	NML625E	RML 2715	SMK715F
RML 2277	CUV277C	RML 2344	CUV344C	RML 2394	JJD394D	RML 2504	JJD504D	RML 2549	JJD549D	RML 2628	NML628E	RML 2716	SMK716F
RML 2280	CUV280C	RML 2346	CUV346C	RML 2401	JJD401D	RML 2505	JJD505D	RML 2552	JJD552D	RML 2632	NML632E	RML 2718	SMK718F
RML 2287	CUV287C	RML 2347	CUV347C	RML 2406	JJD406D	RML 2510	JJD510D	RML 2562	JJD562D	RML 2635	NML635E	RML 2726	SMK726F
RML 2292	CUV292C	RML 2350	CUV350C	RML 2407	JJD407D	RML 2412	JJD512D	RML 2567	JJD567D	RML 2636	NML636E	RML 2730	SMK730F
RML 2294	CUV294C	RML 2351	CUV351C	RML 2408	JJD408D	RML 2514	JJD514D	RML 2571	JJD571D	RML 2638	NML638E	RML 2741	SMK741F
RML 2301	CUV301C	RML 2354	CUV354C	RML 2409	JJD409D	RML 2518	JJD518D	RML 2572	JJD572D	RML 2643	NML643E	RML 2742	SMK742F
RML 2304	CUV304C	RML 2355	CUV355C	RML 2410	JJD410D	RML 2521	JJD521D	RML 2573	JJD573D	RML 2653	NML653E	RML 2746	SMK746F
RML 2307	CUV307C	RML 2356	CUV356C	RML 2416	JJD416D	RML 2523	JJD523D	RML 2574	JJD574D	RML 2655	NML655E	RML 2747	SMK747F
RML 2315	CUV315C	RML 2359	CUV359C	RML 2418	JJD418D	RML 2524	JJD524D	RML 2577	JJD577D	RML 2658	SMK658F	RML 2750	SMK750F
RML 2323	CUV323C	RML 2366	JJD366C	RML 2434	JJD434D	RML 2525	JJD525D	RML 2586	JJD586D	RML 2660	SMK660F	RML 2753	SMK753F
RML 2324	CUV324C	RML 2370	JJD370D	RML 2452	JJD452D	RML 2526	JJD526D	RML 2588	JJD588D	RML 2666	SMK666F	RML 2754	SMK754F
RML 2325	CUV325C	RML 2372	JJD372D	RML 2457	JJD457D	RML 2528	JJD528D	RML 2589	JJD589D	RML 2675	SMK675F	RML 2758	SMK758F
RML 2326	CUV326C	RML 2373	JJD373D	RML 2460	JJD460D	RML 2431	JJD531D	RML 2591	JJD591D	RML 2678	SMK678F	RML 2759	SMK759F
RML 2328	CUV328C	RML 2375	JJD375D	RML 2468	JJD468D	RML 2533	JJD533D	RML 2595	JJD595D	RML 2682	SMK682F		
RML 2329	CUV329C	RML 2380	JJD380D	RML 2477	JJD477D	RML 2534	JJD534D	RML 2597	JJD597D	RML 2684	SMK684F		
RML 2330	CUV330V	RML 2382	JJD382D	RML 2483	JJD483D	RML 2536	JJD536D	RML 2608	NML608E	RML 2685	SMK685F		

RV 1x	GJG750D	AEC Regent V 2D3RA	Park Royal	H40/32F	1966	Ex Arriva EH & E, 1997

SLW 1-14		Scania N113CRL	Wright Pathfinder 320	B37D	1994	Ex London Buses, 1994

SLW 1	RDZ1701	SLW 3	RDZ1703	SLW 5	RDZ1705	SLW 7	RDZ1707	SLW 9	RDZ1709	SLW 11	RDZ1711	SLW 13	RDZ1713
SLW 2	RDZ1702	SLW 4	RDZ1704	SLW 6	RDZ1706	SLW 8	RDZ1708	SLW 10	RDZ1710	SLW 12	RDZ1712	SLW 14	RDZ1714

Fleet	Reg	Chassis	Body	Layout	Year	Notes
T 69†	UJN335V	Leyland Titan TNLXB2RRsp	Park Royal	O44/26D	1979	Ex Arriva EH & E, 1998
T 83†	CUL83V	Leyland Titan TNLXB2RRsp	Park Royal	O44/26D	1979	Ex Arriva EH & E, 1998
T 100†	CUL100V	Leyland Titan TNLXB2RRsp	Park Royal	O44/26D	1979	Ex Arriva EH & E, 1998
TDL 54†u	C254SPC	Leyland Tiger TRCTL11/3RH	Duple 320	C53F	1986	Ex Arriva EH & E, 1998
TPL 1†	124CLT	Leyland Tiger TRCTL11/3ARZM	Plaxton Paramount 3200 III	C53F	1989	Ex Arriva EH & E, 1998
TPL 2†	361CLT	Leyland Tiger TRCTL11/3ARZM	Plaxton Paramount 3200 III	C53F	1989	Ex Arriva EH & E, 1998
TPL 8†	70CLT	Leyland Tiger TRCL10/3ARZA	Plaxton Paramount 3200 III	C53F	1991	Ex Arriva EH & E, 1998
TPL 518†	530MUY	Leyland Tiger TRCTL11/3ARZ	Plaxton Paramount 3500 III	C51FT	1988	Ex Arriva EH & E, 1998

x Special events fleet † Leaside Travel livery (maroon and blue)

VA 116-124		Volvo Citybus B10M-50		Alexander RV			H46/29D	1989	Ex Grey-Green, 1998
VA 116 F116PHM		**VA 117** F117PHM		**VA 118** F118PHM	**VA 123** F123FHM	**VA 124** F124PHM			

VPL 3†	185CLT	Volvo B10M-61	Plaxton Paramount 3200 II	C53F	1986	Ex Arriva EH & E, 1998
VPL 4†	205CLT	Volvo B10M-61	Plaxton Paramount 3200 II	C53F	1986	Ex Arriva EH & E, 1998
VPL 503†	H903AHS	Volvo B10M-60	Plaxton Paramount 3500 III	C53F	1991	Ex Arriva EH & E, 1998

The following vehicles are those with Arriva London North East, formerly Grey-Green. At the time of going to press, none carried any class prefixes but plans were in hand to allocate class letters to bring them in line with the rest of the Arriva London vehicles.

104	E104JYV	Volvo Citybus B10M-50	Alexander RV	H43/35F	1987
105	E105JYV	Volvo Citybus B10M-50	Alexander RV	H43/35F	1987
107	E107JYV	Scania K92CRB	East Lancs	H45/31F	1987

109-114		Scania N112DRB		East Lancs			H46/29F		1988	
109	E109JYV	110	E110JYV	111	E111JYV	112	E112JYV	113	E113JYV	114	E114JYV

115-148		Volvo Citybus B10M-50		Alexander RV			H46/29D		1988-90	
			(136 is fitted with an East Lancs upper deck following accident damage)							
115	F115PHM	125	F125PHM	130	F130PHM	135	F135PHM	140	F140PHM	145	G145TYT
119	F119PHM	126	F126PHM	131	F131PHM	136	F136PHM	141	F141PHM	146	G146TYT
120	F120PHM	127	F127PHM	132	F132PHM	137	F137PHM	142	F142PHM	147	G147TYT
121	F121PHM	128	F128PHM	133	F133PHM	138	F138PHM	143	F143PHM	148	G148TYT
122	F122PHM	129	F129PHM	134	F134PHM	139	F139PHM	144	F144PHM		

149-158		Volvo Citybus B10M-50		Alexander RV			H46/29D*		1990	*149-154 are H46/33F
149	G149TYT	151	G151TYT	153	G153TYT	155	H155XYU	157	H157XYU	
150	G150TYT	152	G152TYT	154	G154TYT	156	H156XYU	158	H158XYU	

159	L159GYL	Scania N113DRB	Northern Counties Palatine I	H42/25D	1994
160	L160GYL	Scania N113DRB	Northern Counties Palatine I	H42/25D	1994
161	L161GYL	Scania N113DRB	Northern Counties Palatine I	H42/25D	1994

163-172		Volvo B10M-61		East Lancs EL2000 (1992)			H44/30D		1985	
163	B863XYR	165	B865XYR	167	B867XYR	170	B870XYR	172	B872XYR	
164	B864XYR	166	B866XYR	168	B868XYR	171	B871XYR			

178-183		Scania N113DRB		Northern Counties Palatine I			H42/25D		1995/6	
178	M178LYP	179	M179LYP	180	M180LYP	181	N181OYH	182	N182OYH	183	N183OYH

401-415		Leyland Olympian ON2R50C13Z4		Northern Counties			H47/30F		1990	Ex County, 1991		
401	H101GEV	403	H103GEV	405	H105GEV	407	H107GEV	409	H109GEV	412	H112GEV	414	H114GEV
402	H102GEV	404	H104GEV	406	H106GEV	408	H108GEV	410	H110GEV	413	H113GEV	415	H115GEV

† Leaside Travel livery (maroon and blue)

721-733			Volvo Citybus B10M-50		Alexander RV			H47/29D		1989	Ex Leaside, 1998
721	F101TML	724	F104TML	726	F106TML	728	F108TML	730	F110TML	733	F113TML
723	F103TML	725	F105TML	727	F107TML	729	F109TML	732	F112TML		

912-925			Volvo B10M-55		East Lancs EL2000 (1992)			B41F		1990	

This batch of vehicles was on loan to Independent Way Ltd (Limebourne) at the beginning of 1999.

912	H912XYT	914	H914XYT	916	H916XYT	918	H918XYT	920	H920XYT	922	H922XYT	925	H925XYT
913	H913XYT	915	H915XYT	917	H917XYT	919	H919XYT	921	H921XYT	923	H923XYT		

934-941			Dennis Dart 9SDL3024		Plaxton Pointer 9m			B31F		1993	
934	L934GYL	936	L936GYL	938	L938GYL	940	L940GYL
935	L935GYL	937	L937GYL	939	L939GYL	941	L941GYL

950	M950LYR	Dennis Dart 9.8SDL3040	Plaxton Pointer 9.8m	B40F	1995

952-968			Dennis Dart SLF SFD212BR1TGW1	Alexander ALX 200 10.25m			B36F		1997	
952	P952RUL	955	P955RUL	958	P958RUL	961	P961RUL	964	P964RUL	967	P967RUL
953	P953RUL	956	P956RUL	959	P959RUL	962	P962RUL	965	P965RUL	968	P968RUL
954	P954RUL	957	P957RUL	960	P960RUL	963	P963RUL	966	P966RUL		

969-983			Dennis Dart SLF SLD212		Alexander ALX 200 10.25m			B27D		1998	
969	S169JUA	972	S172JUA	975	S175JUA	978	S178JUA	981	S181JUA
970	S170JUA	973	S173JUA	976	S176JUA	979	S179JUA	982	S182JUA
971	S171JUA	974	S174JUA	977	S177JUA	980	S180JUA	983	S183JUA

Previous Registrations:

7CLT	D170FYM	324CLT	324CLT,	530MUY	E118KFV	KGJ142A	WLT311	VLT12	C437BUV	VLT244	D244FYM	WLT916	C816BYY
70CLT	H643GRO		VYJ807	656DYE	D156FYM	KGJ975A	330CLT	VLT13	C813BYY	VYJ806	124CLT	WLT954	A954SUL
124CLT	G661WMD	330CLT	C32CHM	815DYE	D215FYM	R151GNW	R152GNW	VLT27	C27CHM	VYJ808	361CLT	XYJ418	WLT736
185CLT	E892KYW	361CLT	G662WMD	EGF220B	811DYE	R152GNW	R151GNW	VLT32	J354BSH	WLT372	D172FYM	XVS651	WLT467
205CLT	E893KYW	398CLT	GYE398W	JIW3696	E908UOH	SVS617	WLT432	VLT47	C47CHM	WLT554	D154FYM		
217CLT	D217FYM	480CLT	D180FYM	KGH858A	125CLT	UJN335V	CUL69V,	VLT88	C379BUV	WLT751	D151FYM		
319CLT	D190FYM	519CLT	D219FYM	KGJ118A	398CLT		70CLT	VLT173	D173FYM	WLT807	C808BYY		

ARRIVA KENT THAMESIDE

Following reductions in requirements for LT work, those vehicles assumed to be withdrawn or transferred away are omitted. Therefore, vehicles listed below are those most likely to be seen on LT supported services. Other vehicles of similar types may be seen on peripheral routes in west Kent.

1444-1814		Optare MetroRider MR17		Optare			B29F	1994/6/8		
1444	M444HPF	1448	M448HPF	1452	M452HPG	1803	N803BKN	1807	N807BKN	1811	R811TKO
1445	M445HPF	1449	M449HPF	1453	M453HPG	1804	N804BKN	1808	N808BKN	1812	R812TKO
1446	M446HPF	1450	M450HPF	1801	N801BKN	1805	N805BKN	1809	R809TKO	1813	R813TKO
1447	M447HPF	1451	M451HPF	1802	N802BKN	1806	N806BKN	1810	R810TKO	1814	R814TKO

1852-1975		Optare MetroRider MR03*		Optare			B25F*	1991/5	*1886-90 are B26F (1852 is MR13)
1852	N852YKE	1887	H887CCU	1890	H890CCU	1970	J970JNL	1975	J975JNL
1886	H886CCU	1889	H889CCU	1962	J962JNL	1974	J974JNL		

3112-3159		Dennis Dart 9SDL3034		Northern Counties Paladin 9m			B35F	1994				
3112	L112YVK	3131	L131YVK	3136	L136YVK	3141	L141YVK	3146	L146YVK	3153	L153YVK	3158	L158YVK
3113	L113YVK	3132	L132YVK	3137	L137YVK	3142	L142YVK	3148	L148YVK	3154	L154YVK	3159	L159YVK
3128	L128YVK	3133	L133YVK	3138	L138YVK	3143	L143YVK	3149	L149YVK	3155	L155YVK		
3129	L129YVK	3134	L134YVK	3139	L139YVK	3144	L144YVK	3150	L150YVK	3156	L156YVK		
3130	L130YVK	3135	L135YVK	3140	L140YVK	3145	L145YVK	3152	L152YVK	3157	L157YVK		

3179	P179LKL	Dennis Dart SLF SFD322BR1TGW1 Plaxton Pointer 10.6m	B40F	1997	Ex Maidstone & District, 1997
3217	P217MKL	Dennis Dart SLF SFD322BR1TGW1 Plaxton Pointer 10.6m	B40F	1997	Ex Maidstone & District, 1997

3261-3272		Dennis Dart SLF SFD322BR1VGW1 Plaxton Pointer 10.6m					B39F	1998		
3261	R261EKO	3263	R263EKO	3265	R265EKO	3267	R267EKO	3269	R269EKO	3271	R271EKO
3262	R262EKO	3264	R264EKO	3266	R266EKO	3268	R268EKO	3270	R270EKO	3272	R272EKO

3492	RUF42R	Leyland National 11351/2R	B25DL	1977	Ex London Buses, 1993
3493	THX202S	Leyland National 10351A/2R	B21DL	1978	Ex London Buses, 1993
3494	YYE290T	Leyland National 10351A/2R	B21DL	1979	Ex London Buses, 1993

7702-7709		Volvo Citybus B10M-50		East Lancs			H49/39F	1989/90	Ex North Western, 1996
7702	G641CHF	7703	G642CHF	7706	G648EKA	7707	G649EKA	7708	G659DTJ	7709	G660DTJ

On order: Dennis Darts; Plaxton Pointer 2

ARRIVA KENT & SUSSEX (Route 402 vehicles)

5901-05		Leyland Olympian ON2R50G13Z4*		Northern Counties			H45/30F	1990	*5902/4 are ON2R50C13Z4
5901	G901SKP	5902	G902SKP	5903	G903SKP	5904	G904SKP	5905	G905SKP	

ARRIVA CROYDON & NORTH SURREY, ARRIVA GUILDFORD & WEST SURREY, ARRIVA WEST SUSSEX

These are the former London & Country and Londonlinks group fleets, which are regarded as interchangeable as required. The vast majority remain in London & Country style livery. Only those vehicles regularly used on LT supported services are included below, although other vehicles of similar types may be seen at times. The fleets come under the control of the Arriva Southern Counties headquarters at Maidstone and it is expected that these fleets will be renumbered during 1999 into the same sequence as Arriva Kent Thameside and Kent & Sussex.

AN 262 KPJ262W	Leyland Atlantean AN68B/1R	Roe	H43/30F	1981	Ex Maidstone & District, 1995

DFD 1-13	DAF DE23RSDB250	Northern Counties Palatine II	H43/24D	1998	

DFD 1 R201CKO	DFD 3 R203CKO	DFD 5 R205CKO	DFD 7 R207CKO	DFD 9 R209CKO	DFD 11 R211CKO	DFD 13 R213CKO
DFD 2 R202CKO	DFD 4 R204CKO	DFD 6 R206CKO	DFD 8 R208CKO	DFD 10 R210CKO	DFD 12 R212CKO	

DS 10-18	Dennis Dart 9SDL3053	East Lancs EL2000 9m	B30FL	1995	

DS 10 M521MPF	DS 11 M522MPF	DS 12 M523MPF	DS 13 M524MPF	DS 16 N528SPA	DS 17 N529SPA	DS 18 N530SPA

DSL 90-96	Dennis Dart SLF SFD322	Plaxton Pointer 10.6m	B39F	1997	

DSL 90 P290FPK	DSL 91 P291FPK	DSL 92 P292FPK	DSL 93 P293FPK	DSL 94 P294FPK	DSL 95 P295FPK	DSL 96 P296FPK

DS 120-151	Dennis Dart 9SDL3034	Northern Counties Paladin 9m	B35F	1994	Ex Kentish Bus, 1997

DS 120 L120YVK	DS 122 L122YVK	DS 124 L124YVK	DS 126 L126YVK
DS 121 L121YVK	DS 123 L123YVK	DS 125 L125YVK	DS 151 L151YVK

DP 160-163	Dennis Dart 9SDL3053	Plaxton Pointer 9m	B35F	1995	

DP 160 M160SKR	DP 161 M161SKR	DP 162 M162SKR	DP 163 M163SKR

DS 164-172	Dennis Dart 9SDL3053	Plaxton Pointer 9m	B34F	1995	Ex Leaside, 1997

DS 164 N701GUM	DS 166 N703GUM	DS 168 N705GUM	DS 170 N707GUM	DS 172 N709GUM
DS 165 N702GUM	DS 167 N704GUM	DS 169 N706GUM	DS 171 N708GUM	

LSL 5-9	Dennis Lance SLF 11SDA3201	Wright Pathfinder 320	B40F*	1994/5	*LSL 9 is B39F

LSL 5 M517KPA	LSL 6 M518KPA	LSL 7 M519KPA	LSL 8 M520KPA	LSL 9 N527SPA

LS 10-19	Dennis Lance 11SDA3113	East Lancs EL2000	B49F	1996	

LS 10 N210TPK	LS 12 N212TPK	LS 14 N214TPK	LS 16 N216TPK	LS 18 N218TPK
LS 11 N211TPK	LS 13 N213TPK	LS 15 N215TPK	LS 17 N217TPK	LS 19 N219TPK

MR 472 P472APJ	Optare MetroRider MR17	Optare	B29F	1996	
MM 473 P473APJ	Mercedes-Benz 711D	Plaxton Beaver	B27F	1996	
MM 474 P474APJ	Mercedes-Benz 811D	Plaxton Beaver	B18FL	1996	

Fleet no.	Reg.	Chassis	Body	Seating	Year	Notes
189	G689OHE	Mercedes-Benz 811D	Reeve Burgess Beaver	B20FL	1990	Ex Metrowest, Warley, 1992
190	G690OHE	Mercedes-Benz 811D	Reeve Burgess Beaver	B20FL	1990	Ex Metrowest, Warley, 1992
402	K402VPK	Mercedes-Benz 709D	Dormobile Routemaker	B25FL	1992	
405	K405VPK	Mercedes-Benz 709D	Dormobile Routemaker	B25FL	1992	

430-438		Mercedes-Benz 811D	Plaxton Beaver	B31F	1994/6	

430	L430CPJ	433	L433CPJ	435	L435CPJ	437	L437CPJ
431	L431CPJ	434	L434CPJ	436	L436CPJ	438	P438HKN

440-443		Optare MetroRider MR17	Optare	B29F	1994	

440	M440HPF	441	M441HPF	442	M442HPF	443	M443HPF

610-622		Volvo Citybus B10M-50	East Lancs	H49/39F	1989	

610	G610BPH	612	G612BPH	614	G614BPH	616	G616BPH	618	G618BPH	620	G620BPH	622	G622BPH
611	G611BPH	613	G613BPH	615	G615BPH	617	G617BPH	619	G619BPH	621	G621BPH		

623-630		Volvo Citybus B10M-50	Northern Counties	H45/35F	1989	

623	G623BPH	625	G625BPH	627	G627BPH	629	G629BPH
624	G624BPH	626	G626BPH	628	G628BPH	630	G630BPH

640	G640CHF	Volvo Citybus B10M-50	East Lancs	H49/39F	1989	Ex North Western, 1996
643	G643CHF	Volvo Citybus B10M-50	East Lancs	H49/39F	1989	Ex North Western, 1996

694-704		Volvo Olympian YN2RV16Z4	East Lancs	H44/30F	1994	

694	M694HPF	696	M696HPF	698	M698HPF	700	M700HPF	702	M702HPF	704	M704HPF
695	M695HPF	697	M697HPF	699	M699HPF	701	M701HPF	703	M703HPF		

969	J969JNL	Optare MetroRider MR03	Optare	B33F	1991	Ex Kentish Bus, 1997

CAPITAL CITYBUS (Part of the First Group)

100	JHE144W	MCW Metrobus DR104/6	MCW	H46/31F	1981	Ex MTL, 1996
101	JHE171W	MCW Metrobus DR104/6	MCW	H46/31F	1981	Ex South Yorkshire, 1991
102u	JHE172W	MCW Metrobus DR104/6	MCW	H46/31F	1981	Ex South Yorkshire, 1991
104	JHE194W	MCW Metrobus DR104/6	MCW	H46/31F	1981	Ex Mainline, 1994
105	JHE138W	MCW Metrobus DR104/6	MCW	H46/31F	1981	Ex MTL, 1995
106	JHE157W	MCW Metrobus DR104/6	MCW	H46/31F	1981	Ex South Yorkshire, 1991
107	G107FJW	MCW Metrobus DR102/70	MCW	H43/30F	1989	Ex Optare, Leeds, 1992
109	JHE152W	MCW Metrobus DR104/6	MCW	H46/31F	1981	Ex MTL, 1996
110	JHE170W	MCW Metrobus DR104/6	MCW	H46/31F	1981	Ex South Yorkshire, 1991
111u	JHE156W	MCW Metrobus DR104/6	MCW	H46/31F	1981	Ex MTL, 1996

113-120		MCW Metrobus DR104/6	MCW	H46/31F	1981	Ex South Yorkshire, 1991

113	JHE169W	115	JHE182W	117	JHE147W	119	JHE149W
114	JHE162W	116	JHE146W	118	JHE148W	120	JHE150W

121-128		Leyland Olympian ONCL10/1RZ	Alexander RL	H47/30F	1990

121	G121YEV	122	G122YEV	123	G123YEV	125	G125YEV	126	G126YEV	128	G128YEV

129-132		Leyland Olympian ON2R50C13Z4	Northern Counties	H47/30F	1991

129	J129YRM	130	J130YRM	131	J131YRM	132	J132YRM

133	G133ATW	Leyland Olympian ONCL10/1RZ	Northern Counties	H45/30F	1989
134	J134YRM	Leyland Olympian ON2R50C13Z4	Northern Counties	H47/30F	1991
135	J135YRM	Leyland Olympian ON2R50C13Z4	Northern Counties	H47/30F	1991

136-158		Leyland Olympian ON2R50C13Z4	Leyland	H47/29F	1991

136	J136YRM	140	J140YRM	144	J144YRM	148	J148YRM	152	J152YRM	156	J156YRM
137	J137YRM	141	J141YRM	145	J145YRM	149	J149YRM	153	J153YRM	157	J157YRM
138	J138YRM	142	J142YRM	146	J146YRM	150	J150YRM	154	J154YRM	158	J158YRM
139	J139YRM	143	J143YRM	147	J247YRM	151	J151YRM	155	J155YRM		

159-165		Leyland Olympian ON2R50C13Z4	Northern Counties Palatine I	H47/30F	1992

159	K888TTT	160	K888ELR	161	K888TWY	162	K888LAD	163	K888PFD	164	K888BFG	165	K888BWU

166	K888TKS	Leyland Olympian ON2RC13Z4	Northern Counties Palatine II	H49/29F	1992	
167	L888YTT	Volvo Olympian YN2RV18Z4	Northern Counties Palatine II	H47/29F	1993	
168	L888TTT	Volvo Olympian YN2RV18Z4	Northern Counties Palatine II	H47/29F	1993	
169	E964PME	Leyland Olympian ONLXB/1RH	Optare	H47/29F	1988	Ex Ensign, 1994
170	470SON	MCW Metrobus DR102/63	MCW	H45/30F	1988	Ex London Buses, 1992
171	E461SON	MCW Metrobus DR102/63	MCW	H45/30F	1988	Ex London Buses, 1992

172	C372CAS	Leyland Olympian ONLXB/1RH	Alexander RL		H47/25F	1986	Ex Highland Scottish, 1992
173	C373CAS	Leyland Olympian ONLXB/1RH	Alexander RL		H47/25F	1986	Ex Highland Scottish, 1992
174	C374CAS	Leyland Olympian ONLXB/1RH	Alexander RL		DPH47/25F	1986	Ex Highland Scottish, 1992
175	DAE510W	MCW Metrobus DR103/4	MCW		DPH43/29F	1980	Ex MTL, Liverpool, 1996
176	DAE512W	MCW Metrobus DR103/4	MCW		DPH43/30F	1980	Ex MTL, Liverpool, 1996
177	DAE513W	MCW Metrobus DR103/4	MCW		DPH43/30F	1980	Ex MTL, Liverpool, 1996
178	E478SON	MCW Metrobus DR102/63	MCW		H45/30F	1988	Ex London Buses, 1992
179	E472SON	MCW Metrobus DR102/63	MCW		H45/30F	1988	Ex London Buses, 1992
180	A183WEV	Leyland Olympian ONLXB/1R	Alexander RL		H45/34F	1984	Ex Highland Scottish, 1992
181	J181HME	Dennis Dominator DDA2004	Northern Counties		H45/29F	1991	
182	J182HME	Dennis Dominator DDA2002	Northern Counties		H45/29F	1991	
183	B443CKW	Dennis Dominator DDA901	Alexander RH		H46/32F	1984	Ex Mainline, 1994
184	B444CKW	Dennis Dominator DDA901	Alexander RH		H46/32F	1984	Ex Mainline, 1994
190	B440CKW	Dennis Dominator DDA901	Alexander RH		H46/32F	1984	Ex Mainline, 1994

191-198		Dennis Dominator DDA1023	East Lancs		H45/31F	1988	Ex Southampton Citybus, 1992
191	F291PTP	193	F293PTP	195	F295PTP	197	F297PTP
192	F292PTP	194	F294PTP	196	F296PTP	198	F298PTP

202	B102WUW	Dennis Dominator DDA1001	Northern Counties		H43/31F	1984	Ex London Coaches, 1993
203	B103WUW	Dennis Dominator DDA1001	Northern Counties		H43/31F	1984	Ex London Coaches, 1992

206-222		Volvo Olympian OLY-4953	Northern Counties Palatine 1		H47/27D	1998	
206	S206LLO	209	S209LLO	212	S212LLO	215	S215LLO	218	S218LLO	221	S221LLO
207	S207LLO	210	S210LLO	213	S213LLO	216	S216LLO	219	S219LLO	222	S422LLO
208	S208LLO	211	S211LLO	214	S214LLO	217	S217LLO	220	S220LLO		

223-238		Volvo Olympian OLY-50	Alexander RH (Belfast)		H47/25D	1997	
223	P223MPU	226	P226MPU	229	P229MPU	232	P232MPU	235	P235MPU	238	P238MPU
224	P224MPU	227	P227MPU	230	P230MPU	233	P233MPU	236	P236MPU		
225	P225MPU	228	P228MPU	231	P231MPU	234	P234MPU	237	P237MPU		

239-249		Volvo Olympian YN2RV18Z4	Northern Counties Palatine I		H47/27D	1996	
239	P239HMD	241	N241CMP	243	P243HMD	245	P245HMD	247	N247CMP	249	P249HMD
240	P240HMD	242	P242HMD	244	N244CMP	246	P246HMD	248	P248HMD		

250	J135PVC	Leyland Olympian ON2R50C13Z4	Leyland		H47/25D	1991	Ex Volvo, Warwick, 1991

251-274		Dennis Dominator DDA2001	Northern Counties		H47/29D	1990/1	
251	H251KVX	255	H255KVX	259	H259KVX	263	H263KVX	267	H267KVX	271	H271KVX
252	H252KVX	256	H256KVX	260	H460KVX	264	H264KVX	268	H268KVX	272	H272KVX
253	H253KVX	257	H257KVX	261	H261KVX	265	H265KVX	269	H269KVX	273	H273KVX
254	H254KVX	258	H258KVX	262	H262KVX	266	H266KVX	270	H270KVX	274	H274KVX

| 276t | FUT36V | MCW Metrobus DR102/14 | MCW | | | | H47/27D | 1980 | Ex Leicester Citybus, 1990 |
| 277t | FUT37V | MCW Metrobus DR102/14 | MCW | | | | H47/27D | 1980 | Ex Leicester Citybus, 1990 |

279-294		MCW Metrobus DR102/71	MCW				H46/31F	1988	

279	F279NHJ	282	F282NHJ	285	F285NHJ	288	F288NHJ	291	F291NHJ
280	F280NHJ	283	F283NHJ	286	F286NHJ	289	F289NHJ	293	F293NHJ
281	F281NHJ	284	F284NHJ	287	F287NHJ	290	F290NHJ	294	F294NHJ

295-299		MCW Metrobus DR104/3	MCW				H46/30F	1980	Ex South Yorkshire, 1988

| 295 | JWF495W | 296 | JWF496W | 297 | JWF497W | 298 | JWF498W | 299 | JWF499W |

301	GYE379W	MCW Metrobus DR101/12	MCW				H43/28D	1980	Ex London General, 1998
302	GYE479W	MCW Metrobus DR101/12	MCW				H43/28D	1980	Ex London General, 1998
303	GYE546W	MCW Metrobus DR101/14	MCW				H43/28D	1980	Ex London General, 1998
304	BYX284V	MCW Metrobus DR101/12	MCW				H43/28D	1980	Ex London General, 1998
305	GYE405W	MCW Metrobus DR101/12	MCW				H43/28D	1980	Ex London General, 1998
306	KYO606X	MCW Metrobus DR101/14	MCW				H43/28D	1980	Ex London General, 1998
307	BYX287V	MCW Metrobus DR101/12	MCW				H43/28D	1980	Ex London General, 1998
308	GYE498W	MCW Metrobus DR101/12	MCW				H43/28D	1980	Ex First CentreWest, 1998
309	BYX249V	MCW Metrobus DR101/12	MCW				H43/28D	1980	Ex London General, 1998
310	GYE369W	MCW Metrobus DR101/12	MCW				H43/28D	1980	Ex First CentreWest, 1998
311	BYX311V	MCW Metrobus DR101/12	MCW				H43/28D	1980	Ex First CentreWest, 1998
312	EYE339V	MCW Metrobus DR101/12	MCW				H43/28D	1980	Ex First CentreWest, 1998
313	EYE343V	MCW Metrobus DR101/12	MCW				H43/28D	1980	Ex First CentreWest, 1998
314	GYE434W	MCW Metrobus DR101/12	MCW				H43/28D	1980	Ex First CentreWest, 1998
315	GYE355W	MCW Metrobus DR101/12	MCW				H43/28D	1980	Ex London General, 1998
316	GYE416W	MCW Metrobus DR101/12	MCW				H43/28D	1980	Ex London General, 1998
317	GYE457W	MCW Metrobus DR101/12	MCW				H43/28D	1980	Ex London General, 1998
318	KYV668X	MCW Metrobus DR101/14	MCW				H43/28D	1980	Ex London General, 1998
319	KYV769X	MCW Metrobus DR101/14	MCW				H43/28D	1980	Ex London General, 1998
321	GYE451W	MCW Metrobus DR101/12	MCW				H43/28D	1980	Ex First CentreWest, 1998
322	GYE487W	MCW Metrobus DR101/12	MCW				H43/28D	1980	Ex First CentreWest, 1998
323	OJD843Y	MCW Metrobus DR101/16	MCW				H43/28D	1983	Ex First CentreWest, 1998
328	GYE418W	MCW Metrobus DR101/12	MCW				H43/28D	1980	Ex First CentreWest, 1998
330	EYE330V	MCW Metrobus DR101/12	MCW				H43/28D	1980	Ex First Leicester, 1998
332	EYE332V	MCW Metrobus DR101/12	MCW				H43/28D	1980	Ex First Leicester, 1998
333	GYE413W	MCW Metrobus DR101/12	MCW				H43/28D	1980	Ex First Leicester, 1998

340-348		Dennis Dominator DDA1024	East Lancs				H46/33F	1989	Ex Leicester Citybus, 1996

| 340 | F140MBC | 341 | F141MBC | 342 | F142MBC | 344u | F144MBC | 345 | F145MBC | 347 | F147MBC | 348 | F148MBC |

401-412				Dennis Arrow SFD121BR2SGL6*		Northern Counties Palatine II		H47/33F		1996		*408, 410-12 are a SFD121BR2TGL6	
401	P401PLE	403	P403PLE	405	P405PLE	407	P407PLE	409	P409PLE	411	P411PLE		
402	P402PLE	404	P404PLE	406	P406PLE	408	P408PLE	410	P410PLE	412	P412PLE		

413-416				Dennis Arrow SFD121BR2		Northern Counties Palatine II		H47/35F		1996	
413	P413MTW	414	P414MTW	415	P415MTW	416	P416MTW				

417-426				Dennis Arrow SFD121BR3		East Lancs Pyoneer		H49/28D*		1997/8		*418 & 426 are H49/27D	
417	P417PVW	419	P419PVW	421	P421PVW	423	P423PVW	425	P425PVW				
418	P418PVW	420	P420PVW	422	P422PVW	424	P424PVW	426	R426SOY				

427-454				Dennis Arrow SFD121		East Lancs Pyoneer		H49/27D		1998					
427	R427ULE	431	R431ULE	435	R435ULE	439	R439ULE	443	R443ULE	447	R447ULE	451	S451SLL
428	R428ULE	432	R432ULE	436	R436ULE	440	R440ULE	444	R844YLC	448	R448ULE	452	S452SLL
429	R429ULE	433	R433ULE	437	R437ULE	441	R441ULE	445	R445ULE	449	R449ULE	453	453SLL
430	R430ULE	434	R434ULE	438	R438ULE	442	R442ULE	446	R446ULE	450	R450ULE	454	S454SLL

561u	F251NJN	Mercedes-Benz 709D	Reeve Burgess Beaver	B23F	1989	Ex Thamesway, 1998
562u	F255RHK	Mercedes-Benz 709D	Reeve Burgess Beaver	B23F	1990	Ex Thamesway, 1998
563u	F253RHK	Mercedes-Benz 709D	Reeve Burgess Beaver	B23F	1990	Ex Thamesway, 1998
564	D761KWT	Mercedes-Benz 609D	Robin Hood	B20F	1986	Ex Thamesway, 1998
565	F245MVW	Mercedes-Benz 709D	Reeve Burgess Beaver	B23F	1989	Ex Thamesway, 1998
566	F256RHK	Mercedes-Benz 709D	Reeve Burgess Beaver	B23F	1990	Ex Thamesway, 1998
567	F257RHK	Mercedes-Benz 709D	Reeve Burgess Beaver	B23F	1990	Ex Thamesway, 1998
568	F258RHK	Mercedes-Benz 709D	Reeve Burgess Beaver	B23F	1990	Ex Thamesway, 1998
569	F246MVW	Mercedes-Benz 709D	Reeve Burgess Beaver	B23F	1989	Ex Thamesway, 1998
570	F254RHK	Mercedes-Benz 709D	Reeve Burgess Beaver	B23F	1990	Ex Thamesway, 1998

571-579				Mercedes-Benz O814 Vario		Marshall		B28F		1997		Ex Thamesway, 1998	
571	R411VPU	573	R413VPU	575	R415VPU	577	R417VPU	579	R419VPU				
572	R412VPU	574	R414VPU	576	R416VPU	578	R418VPU						

581-595				Mercedes-Benz 709D		Reeve Burgess Beaver		B23F		1990-91		Ex Thamesway, 1998			
581	H301LPU	583	H303LPU	585	H305LPU	588	H388MAR	590	H390MAR	592	H392MAR	594	H394MAR
582	H302LPU	584	H304LPU	586	H306LPU	589	H389MAR	591	H391MAR	593	H393MAR	595	H395MAR

596	K396GHJ	Mercedes-Benz 709D	Plaxton Beaver	B23F	1993	Ex Thamesway, 1998
600	F800RHK	Mercedes-Benz 811D	Reeve Burgess Beaver	B31F	1989	Ex Thamesway, 1998
601	J601HMF	Mercedes-Benz 811D	Plaxton Beaver	B28F	1992	
602	J602HMF	Mercedes-Benz 811D	Plaxton Beaver	B28F	1992	

603	F803RHK	Mercedes-Benz 811D	Reeve Burgess Beaver	B31F	1989	Ex Thamesway, 1998
604	F804RHK	Mercedes-Benz 811D	Reeve Burgess Beaver	B31F	1989	Ex Thamesway, 1998
605	J605HMF	Mercedes-Benz 811D	Plaxton Beaver	B28F	1992	
606	F801RHK	Mercedes-Benz 811D	Reeve Burgess Beaver	B31F	1989	Ex Thamesway, 1998
607	F802RHK	Mercedes-Benz 811D	Reeve Burgess Beaver	B31F	1989	Ex Thamesway, 1998

610-620 Mercedes-Benz 811D — Plaxton Beaver — B28F — 1992

610	J610HMF	612	J612HMF	615	J615HMF	617	J617HMF	620	J620HMF
611	J611HMF	613	J613HMF	616	J616HMF	618	J618HMF		

621-630 Optare MetroRider — Optare — B28F — 1992

621	J621HMH	623	J623HMH	625	J625HMH	627	J627HMH	629	J629HMH
622	J622HMH	624	J624HMH	626	J626HMH	628	J628HMH	630	J630HMH

631	J631HMH	Mercedes-Benz 811D	Alexander AM	B28F	1992	
632	J632HMH	Mercedes-Benz 811D	Alexander AM	B28F	1992	
633	J633HMH	Mercedes-Benz 811D	Alexander AM	B28F	1992	

639-645 Dennis Dart 8.5SDL3003 — Wright Handybus 8.5m — B26F — 1991 — Ex First CentreWest, 1998

639	JDZ2339	640	JDZ2340	641	JDZ2341	642	JDZ2342	643	JDZ2343	644	JDZ2372	645	JDZ2373

669	J459JOW	Dennis Dart 9SDL3011	Wadham Stringer Portsdown 9m	B37F	1991	Ex Wealden PSV, Five Oaks Green, 1995
670	L670SMC	Dennis Dart 9SDL3034	Northern Counties Paladin 9m	B31F	1994	

671-680 Volvo B6-41 — Alexander Dash 9m — B31F — 1994

671	L671RMD	673	L673RMD	675	L675RMD	677	L677RMD	679	L679RMD
672	L672RMD	674	L674RMD	676	L676RMD	678	L678RMD	680	L680RMD

681	L281RML	Volvo B6-50	Northern Counties Paladin	B39F	1994	
682	L888JTC	Volvo B6-50	Northern Counties Paladin	B39F	1994	
683	L888AMY	Volvo B6-50	Northern Counties Paladin	B39F	1994	
684	L4GML	Volvo B6-50	Northern Counties Paladin	B31F	1994	Ex Flightparks, Horley, 1996
685	L5GML	Volvo B6-50	Northern Counties Paladin	B31F	1994	Ex Flightparks, Horley, 1996
686	L6GML	Volvo B6-50	Northern Counties Paladin	B31F	1994	Ex Flightparks, Horley, 1996

691-696 Dennis Dart 9SDL3016 — Plaxton Pointer 9m — B35F — 1992 — Ex First Thamesway, 1998

691	K901CVW	692	K902CVW	693	K903CVW	694	K904CVW	695	K905CVW	696	K906CVW

701-704 Optare Excel L1000 — Optare — B33F — 1996

701	P701HMT	702	P702HMT	703	P703HMT	704	P704HMT

705-717			Dennis Dart SLF SFD212BR1		East Lancs Spryte 10.2m			B37F		1998			
705	R705VLA	707	R707VLA	709	R709VLA	711	R711VLA	713	R713VLA	715	R715VLA	717	R717VLA
706	R706VLA	708	R708VLA	710	R710VLA	712	R712VLA	714	R714VLA	716	R716VLA		

738-742			Leyland National 2 NL106L11/1R					B44F		1980		Ex Bluebird Northern, 1993
738	KRS538V	739u	KRS539V	740	KRS534V	741u	KRS541V	742	MSO11W			

744	GUW454W	Leyland National 2 NL106AL11/2R	B41F	1981	Ex London Buses, 1994
748	B358LOY	Leyland National 2 NL116TL11/3R	B48F	1984	Ex British Airways, 1993
749	B359LOY	Leyland National 2 NL116L11/3R	B49F	1985	Ex British Airways, 1993
750	NLP389V	Leyland National 2 NL116L11/3R	B49F	1980	Ex British Airways, 1993
751	NLP391V	Leyland National 2 NL116L11/3R	B49F	1980	Ex British Airways, 1993

773-786			Dennis Dart SFD412		Plaxton Pointer 9.8m			B40F		1996		Ex Thamesway, 1998
773	N973EHJ	775	N975EHJ	777	N977EHJ	779	N979EHJ	781	N981EHJ	783	N983EHJ	785	N985EHJ
774	N974EHJ	776	N976EHJ	778	N978EHJ	780	N980EHJ	782	N982EHJ	784	N984EHJ	786	N986EHJ

796	M796MPM	Dennis Lance II SDA3101	Alexander PS	B46F	1992	Ex Dennis Development Vehicle, 1998
797	D497NYS	Volvo B10M-61	Duple Dominant	B55F	1986	Ex Eastbourne, 1996
799	D499NYS	Volvo B10M-61	Duple Dominant	B55F	1986	Ex Eastbourne, 1996
913	ALD913B	AEC Routemaster R2RH	Park Royal	H36/28R	1964	Ex preservation, 1996
920	VLT120	AEC Routemaster R2RH	Park Royal	O36/28R	1959	On loan from Allco
931u	D231PPU	Mercedes-Benz L608D	Reeve Burgess	B20F	1986	On loan from Thamesway
932	C230HCV	Mercedes-Benz L608D	Robin Hood	B20F	1986	On loan from Thamesway
934	D234PPU	Mercedes-Benz L608D	Reeve Burgess	B20F	1986	On loan from Thamesway
935	D235PPU	Mercedes-Benz L608D	Dormobile	B20F	1986	On loan from Thamesway
936	H345LJN	Mercedes-Benz 709D	Reeve Burgess Beaver	B23F	1991	On loan from Thamesway
937	H346LJN	Mercedes-Benz 709D	Reeve Burgess Beaver	B23F	1991	On loan from Thamesway

On order for 1999:

1 Dennis Trident- East Lancs Lolyne (as a long term demonstrator);
22 Dennis Trident- Plaxton President low floor dual-door double deckers (for routes 1,N1,W8); approx 30 more low floor double deckers (type unknown) for routes 25,N25;
23 Dennis Dart SLF- Marshall 10.4m dual door (for routes D6,D7); 6 Dennis Dart SLF- Marshall 8.5m for route D8.

Previous Registrations:

A183WEV	A980OST	GYE379W	GYE379W,	KRS534V	GSO1V	P401PLE	P901HMH	P405PLE	P905HMH	P409PLE	P909HMH	D497NYS	C984KHS
BYX284V	BYX284V,		WLT379	KRS538V	GSO4V	P402PLE	P902HMH	P406PLE	P906HMH	P410PLE	P910HMH		
	VLT284	GYE479W	GYE479W,	KRS539V	GSO5V	P403PLE	P903HMH	P407PLE	P907HMH	P411PLE	P911HMH		
D497NYS	C984KHS		VLT179	KRS541V	GSO7V	P404PLE	P904HMH	P408PLE	P908HMH	P412PLE	P912HMH		

Special livery:

691-696 carry blue red and white for use on the Docklands Light Railway service.

CAPITAL LOGISTICS

CS 1	L204ULX	Mercedes-Benz 709D	Plaxton Beaver	B18FL	1993	
CS 2	L205ULX	Mercedes-Benz 709D	Plaxton Beaver	B18FL	1993	
CS 3	L206ULX	Mercedes-Benz 709D	Plaxton Beaver	B18FL	1993	
CS 4	P255MLE	Mercedes-Benz 711D	Plaxton Beaver	B20FL	1997	
CS 5	P456MLE	Mercedes-Benz 711D	Plaxton Beaver	B20FL	1997	
CS 6	H837GLD	Mercedes-Benz 609D	North Western Coach Sales	C13F	1991	Ex Marton, West Drayton, 1992

J801-810KHD	DAF SB220LC550	Ikarus Citibus	DP42F	1992	Ex London Coaches, 1998

J801KHD	J803KHD	J805KHD	J807KHD	J809KHD
J802KHD	J804KHD	J806KHD	J808KHD	J810KHD

M806RCP	DAF SB220LC550	Ikarus Citibus	DP42F	1994	On hire from Arriva Bus & Coach

R985-993EWU	Optare Excel L1000	Optare	B35F	1998

R985EWU	R987EWU	R989EWU	R991EWU	R993EWU
R986EWU	R988EWU	R990EWU	R992EWU	

CENTREWEST (Part of the First Group)

D 33-41	Dennis Dart SFD412BR5TGD1	Plaxton Pointer 9.8m	B37F	1996

D 33	133CLT	D 35	N635ACF	D 37	N637ACF	D 39	P409MLA	D 41 P411MLA
D 34	N634ACF	D 36	N636ACF	D 38	P408MLA	D 40	P410MLA	

DLP 1	P41MLE	Dennis Dart SLF SFD112BR1	Plaxton Pointer 9.2m	B27D	1996	(Currently on loan from London Transport)

DM 117-164, 201-234	Dennis Dart SLF SFD112BR1	Marshall Capital 9.4m	B31F*	1997/8	*201-34 are B23D

DM 117	P117NLW	DM 129	P129NLW	DM 141	P141NLW	DM 153	P153NLW	DM 201	R201TLM	DM 213 R213TLM	DM 225 R225TLM
DM 118	P118NLW	DM 130	P130NLW	DM 142	P142NLW	DM 154	P154NLW	DM 202	R202TLM	DM 214 R214TLM	DM 226 R226TLM
DM 119	P119NLW	DM 131	P131NLW	DM 143	P143NLW	DM 155	P255RFL	DM 203	R203TLM	DM 215 R215TLM	DM 227 R227TLM
DM 120	P120NLW	DM 132	P132NLW	DM 144	P144NLW	DM 156	P156NLW	DM 204	R204TLM	DM 216 R216TLM	DM 228 R228TLM
DM 121	P121NLW	DM 133	P133NLW	DM 145	P145NLW	DM 157	P157NLW	DM 205	R205TLM	DM 217 R217TLM	DM 229 R229TLM
DM 122	P122NLW	DM 134	P134NLW	DM 146	P146NLW	DM 158	R158TLM	DM 206	R206TLM	DM 218 R218TLM	DM 230 R230TLM
DM 123	P123NLW	DM 135	P135NLW	DM 147	P247OEW	DM 159	R159TLM	DM 207	R207TLM	DM 219 R219TLM	DM 231 R231TLM
DM 124	P124NLW	DM 136	P136NLW	DM 148	P148NLW	DM 160	R160TLM	DM 208	R208TLM	DM 220 R220TLM	DM 232 R232TLM
DM 125	P125NLW	DM 137	P137NLW	DM 149	P149NLW	DM 161	R161TLM	DM 209	R209TLM	DM 221 R221TLM	DM 233 R233TLM
DM 126	P126NLW	DM 138	P138NLW	DM 150	P150NLW	DM 162	R162TLM	DM 210	R210TLM	DM 222 R322TLM	DM 234 R234TLM
DM 127	P127NLW	DM 139	P139NLW	DM 151	P151NLW	DM 163	R163TLM	DM 211	R211TLM	DM 223 R223TLM	
DM 128	P128NLW	DM 140	P140NLW	DM 152	P152NLW	DM 164	R164TLM	DM 212	R212TLM	DM 224 R224TLM	

DML 165-200, 235-256 Dennis Dart SLF SFD212BR1 Marshall Capital 10.2m *B35F 1997/8
*DML179-190 are B37F, 249-252 are B24D and 241-248, 253-256 are B29D.

DML 165 R165TLM	DML 174 R174TLM	DML 183 R183TLM	DML 192 R192VLD	DML 235 S235KLM	DML 244 S244KLM	DML 253 S253JLP
DML 166 R166TLM	DML 175 R175TLM	DML 184 R184TLM	DML 193 R193VLD	DML 236 S236KLM	DML 245 S245KLM	DML 254 S254JLP
DML 167 R167TLM	DML 176 R176TLM	DML 185 R185TLM	DML 194 R194VLD	DML 237 S237KLM	DML 246 S246KLM	DML 255 S255JLP
DML 168 R168TLM	DML 177 R177TLM	DML 186 R186TLM	DML 195 R195VLD	DML 238 S238KLM	DML 247 S247KLM	DML 256 S256JLP
DML 169 R169TLM	DML 178 R178TLM	DML 187 R187TLM	DML 196 R196VLD	DML 239 S239KLM	DML 248 S248KLM	
DML 170 R170TLM	DML 179 R179TLM	DML 188 R188TLM	DML 197 S197KLM	DML 240 S240KLM	DML 249 809DYE	
DML 171 R171TLM	DML 180 R180TLM	DML 189 R189TLM	DML 198 S198KLM	DML 241 S241KLM	DML 250 810DYE	
DML 172 R172TLM	DML 181 R181TLM	DML 190 R190TLM	DML 199 S199KLM	DML 242 S242KLM	DML 251 811DYE	
DML 173 R173TLM	DML 182 R182TLM	DML 191 R191VLD	DML 200 S220KLM	DML 243 S243KLM	DML 252 292CLT	

DP 1-32 Dennis Dart 9SDL3053 Plaxton Pointer 9m B32F 1995

DP 1 N801FLW	DP 6 N806FLW	DP 11 N811FLW	DP 16 N816FLW	DP 21 N821FLW	DP 26 N826FLW	DP 31 N831FLW
DP 2 N802FLW	DP 7 N807FLW	DP 12 N812FLW	DP 17 N817FLW	DP 22 N822FLW	DP 27 N827FLW	DP 32 N832FLW
DP 3 N803FLW	DP 8 N808FLW	DP 13 N813FLW	DP 18 N818FLW	DP 23 N823FLW	DP 28 N828FLW	
DP 4 N804FLW	DP 9 N809FLW	DP 14 N814FLW	DP 19 N819FLW	DP 24 N824FLW	DP 29 N829FLW	
DP 5 N805FLW	DP 10 N810FLW	DP 15 N815FLW	DP 20 N820FLW	DP 25 N825FLW	DP 30 N830FLW	

DW 1-91 Dennis Dart 8.5SDL3003 Wright Handybus 8.5m *B26F 1990 Ex London Buses, 1994
*DW1-14 are DP30F, DW26-32 are B30F.

DW 1 JDZ2301	DW 8 JDZ2308	DW 15 JDZ2315	DW 27 JDZ2327	DW 75 JDZ2375	DW 83 JDZ2383	DW 90 JDZ2390
DW 2 JDZ2302	DW 9 JDZ2309	DW 16 JDZ2316	DW 28 JDZ2328	DW 77 JDZ2377	DW 84 JDZ2384	DW 91 JDZ2391
DW 3 JDZ2303	DW 10 JDZ2310	DW 17 JDZ2317	DW 29 JDZ2329	DW 78 JDZ2378	DW 85 JDZ2385	
DW 4 JDZ2304	DW 11 JDZ2311	DW 22 JDZ2322	DW 30 JDZ2330	DW 79 JDZ2379	DW 86 JDZ2386	
DW 5 JDZ2305	DW 12 JDZ2312	DW 23 JDZ2323	DW 31 JDZ2331	DW 80 JDZ2380	DW 87 JDZ2387	
DW 6 JDZ2306	DW 13 JDZ2313	DW 24 JDZ2324	DW 32 JDZ2332	DW 81 JDZ2381	DW 88 JDZ2388	
DW 7 JDZ2307	DW 14 JDZ2314	DW 26 JDZ2326	DW 74 JDZ2374	DW 82 JDZ2382	DW 89 JDZ2389	

DW 92-99 Dennis Dart 8.5SDL3010 Wright Handybus 8.5m B26F 1990 Ex London Buses, 1994

DW 92 JDZ2392	DW 94 JDZ2394	DW 96 JDZ2396	DW 98 JDZ2398
DW 93 JDZ2393	DW 95 JDZ2395	DW 97 JDZ2397	DW 99 JDZ2399

DW 100 JDZ2300 Dennis Dart 8.5SDL3003 Wright Handybus 8.5m B26F 1990 Ex London Buses, 1994

DW 101-114 Dennis Dart 8.5SDL3010 Wright Handybus 8.5m B26F 1991/2 Ex London Buses, 1994

DW 101 KDZ5101	DW 103 KDZ5103	DW 105 KDZ5105	DW 107 KDZ5107	DW 109 KDZ5109	DW 111 KDZ5111	DW 113 LDZ9113
DW 102 KDZ5102	DW 104 KDZ5104	DW 106 KDZ5106	DW 108 KDZ5108	DW 110 KDZ5110	DW 112 KDZ5112	DW 114 LDZ9114

DW 115-125 Dennis Dart 8.5SDL3015 Wright Handybus 8.5m B26F 1992 Ex London Buses, 1994

DW 115 LDZ9115	DW 117 LDZ9117	DW 119 LDZ9119	DW 121 LDZ9121	DW 123 LDZ9123	DW 125 LDZ9125
DW 116 LDZ9116	DW 118 LDZ9118	DW 120 LDZ9120	DW 122 LDZ9122	DW 124 LDZ9124	

DW 126 LDZ9126	Dennis Dart 8.5SDL3018	Wright Handybus 8.5m	B26F	1992	Ex London Buses, 1994

DW 162-168	Dennis Dart 8.5SDL3015	Wright Handybus 8.5m	B29F	1993	Ex London Buses, 1994

DW 162 NDZ3162	**DW 163** NDZ3163	**DW 164** NDZ3164	**DW 165** NDZ3165	**DW 166** NDZ3166	**DW 167** NDZ3167	**DW 168** NDZ3168

DW 169 NDZ3169	Dennis Dart 8.5SDL3015	Wright Handybus 8.5m	B26F	1992	Ex London Buses, 1994
DW 170 NDZ3170	Dennis Dart 8.5SDL3015	Wright Handybus 8.5m	B26F	1992	Ex London Buses, 1994

L 1-6	Dennis Dart SLF SFD212BR1	Plaxton Pointer 10m	B34F	1996	

L 1 P401MLA	**L 2** P402MLA	**L 3** P403MLA	**L 4** P404MLA	**L 5** P405MLA	**L 6** P406MLA

LA 24-28	Leyland Olympian ON2R50C13Z4	Alexander RH	H45/29F	1993	Ex London Buslines, 1997

LA 24 L24GAN	**LA 25** L25GAN	**LA 26** L26GAN	**LA 27** L27GAN	**LA 28** L28GAN

LA 46-54	Leyland Olympian ONCL10/1RZ	Alexander RL	H47/28F	1989	Ex London Buslines, 1997

LA 46 G46XLO	**LA 48** G48XLO	**LA 50** G50XLO	**LA 52** G52XLO	**LA 54** G54XLO
LA 47 G47XLO	**LA 49** G49XLO	**LA 51** G51XLO	**LA 53** G53XLO	

LC 1-3	LDV 400	Crystals	DP10FL	1995	

LC 1 N921LUF	**LC 2** N922LUF	**LC 3** N923LUF

LLW 11-24	Dennis Lance SLF 11SDA3201	Wright Pathfinder 320	B34D	1993/4	Ex London Buses, 1994

LLW 11 ODZ8911	**LLW 13** ODZ8913	**LLW 15** ODZ8915	**LLW 17** ODZ8917	**LLW 19** ODZ8919	**LLW 21** ODZ8921	**LLW 23** ODZ8923
LLW 12 ODZ8912	**LLW 14** ODZ8914	**LLW 16** ODZ8916	**LLW 18** ODZ8918	**LLW 20** ODZ8920	**LLW 22** ODZ8922	**LLW 24** ODZ8924

LLW 31 M221EAF	Dennis Lance SLF 11SDA3202	Wright Pathfinder 320	B40F	1995	Ex Leeds Citylink, 1998

LN 29-45	Leyland Olympian ON2R50C13Z4	Northern Counties	H47/30F	1990	Ex London Buslines, 1996/7

LN 29 H129FLX	**LN 32** H132FLX	**LN 35** H135FLX	**LN 38** H138FLX	**LN 41** H141FLX	**LN 44** H144FLX
LN 30 H130FLX	**LN 33** H133FLX	**LN 36** H136FLX	**LN 39** H139FLX	**LN 42** H142FLX	**LN 45** H145FLX
LN 31 H131FLX	**LN 34** H134FLX	**LN 37** H137FLX	**LN 40** H140FLX	**LN 43** H143FLX	

LS 444-504	Leyland National 2 NL106AL11/2R (Volvo)		DP43F	1981	Ex London Buses, 1994

LS 444t GUW444W	**LS 472t** GUW472W	**LS 503t** 503CLT	**LS 504t** GUW504W

LX 11 D876ELL	Leyland Lynx LX112TL11ZR1R		DP48F	1987	Ex London Buses, 1994

M 285-505 MCW Metrobus DR101/12 MCW H43/28D 1980 Ex London Buses, 1994

M 285 BYV285V	**M 329** EYE329V	**M 358** GYE358W	**M 371** GYE371W	**M 397** GYE397W	**M 442** GYE442W	**M 494** GYE494W
M 291 BYV291V	**M 337** EYE337V	**M 360** GYE360W	**M 374** GYE374W	**M 406** GYE406W	**M 452** GYE452W	**M 497** GYE497W
M 305 BYV305V	**M 338** EYE338V	**M 362** GYE362W	**M 383** GYE383W	**M 414** GYE414W	**M 465** GYE465W	**M 499** GYE499W
M 308 BYV308V	**M 340** EYE340V	**M 364** GYE364W	**M 385** GYE385W	**M 421**w GYE421W	**M 470** GYE470W	**M 504** GYE504W
M 316 EYE316V	**M 347** GYE347W	**M 368** GYE368W	**M 390** GYE390W	**M 425** GYE425W	**M 486** GYE486W	**M 505** GYE505W
M 319 EYE319V	**M 349** GYE349W	**M 370** GYE370W	**M 393** GYE393W	**M 427** GYE427W	**M 489** GYE489W	

M 523 GYE523W	MCW Metrobus DR101/14	MCW	H43/28D	1980	Ex London Buses, 1994
M 583 GYE583W	MCW Metrobus DR101/14	MCW	H43/28D	1980	Ex London Buses, 1994

M 851-952 MCW Metrobus DR101/16 MCW H43/28D 1983 Ex London Buses, 1994

M 851 OJD851Y	**M 861** OJD861Y	**M 875** OJD875Y	**M 885** OJD885Y	**M 893** A893SUL	**M 941** A941SUL
M 857 OJD857Y	**M 866** OJD866Y	**M 882** OJD882Y	**M 886** OJD886Y	**M 898** A898SUL	**M 943** A943SUL
M 859 OJD859Y	**M 872** OJD872Y	**M 883** OJD883Y	**M 887** OJD887Y	**M 901** A901SUL	**M 952** A952SUL
M 860 OJD860Y	**M 874** OJD874Y	**M 884** OJD884Y	**M 892** A892SUL	**M 938** A938SUL	

M 979 A979SYF	MCW Metrobus DR101/17	MCW	H43/28D	1984	Ex London Buses, 1994
M 1049 A749THV	MCW Metrobus DR101/19	MCW	H43/28D	1984	Ex London Buses, 1994
M 1051 A751THV	MCW Metrobus DR101/19	MCW	H43/28D	1984	Ex London Buses, 1994
M 1054 A754THV	MCW Metrobus DR101/19	MCW	H43/28D	1984	Ex London Buses, 1994

M 1144-1438 MCW Metrobus DR101/17 MCW H43/28D 1985/6 Ex London Buses, 1994

M 1144 B144WUL	**M 1246** B246WUL	**M 1260**t B260WUL	**M 1340**t C340BUV	**M 1380**t C380BUV	**M 1415** C415BUV	**M 1422**t C422BUV
M 1199 B199WUL	**M 1247** B247WUL	**M 1267** B267WUL	**M 1375** C375BUV	**M 1382** C382BUV	**M 1418**t C418BUV	**M 1438** C438BUV
M 1201 B201WUL	**M 1256** B256WUL	**M 1328**t C328BUV	**M 1376** C376BUV	**M 1384**t C384BUV	**M 1419**t C419BUV	
M 1244 B244WUL	**M 1258** B258WUL	**M 1335**t C335BUV	**M 1377** C377BUV	**M 1400** C400BUV	**M 1420**t C420BUV	
M 1245 B245WUL	**M 1259** B259WUL	**M 1338**t C338BUV	**M 1378** C378BUV	**M 1412**t C412BUV	**M 1421** C421BUV	

MA 1-86 Mercedes-Benz 811D Alexander AM *B28F 1988/9 Ex London Buses, 1994 *(1 and 51 are B26F)

MA 1w F601XMS	**MA 70**w F670XMS	**MA 73**w F673XMS	**MA 78**w F678XMS	**MA 85**w F685XMS
MA 51w F951XMS	**MA 72**w F672XMS	**MA 74**w F674XMS	**MA 81**w F681XMS	**MA 86**w F686XMS

ML 101-116 Marshall Minibus Marshall B26F 1997/8

ML 101 R101VLX	**ML 104** R104VLX	**ML 107** R107VLX	**ML 110** R110VLX	**ML 113** R113VLX	**ML 116** R116VLX
ML 102 R102VLX	**ML 105** R105VLX	**ML 108** R108VLX	**ML 111** R211VLX	**ML 114** R114VLX	
ML 103 R103VLX	**ML 106** R706VLX	**ML 109** R109VLX	**ML 112** R112VLX	**ML 115** R115VLX	

MM 1-10 Mercedes-Benz 811D Marshall C16 B28F 1995/6

MM 1 N521REW	**MM 3** N523REW	**MM 5** N525REW	**MM 7** N527REW	**MM 9** P489CEG
MM 2 N522REW	**MM 4** N524REW	**MM 6** N526REW	**MM 8** P488CEG	**MM 10** P490CEG

MM 25	P825NAV	Mercedes-Benz O814 Vario	Marshall Master	B29F	1997	
MM 26	P826NAV	Mercedes-Benz O814 Vario	Marshall Master	B29F	1997	
MT 8	G538GBD	Mercedes-Benz 709D	Reeve Burgess Beaver	B18FL	1989	Ex London Buses, 1994
MW 17w	LDZ9017	Mercedes-Benz 811D	Wright Nimbus	B26F	1992	Ex London Buses, 1994
RF 326u	MLL963	AEC Regal IV 9821LT	Metro-Cammell	B39F	1952	Ex preservation, 1996
RM 1292w	NVS485	AEC Routemaster R2RH	Park Royal	H36/28R	1962	Ex London Transport, 1997
RM 1676w	676DYE	AEC Routemaster R2RH	Park Royal	H36/28R	1963	Ex London Transport, 1997
RMC 1492w	492CLT	AEC Routemaster R2RH	Park Royal	H32/25RD	1962	Ex London Buses, 1994
RMC 1510	510CLT	AEC Routemaster R2RH	Park Royal	O32/25RD	1962	Ex London Buses, 1994
RML 885	WLT885	AEC Routemaster R2RH	Park Royal	H40/32R	1961	Ex London Buses, 1994
RML 2268-2740		AEC Routemaster R2RH/1	Park Royal	H40/32R	1965-7	Ex London Buses, 1994

RML 2268	CUV268C	RML 2357	CUV357C	RML 2390	JJD390D	RML 2480	JJD480D	RML 2530	JJD530D	RML 2623	NML623E	RML 2687	SMK687F
RML 2278	CUV278C	RML 2365	JJD365D	RML 2405	JJD405D	RML 2486	JJD486D	RML 2542	JJD542D	RML 2647	NML647E	RML 2717	SMK717F
RML 2281	CUV281C	RML 2369	JJD369D	RML 2428	JJD428D	RML 2490	JJD490D	RML 2553	JJD553D	RML 2656	NML656E	RML 2724	SMK724F
RML 2291	CUV291C	RML 2374	JJD374D	RML 2442	JJD442D	RML 2498	JJD498D	RML 2555	JJD555D	RML 2664	SMK664F	RML 2735	SMK735F
RML 2309	CUV309C	RML 2378	JJD378D	RML 2467	JJD467D	RML 2501	JJD501D	RML 2559	JJD559D	RML 2667	SMK667F	RML 2740	SMK740F
RML 2313	CUV313C	RML 2379	JJD379D	RML 2473	JJD473D	RML 2506	JJD506D	RML 2602	NML602E	RML 2672	SMK672F		
RML 2352	CUV352C	RML 2388	JJD388D	RML 2476	JJD476D	RML 2522	JJD522D	RML 2609	NML609E	RML 2677	SMK677F		

RW 58	HDZ5458	Renault-Dodge S75	Wright Nimbus	B28F	1990	Ex London Buses, 1994
RW 60	HDZ5460	Renault-Dodge S75	Wright Nimbus	B28F	1990	Ex London Buses, 1994
RW 83	HDZ5483	Renault-Dodge S75	Wright Nimbus	B28F	1990	Ex London Buses, 1994
V 1-55		Volvo Olympian YN2RV18Z4	*Northern Counties Palatine II	H43/29F	1995/6	*V41–55 are OLY-50

V 1	N301JBV	V 5	N305JBV	V 9	N309JBV	V 41	P241UCW	V 45	P245UCW	V 49	P249UCW	V 53	P253UCW
V 2	N302JBV	V 6	N306JBV	V 10	N310JBV	V 42	P242UCW	V 46	P246UCW	V 50	P250UCW	V 54	P254UCW
V 3	N303JBV	V 7	N307JBV	V 11	N311JBV	V 43	P243UCW	V 47	P247UCW	V 51	P251UCW	V 55	P255UCW
V 4	N304JBV	V 8	N308JBV	V 12	N312JBV	V 44	P244UCW	V 48	P248UCW	V 52	P252UCW		

On order:

30 x Dennis Trident/Plaxton President low floor double deckers for mid-1999 delivery for routes 18, N18 and Sunday 23;
13 x 8.8 metre Dennis Dart SLF MPD/Marshall Capital for early 1999 delivery.

Special liveries:

The training buses are predominantly yellow.
DML 249-252 carry silver livery and are dedicated to the Paddington Station/Hotel Shuttle link.

Previous registrations:

133CLT N633ACF	**292CLT** R680MEW	**503CLT** GUW503W	**809DYE** R677MEW	**810DYE** R678MEW	**811DYE** R679MEW	**NVS485** 292CLT

CRYSTALS

K286ESF	Mercedes-Benz 709D	Dormobile Routemaker	B27F	1993	Ex Dennis's, Dunkinfield, 1998
L67DPE	Mercedes-Benz 709D	Crystals	DP19FL	1994	
L76DPE	Mercedes-Benz 709D	Crystals	DP18FL	1994	
L168EKR	Mercedes-Benz 711D	Crystals	B18FL	1994	Ex Crystals demonstrator, 1994
M569TJL	Mercedes-Benz 709D	Crystals	B19FL	1995	
N601JGP	Mercedes-Benz 709D	Crystals	B25F	1995	
N602JGP	Mercedes-Benz 709D	Crystals	B25F	1995	
N603JGP	Mercedes-Benz 709D	Crystals	B25F	1995	
N604JGP	Mercedes-Benz 811D	Crystals	B29F	1995	
N605JGP	Mercedes-Benz 811D	Crystals	B29F	1995	
N606JGP	Mercedes-Benz 811D	Crystals	B29F	1995	
P347HKU	Mercedes-Benz 711D	Crystals	B20FL	1997	
P348HKU	Mercedes-Benz 711D	Crystals	B20FL	1997	

Special Liveries:

N601-606JGP are blue for use in the Orpington area.

EPSOM BUSES

E204YGC	Mercedes-Benz 709D	Reeve Burgess Beaver	DP25F	1988	
E205YGC	Mercedes-Benz 709D	Reeve Burgess Beaver	DP25F	1988	
F207DGT	Mercedes-Benz 709D	Reeve Burgess Beaver	DP25F	1988	
F208GGH	Mercedes-Benz 709D	Robin Hood	B26F	1988	
F209GGH	Mercedes-Benz 709D	Robin Hood	B26F	1988	
H210UGO	Mercedes-Benz 709D	Pheonix	B26F	1990	
H947JPA	Mercedes-Benz 709D	Reeve Burgess Beaver	B25F	1990	Ex Bookham Coaches, Little Bookham, 1997

H679-689YGO	Optare MetroRider MR03	Optare	B26F	1991	Ex London General, 1997

H679YGO	H681YGO	H683YGO	H685YGO	H687YGO	H689YGO
H680YGO	H682YGO	H684YGO	H686YGO	H688YGO	

K593BEG	Mercedes-Benz 709D	Marshall C19	B27F	1992	
K892CSX	Dennis Dart 9.8SDL3017	Alexander Dash 9.8m	B40F	1992	
K321GEW	Dennis Dart 9.8SDL3017	Marshall C27 9.8m	B40F	1993	
K112NGK	Dennis Dart 9.8SDL3012	Plaxton Pointer 9.8m	B40F	1993	
K113NGK	Dennis Dart 9.8SDL3012	Plaxton Pointer 9.8m	B40F	1993	
L894GAV	Mercedes-Benz 709D	Marshall C19	B27F	1993	
M960CGF	Dennis Dart 9.8SDL3040	Plaxton Pointer 9.8m	B40F	1994	
N401SPA	Dennis Dart 9.8SDL3054	Plaxton Pointer 9.8m	B40F	1995	
N402SPA	Dennis Dart 9.8SDL3054	Plaxton Pointer 9.8m	B40F	1995	
P570APJ	Mercedes-Benz 709D	Plaxton Beaver	B27F	1997	
R211MGT	Mercedes-Benz O814Vario	U.V.G.Citistar	B27F	1997	
R212MGT	Mercedes-Benz O814 Vario	U.V.G.Citistar	B27F	1997	
R213MGT	Mercedes-Benz O814 Vario	U.V.G.Citistar	B27F	1997	
S451LGN	Mercedes-Benz O814 Vario	Plaxton Beaver 2	B31F	1998	
S452LGN	Mercedes-Benz O814 Vario	Plaxton Beaver 2	B31F	1998	
S453LGN	Mercedes-Benz O814 Vario	Plaxton Beaver 2	B31F	1998	
S454LGN	Mercedes-Benz O814 Vario	Plaxton Beaver 2	B31F	1998	
S455LGN	Mercedes-Benz O814 Vario	Plaxton Beaver 2	B31F	1998	

S456-466LGN	Dennis Dart SLF MPD	Plaxton Pointer 2 8.8m	B29F	1998-99	

S456LGN	S458LGN	S460LGN	S462LGN	S464LGN	S466LGN
S457LGN	S459LGN	S461LGN	S463LGN	S465LGN	

S467LGN	Dennis Dart SLF SFD	Plaxton Pointer 2 10.1m	B33F	1999	
S468LGN	Dennis Dart SLF SFD	Plaxton Pointer 2 10.1m	B33F	1999	

The coach fleet is included in the London Coach Handbook

HARRIS BUS

302	J582WVX	Mercedes-Benz 709D	Alexander AM	B25F	1991	In LTS Rail advert livery
303	J583WVX	Mercedes-Benz 790D	Alexander AM	B25F	1991	In Gala Bingo advert livery
310	F310OVW	MCW Metrorider MF150/112	MCW	B24F	1988	
315	J51GCX	DAF SB220LC550	Ikarus Citibus	B48F	1992	Ex Strathclyde, 1994
316	J52GCX	DAF SB220LC550	Ikarus Citibus	B48F	1992	Ex Strathclyde, 1994
317	P317KTW	DAF DE02RSDB250	Northern Counties Palatine II	H47/30F	1996	
318	P318KTW	DAF DE02RSDB250	Northern Counties Palatine II	H47/30F	1996	
319	M649RCP	DAF DB250RS505	Northern Counties Palatine II	H47/30F	1995	Ex Beeline, Manchester, 1996

320-334		Optare Excel L1070	Optare	B35F	1996

320	P320KAR	323	P323KAR	326	P326NHJ	329	P329NHJ	332	P332NHJ
321	P321KAR	324	P324NHJ	327	P327NHJ	330	P330NHJ	333	P333HBC
322	P322KAR	325	P325NHJ	328	P328NHJ	331	P331NHJ	334	P334NHJ

335	P335ROO	DAF DE02RSDB250	Northern Counties Palatine II	H43/25D	1997
336	P336ROO	DAF DE02RSDB250	Northern Counties Palatine II	H43/25D	1997
337	P337ROO	DAF DE02RSDB250	Northern Counties Palatine II	H43/25D	1997

338-372		Volvo Olympian OLY-56	East Lancs Pyoneer	*H51/28D	1997/8	*(351-359 are H51/35F)

338	P338ROO	343	P343ROO	348	P348ROO	353	P353ROO	358	R358XVX	363	R363DJN	368	R368DJN
339	P339ROO	344	P344ROO	349	P349ROO	354	R354XVX	359	R359XVX	364	R364DJN	369	R369DJN
340	P340ROO	345	P345ROO	350	P350ROO	355	R355XVX	360	R360DJN	365	R365DJN	370	R370DJN
341	P341ROO	346	P346ROO	351	P351ROO	356	R356XVX	361	R361DJN	366	R366DJN	371	R371DJN
342	P342ROO	347	P347ROO	352	P352ROO	357	R357XVX	362	R362DJN	367	R367DJN	372	R372DJN

373-380		Optare Excel L1070	Optare	B35F	1998

373	R373DJN	375	R375DJN	377	R377DJN	379	R379DJN
374	R374DJN	376	R376DJN	378	R378DJN	380	R380DJN

381	R381GTW	DAF DE02RSDB250	Northern Counties Palatine II	H43/25D	1998
382	R382GTW	DAF DE02RSDB250	Northern Counties Palatine II	H43/25D	1998

Special liveries:

Ilford Link (317/8,335-359), Lewisham Link (324-334,360-372), Eltham Link (373-380), Thurrock Link (315/6,320-3), Lakeside Link (381/2).

INTERNATIONAL COACH LINES (vehicles used on route 709)

RMA 52	NMY637E	AEC Routemaster R2RH/2	Park Royal	H32/24F	1967	Ex Time Travel, Thornton Heath, 1996
RMA 57	NMY654E	AEC Routemaster R2RH/2	Park Royal	H32/24F	1967	Ex preservation, 1996

LIMEBOURNE (Independent Way Ltd)

	Dennis Dart 8.5SDL3003		Carlyle Dartline 8.5m		B28F	1990-1	Ex Metroline, 1998
H89MOB	H124MOB	H126MOB	H136MOB	H142MOB	H157NON		
H93MOB	H125MOB	H134MOB	H141MOB	H156MOB			

On hire at early 1999:

13 x Volvo B10M/East Lancs B41F (H912-923/5XYT) from Arriva London North East; 6 x Marshall Minibus B29F (P501-6HEG) from London General.

On order for early 1999 to replace the above:

17 x Dennis Dart SLF/ Caetano Compass dual-door single deckers.

LONDON BUSLINES (Part of the First Group)

D 601-610		Dennis Dart 9.8SDL3054		Plaxton Pointer 9.8m		B37F	1996		
D 601 N601XJM	**D 603** N603XJM	**D 605** N605XJM	**D 607** N607XJM	**D 609** N609XJM					
D 602 N602XJM	**D 604** N604XJM	**D 606** N606XJM	**D 608** N608XJM	**D 610** N610XJM					

D 611-632		Dennis Dart SFD412BR5		Plaxton Pointer 9.8m		B37F	1996		
D 611 N611XJM	**D 615** N615XJM	**D 619** N619XJM	**D 623** N623XJM	**D 627** P627CGM	**D 631** P631CGM
D 612 N612XJM	**D 616** N616XJM	**D 620** N620XJM	**D 624** N624XJM	**D 628** P628CGM	**D 632** P632CGM
D 613 N613XJM	**D 617** N617XJM	**D 621** N621XJM	**D 625** N625XJM	**D 629** P629CGM	
D 614 N614XJM	**D 618** N618XJM	**D 622** N622XJM	**D 626** N626XJM	**D 630** P630CGM	

DML 633-653	Dennis Dart SLF SFD212BR1	Marshall Capital 10.2m		B37F	1997/8		
DML 633 R633VLX	**DML 636** R636VLX	**DML 639** R639VLX	**DML 642** R642TLM	**DML 645** R645TLM	**DML 648** R648TLM	**DML 651** R651TLM
DML 634 R634VLX	**DML 637** R637VLX	**DML 640** R640VLX	**DML 643** R643TLM	**DML 646** R646TLM	**DML 649** R649TLM	**DML 652** R652TLM
DML 635 R835VLX	**DML 638** R638VLX	**DML 641** R641VLX	**DML 644** R644TLM	**DML 647** R647TLM	**DML 650** R650TLM	**DML 653** R653TLM

L 7	P407MLA	Dennis Dart SLF SFD212BR1	Plaxton Pointer 10m	B34F	1996	Ex First CentreWest, 1997
L 237	P237NLW	Dennis Dart SLF SFD212BR1	Plaxton Pointer 10m	B35F	1996	Ex First CentreWest, 1997
L 238	P238NLW	Dennis Dart SLF SFD212BR1	Plaxton Pointer 10m	B35F	1996	Ex First CentreWest, 1997
L 239	P239NLW	Dennis Dart SLF SFD212BR1	Plaxton Pointer 10m	B35F	1996	Ex First CentreWest, 1997
RB 551	K651DBL	Renault-Dodge S75	Plaxton Beaver	B18FL	1992	
RB 552	K652DBL	Renault-Dodge S75	Plaxton Beaver	B18FL	1992	
RB 553	K653DBL	Renault-Dodge S75	Plaxton Beaver	B18FL	1992	

LONDON CENTRAL & LONDON GENERAL (Part of the Go Ahead Group)

AV 1-9 Volvo Olympian YN2RC16Z4 Alexander Royale H45/29F 1995

AV 1 M81MYM	**AV 3** M83MYM	**AV 5** M85MYM	**AV 7** M87MYM	**AV 9** WLT789
AV 2 M82MYM	**AV 4** M84MYM	**AV 6** M86MYM	**AV 8** M91MYM	

DEL 1-11 Dennis Dart 9SDL3034 East Lancs EL2000 9m B34F 1994 Ex London Buses, 1994

DEL 1 L901JRN	**DEL 3** L903JRN	**DEL 5** L905JRN	**DEL 7** L907JRN	**DEL 9** L909JRN	**DEL 11** L911JRN
DEL 2 L902JRN	**DEL 4** L904JRN	**DEL 6** L906JRN	**DEL 8** L908JRN	**DEL 10** L910JRN	

DPL 1-16 Dennis Dart 9SDL3053 Plaxton Pointer 9m B35F 1995

DPL 1 M201EGF	**DPL 4** M204EGF	**DPL 7** M207EGF	**DPL 10** M210EGF	**DPL 13** M213EGF	**DPL 16** M216EGF
DPL 2 M202EGF	**DPL 5** M205EGF	**DPL 8** M208EGF	**DPL 11** M211EGF	**DPL 14** M214EGF	
DPL 3 M203EGF	**DPL 6** M206EGF	**DPL 9** M209EGF	**DPL 12** M212EGF	**DPL 15** M215EGF	

DR 32-52 Dennis Dart 8.5SDL3003 Plaxton Pointer 8.5m B28F 1991 Ex London Buses, 1994

DR 32 WLT532	**DR 35** H835XGK	**DR 38** H538XGK	**DR 43** H543XGK	**DR 46** 46CLT	**DR 49** H549XGK	**DR 52** H552XGK
DR 33 H533XGK	**DR 36** H536XGK	**DR 39** H539XGK	**DR 44** H544XGK	**DR 47** H547XGK	**DR 50** H550XGK	
DR 34 H534XGK	**DR 37** H537XGK	**DR 41** H541XGK	**DR 45** H545XGK	**DR 48** H548XGK	**DR 51** H551XGK	

DR 149-153 Dennis Dart 8.5SDL3015 Plaxton Pointer 8.5m B28F 1992 Ex London Buses, 1994

DR 149 K149LGO	**DR 150** K150LGO	**DR 151** K151LGO	**DR 152** K152LGO	**DR 153** K153LGO

DRL 1-16 Dennis Dart 9SDL3011 Plaxton Pointer 9m B34F 1991 Ex London Buses, 1994

DRL 1 J601XHL	**DRL 4** J604XHL	**DRL 7** J607XHL	**DRL 10** J610XHL	**DRL 13** J613XHL	**DRL 16** J616XHL
DRL 2 J602XHL	**DRL 5** J605XHL	**DRL 8** J608XHL	**DRL 11** J611XHL	**DRL 14** J614XHL	
DRL 3 J603XHL	**DRL 6** J606XHL	**DRL 9** J609XHL	**DRL 12** J612XHL	**DRL 15** J615XHL	

DRL 53-73 Dennis Dart 9SDL3016 Plaxton Pointer 9m B34F 1992 Ex London Buses, 1994

DRL 53 K853LGN	**DRL 56** K856LGN	**DRL 59** K859LGN	**DRL 62** K862LGN	**DRL 65** K865LGN	**DRL 68** K868LGN	**DRL 71** K871LGN
DRL 54 K854LGN	**DRL 57** K857LGN	**DRL 60** K860LGN	**DRL 63** K863LGN	**DRL 66** K866LGN	**DRL 69** K869LGN	**DRL 72** K872LGN
DRL 55 K855LGN	**DRL 58** K858LGN	**DRL 61** K861LGN	**DRL 64** K864LGN	**DRL 67** K867LGN	**DRL 70** K870LGN	**DRL 73** K873LGN

DRL 74-95 Dennis Dart 9SDL3024 Plaxton Pointer 9m B32F 1993 Ex London Buses, 1994

DRL 74 K574MGT	**DRL 78** K578MGT	**DRL 82** K582MGT	**DRL 86** K586MGT	**DRL 90** K590MGT	**DRL 94** K767OGK
DRL 75 K575MGT	**DRL 79** K579MGT	**DRL 83** K583MGT	**DRL 87** K587MGT	**DRL 91** K591MGT	**DRL 95** WLT395
DRL 76 K576MGT	**DRL 80** K580MGT	**DRL 84** K584MGT	**DRL 88** K588MGT	**DRL 92** K592MGT	
DRL 77 K577MGT	**DRL 81** K581MGT	**DRL 85** K585MGT	**DRL 89** K589MGT	**DRL 93** K593MGT	

DW 44-70   Dennis Dart 8.5SDL3003   Wright Handybus 8.5m   B30F   1990/1   Ex London Buses, 1994

DW 44 JDZ2344	**DW 47** G560SGT	**DW 50** JDZ2350	**DW 53** JDZ2353	**DW 56** JDZ2356	**DW 66** H881BGN	**DW 69** H369XGC
DW 45 G554SGT	**DW 48** G551SGT	**DW 51** JDZ2351	**DW 54** JDZ2354	**DW 57** JDZ2357	**DW 67** H367XGC	**DW 70** H370XGC
DW 46 G552SGT	**DW 49** JDZ2349	**DW 52** G570SGT	**DW 55** JDZ2355	**DW 58** JDZ2358	**DW 68** H368XGC	

DW 127-161   Dennis Dart 8.5SDL3015   Wright Handybus 8.5m   B30F   1992/3   Ex London Buses, 1994

DW 127 K127LGO	**DW 129** K129LGO	**DW 131** K131LGO	**DW 160** NDZ3160
DW 128 K128LGO	**DW 130** K130LGO	**DW 132** K132LGO	**DW 161** NDZ3161

GLS 1-506   Leyland National 2 NL106AL11/2R   East Lancs Greenway (1992-4)   *B24D   1981   Ex London Buses, 1994
*448, 483-87/96 are B38D, 459 & 473 are B36D

GLS 1 GUW466W	**GLS 446** GUW446W	**GLS 459** GUW459W	**GLS 471** GUW471W	**GLS 479** GUW479W	**GLS 490** GUW490W
GLS 438 GUW438W	**GLS 448** WLT648	**GLS 460** GUW460W	**GLS 473** GUW473W	**GLS 480** VLT180	**GLS 491** GUW491W
GLS 439 GUW439W	**GLS 449** GUW449W	**GLS 463** GUW463W	**GLS 474** GUW474W	**GLS 481** GUW481W	**GLS 492** GUW492W
GLS 440 GUW440W	**GLS 450** GUW450W	**GLS 467** WLT467	**GLS 476** GUW476W	**GLS 483** 83CLT	**GLS 493** GUW493W
GLS 442 GUW442W	**GLS 452** GUW452W	**GLS 468** GUW468W	**GLS 477** GUW477W	**GLS 486** 186CLT	**GLS 496** WLT696
GLS 443 WLT843	**GLS 455** GUW455W	**GLS 469** GUW469W	**GLS 478** GUW478W	**GLS 487** WLT487	**GLS 498** WLT598

GLS 499 GUW499W	
GLS 500 GUW500W	
GLS 501 GUW501W	
GLS 502 GUW502W	
GLS 505 GUW505W	
GLS 506 GUW506W	

LDP 1-17   Dennis Dart SLF SFD112BR1   Plaxton Pointer 9.2m   B32F   1996

LDP 1 P501RYM	**LDP 4** P504RYM	**LDP 7** P507RYM	**LDP 10** P510RYM	**LDP 13** P513RYM	**LDP 16** P516RYM
LDP 2 P502RYM	**LDP 5** P505RYM	**LDP 8** 188CLT	**LDP 11** P511RYM	**LDP 14** P514RYM	**LDP 17** P517RYM
LDP 3 P503RYM	**LDP 6** P506RYM	**LDP 9** WLT379	**LDP 12** P512RYM	**LDP 15** P515RYM	

LDP 18-44   Dennis Dart SLF SFD212BR1   Plaxton Pointer 10m   B36F   1996

LDP 18 P718RYL	**LDP 22** P722RYL	**LDP 26** P726RYL	**LDP 30** P730RYL	**LDP 34** P734RYL	**LDP 38** P738RYL	**LDP 42** P742RYL
LDP 19 P719RYL	**LDP 23** P723RYL	**LDP 27** P727RYL	**LDP 31** P731RYL	**LDP 35** P735RYL	**LDP 39** P739RYL	**LDP 43** P743RYL
LDP 20 P720RYL	**LDP 24** P724RYL	**LDP 28** P728RYL	**LDP 32** P732RYL	**LDP 36** P736RYL	**LDP 40** P740RYL	**LDP 44** P744RYL
LDP 21 P721RYL	**LDP 25** P725RYL	**LDP 29** P729RYL	**LDP 33** P733RYL	**LDP 37** P737RYL	**LDP 41** P741RYL	

LDP 45-89   Dennis Dart SLF SFD212BR1   Plaxton Pointer 10m   B36F   1997

LDP 45 R445LGH	**LDP 53** R453LGH	**LDP 60** R460LGH	**LDP 67** R467LGH	**LDP 74** 174CLT	**LDP 82** R482LGH	**LDP 89** R489LGH
LDP 46 R446LGH	**LDP 54** R454LGH	**LDP 61** R461LGH	**LDP 68** R468LGH	**LDP 75** R475LGH	**LDP 83** R483LGH	
LDP 47 R447LGH	**LDP 55** R455LGH	**LDP 62** R462LGH	**LDP 69** R469LGH	**LDP 76** 176CLT	**LDP 84** R484LGH	
LDP 48 R448LGH	**LDP 56** R456LGH	**LDP 63** R463LGH	**LDP 70** R470LGH	**LDP 77** R477LGH	**LDP 85** R485LGH	
LDP 49 R449LGH	**LDP 57** R457LGH	**LDP 64** R464LGH	**LDP 71** R471LGH	**LDP 78** R478LGH	**LDP 86** R486LGH	
LDP 51 R451LGH	**LDP 58** R458LGH	**LDP 65** R465LGH	**LDP 72** WLT872	**LDP 79** R479LGH	**LDP 87** R487LGH	
LDP 52 R452LGH	**LDP 59** R459LGH	**LDP 66** R466LGH	**LDP 73** R473LGH	**LDP 81** R481LGH	**LDP 88** R488LGH	

LDP 90-117 Dennis Dart SLF SFD Plaxton Pointer 2 10.2m B29D 1998/9

LDP 90 WLT990	**LDP 94** S94EGK	**LDP 98** S98EGK	**LDP 103** S103EGK	**LDP 107** S107EGK	**LDP 111** WLT311	**LDP 115** S115EGK
LDP 91 S91EGK	**LDP 95** S95EGK	**LDP 99** WLT599	**LDP 104** S104EGK	**LDP 108** S108EGK	**LDP 112** S112EGK	**LDP 116** S116EGK
LDP 92 S92EGK	**LDP 96** S96EGK	**LDP 101** S101EGK	**LDP 105** S105EGK	**LDP 109** S109EGK	**LDP 113** S113EGK	**LDP 117** S117EGK
LDP 93 S93EGK	**LDP 97** S97EGK	**LDP 102** S102EGK	**LDP 106** S106EGK	**LDP 110** S110EGK	**LDP 114** S114EGK	

M 11 WYW11T MCW Metrobus DR101/8 MCW H43/28D 1978 Ex London Buses, 1994
M 47t WYW47T MCW Metrobus DR101/6 MCW H43/28D 1978 Ex London Buses, 1994

M 120-202 MCW Metrobus DR101/9 MCW *H43/28D 1979 Ex London Buses, 1994 *OM171 is O43/27D

M 120u BYX120V	**M 158u** BYX158V	**OM 171** VLT71	**M 177** BYX177V	**M 197u** BYX197V	**M 202t** BYX202V
M 144u BYX144V	**M 164u** BYX164V	**M 174u** BYX174V	**M 188u** BYX188V	**M 198** SGK374V	
M 156u BYX156V	**M 165u** BYX165V	**M 176u** BYX176V	**M 196** BYX196V	**M 201** BYX201V	

M 207-502 MCW Metrobus DR101/12 MCW *H43/28D 1980 Ex London Buses, 1994
*OM 241 is O43/27D. OM 420 is O43/28D

M 207 BYX207V	**M 256** BYX256V	**M 278u** 78CLT	**M 307** BYX307V	**M 361** GYE361W	**M 430** GYE430W	**M 480** GYE480W
M 211 BYX211V	**M 257** BYX257V	**M 279** BYX279V	**M 318u** EYE318V	**M 375** GYE375W	**M 431** GYE431W	**M 483** GYE483W
M 212 BYX212V	**M 258** BYX258V	**M 286** BYX286V	**M 323** EYE323V	**M 392** GYE392W	**M 433** GYE433W	**M 484** GYE484W
M 214 BYX214V	**M 260** BYX260V	**M 288** BYX288V	**M 331** EYE331V	**M 401** GYE401W	**M 435** GYE435W	**M 488** GYE488W
M 226 BYX226V	**M 265** BYX265V	**M 289** BYX289V	**M 333** EYE333V	**M 404** GYE404W	**M 463** WLT463	**M 490** GYE490W
M 237 BYX237V	**M 269** BYX269V	**M 292** BYX292V	**M 348** GYE348W	**M 408** GYE408W	**M 466** GYE466W	**M 502** GYE502W
M 239 BYX239V	**M 270** BYX270V	**M 293t** BYX293V	**M 350** GYE350W	**M 411** GYE411W	**M 472u** GYE472W	
OM 241 BYX241V	**M 271t** BYX271V	**M 295** BYX295V	**M 354** GYE354W	**M 412** GYE412W	**M 475** GYE475W	
M 246 BYX246V	**M 273** BYX273V	**M 297** BYX297V	**M 357l** GYE357W	**OM 420** GYE420W	**M 476** GYE476W	
M 254u BYX254V	**M 274** BYX274V	**M 302** BYX302V	**M 359** GYE359W	**M 423** GYE423W	**M 477** GYE477W	

M 513-794 MCW Metrobus DR101/14 MCW H43/28D 1980-1 Ex London Buses, 1994

M 513 GYE513W	**M 532** GYE532W	**M 566** GYE566W	**M 607** KYO607X	**M 670** KYV670X	**M 706** KYV706X	**M 763** KYV763X
M 514 GYE514W	**M 542** 542CLT	**M 589** GYE589W	**M 662** KYV662X	**M 690** KYV690X	**M 725** KYV725X	**M 779** KYV779X
M 516 GYE516W	**M 556** GYE556W	**M 597** GYE597W	**M 667** KYV667X	**M 695** KYV695X	**M 760** KYV760X	**M 794** KYV794X

M 806-953 MCW Metrobus DR101/16 MCW H43/28D 1983 Ex London Buses, 1994

M 806 OJD806Y	**M 820** OJD820Y	**M 837** OJD837Y	**M 853** SGC671Y	**M 877** OJD877Y	**M 908** A908SUL	**M 933** A933SUL
M 807 OJD807Y	**M 821** OJD821Y	**M 838** OJD838Y	**M 854** OJD854Y	**M 880** OJD880Y	**M 909** A909SUL	**M 940** A940SUL
M 808 OJD808Y	**M 822** OJD822Y	**M 842** OJD842Y	**M 855** OJD855Y	**M 888** OJD888Y	**M 913** A913SUL	**M 942** A942SUL
M 811 OJD811Y	**M 823** OJD823Y	**M 845** OGK708Y	**M 862** OJD862Y	**M 897** A897SUL	**M 914** A914SUL	**M 944** A944SUL
M 812 OJD812Y	**M 826** OJD826Y	**M 846** OJD846Y	**M 867** OJD867Y	**M 900** A900SUL	**M 918** A918SUL	**M 946** A946SUL
M 814 OJD814Y	**M 828** OJD828Y	**M 847** OJD847Y	**M 868** OJD868Y	**M 902** A902SUL	**M 922** A922SUL	**M 947** A947SUL
M 816 OJD816Y	**M 830** OJD830Y	**M 848** OJD848Y	**M 870** OJD870Y	**M 904** A904SUL	**M 923** A923SUL	**M 949** A949SUL
M 817 OJD817Y	**M 833** OJD833Y	**M 849** OJD849Y	**M 871** OJD871Y	**M 905** A905SUL	**M 926** A926SUL	**M 953** A953SUL
M 818 OJD818Y	**M 834** OJD834Y	**M 852** OJD852Y	**M 873** OJD873Y	**M 907** A907SUL	**M 931** A931SUL	

M 965-1440 — MCW Metrobus DR101/17 — MCW H43/28D (1432/5/40 are DPH43/28D) — 1984-6 — Ex London Buses, 1994

M 965	A965SYF	M 1002	A702THV	M 1203	B203WUL	M 1226	B226WUL	M 1302	B302WUL	M 1364	C364BUV
M 970	A970SYF	M 1005	A705THV	M 1206	B206WUL	M 1230	B230WUL	M 1304	304CLT	M 1370	C370BUV
M 975	A975SYF	M 1046	VLT46	M 1211	B211WUL	M 1232	B232WUL	M 1305	B305WUL	M 1371t	C371BUV
M 976	A976SYF	M 1055t	A755THV	M 1215	B215WUL	M 1235	B235WUL	M 1306	C306BUV	M 1372t	772DYE
M 977	A977SYF	M 1107	B107WUL	M 1220t	B220WUL	M 1237	B237WUL	M 1311	C311BUV	M 1373t	C373BUV
M 978t	A978SYF	M 1108	B108WUL	M 1222u	B222WUL	M 1241	B241WUL	M 1315	C109NGH	M 1386	C386BUV
M 983	A983SYF	M 1177	B177WUL	M 1223	B223WUL	M 1264	B264WUL	M 1337	C337BUV	M 1387	C387BUV
M 991	A991SYF	M 1180	B180WUL	M 1224	B224WUL	M 1268	B268WUL	M 1347	C347BUV	M 1388	C388BUV
M 992	A992SYF	M 1196u	B196WUL	M 1225	B225WUL	M 1301	B301WUL	M 1357	C357BUV	M 1389t	89CLT

M 1391	C391BUV
M 1410t	C410BUV
M 1411t	C411BUV
M 1432	WLT432
M 1433	C433BUV
M 1434t	WLT434
M 1435	435CLT
M 1436t	VLT136
M 1440	C440BUV

ML 1-15 — Marshall Minibus — Marshall — B29F — 1996/7 — (ML 1-6 currently on loan to Limebourne)

ML 1	P501HEG	ML 4	P504HEG	ML 7	P407KAV	ML 10	P410KAV	ML 13	P403KAV	
ML 2	P502HEG	ML 5	P505HEG	ML 8	P408KAV	ML 11	P401KAV	ML 14t	P404KAV	
ML 3	P503HEG	ML 6	P506HEG	ML 9	P409KAV	ML 12	P402KAV	ML 15	P405KAV	

MRL 136-241 — Optare MetroRider MR03 — Optare — B26F — 1990-3 — Ex London Buses, 1994

MRL 136	H136UUA	MRL 159	H159UUA	MRL 206	J706CGK	MRL 227	K427HWY	MRL 231	K431HWY	MRL 235	K435HWY
MRL 137	H137UUA	MRL 178	H678YGO	MRL 224	K424HWY	MRL 228	K428HWY	MRL 232	K432HWY	MRL 236	K436HWY
MRL 155	H155UUA	MRL 190	H690YGO	MRL 225	K425HWY	MRL 229	K429HWY	MRL 233	K433HWY	MRL 237	K437HWY
MRL 157	H157UUA	MRL 196	J696CGK	MRL 226	K426HWY	MRL 230	K430HWY	MRL 234	K434HWY	MRL 238	K438HWY

MRL 239	K439HWY
MRL 240	K440HWY
MRL 241	K441HWY

NV 1-27 — Volvo Olympian YN2RV18Z4 — Northern Counties Palatine I — H47/30F — 1995

NV 1	M401RVU	NV 5	M405RVU	NV 9	M409RVU	NV 13	N413JBV	NV 17	N417JBV	NV 21	N421JBV
NV 2	2CLT	NV 6	M406RVU	NV 10	M410RVU	NV 14	N414JBV	NV 18	N418JBV	NV 22	N422JBV
NV 3	M403RVU	NV 7	M407RVU	NV 11	WLT411	NV 15	WLT815	NV 19	N419JBV	NV 23	N423JBV
NV 4	M404RVU	NV 8	WLT838	NV 12	N412JBV	NV 16	N416JBV	NV 20	N420JBV	NV 24	N424JBV

NV 25	N425JBV
NV 26	N426JBV
NV 27	WLT527

NV 28-48 — Volvo Olympian YN2RV18Z4 — Northern Counties Palatine I — H48/27D — 1996

NV 28	N528LHG	NV 31	N531LHG	NV 34	N534LHG	NV 37	N537LHG	NV 40	N540LHG	NV 43	N543LHG
NV 29	VLT29	NV 32	N532LHG	NV 35	N535LHG	NV 38	WLT688	NV 41	N541LHG	NV 44	N544LHG
NV 30	N530LHG	NV 33	N533LHG	NV 36	N536LHG	NV 39	N539LHG	NV 42	N542LHG	NV 45	N545LHG

NV 46	N546LHG
NV 47	N547LHG
NV 48	N548LHG

NV 49-99 — Volvo Olympian OLY-4953 — Northern Counties Palatine I — H47/27D* — 1997/8 — *NV 58 & 60 are DPH47/27D

NV 49	P549WGT	NV 57	R257LGH	NV 65	R265LGH	NV 73	R273LGH	NV 82	R282LGH	NV 90	R390LGH
NV 50	P550WGT	NV 58	R258LGH	NV 66	R266LGH	NV 74	R274LGH	NV 83	R283LGH	NV 91	R391LGH
NV 51	R251LGH	NV 59	R259LGH	NV 67	R267LGH	NV 75	R275LGH	NV 84	R284LGH	NV 92	R392LGH
NV 52	R252LGH	NV 60	260CLT	NV 68	WLT868	NV 76	R276LGH	NV 85	R285LGH	NV 93	R393LGH
NV 53	R253LGH	NV 61	R261LGH	NV 69	R269LGH	NV 77	R277LGH	NV 86	R286LGH	NV 94	R394LGH
NV 54	R254LGH	NV 62	R262LGH	NV 70	R270LGH	NV 78	R278LGH	NV 87	R287LGH	NV 95	R395LGH
NV 55	R255LGH	NV 63	R263LGH	NV 71	R271LGH	NV 79	R279LGH	NV 88	R288LGH	NV 96	R396LGH
NV 56	R256LGH	NV 64	R264LGH	NV 72	R272LGH	NV 81	R281LGH	NV 89	R389LGH	NV 97	R397LGH

NV 98	R398LGH
NV 99	R399LGH

NV 101-159 Volvo Olympian YN2RV18Z4* Northern Counties Palatine I H47/27D 1997/8 *NV 131-159 are OLY-4953

NV 101 P901RYO	NV 110 P910RYO	NV 119 P919RYO	NV 128 P928RYO
NV 102 P902RYO	NV 111 P911RYO	NV 120 P920RYO	NV 129 P929RYO
NV 103 P903RYO	NV 112 P912RYO	NV 121 P921RYO	NV 130 P930RYO
NV 104 P904RYO	NV 113 P913RYO	NV 122 P922RYO	NV 131 R331LGH
NV 105 P905RYO	NV 114 P914RYO	NV 123 P923RYO	NV 132 R332LGH
NV 106 P906RYO	NV 115 P915RYO	NV 124 P924RYO	NV 133 R433LGH
NV 107 P907RYO	NV 116 P916RYO	NV 125 P925RYO	NV 134 R334LGH
NV 108 698DYE	NV 117 P917RYO	NV 126 P926RYO	NV 135 R335LGH
NV 109 P909RYO	NV 118 P918RYO	NV 127 P927RYO	NV 136 R336LGH

NV 137 R337LGH	NV 147 R347LGH	NV 156 R556LGH
NV 138 R338LGH	NV 148 WLT548	NV 157 R557LGH
NV 139 R339LGH	NV 149 R549LGH	NV 158 R558LGH
NV 141 R341LGH	NV 150 R550LGH	NV 159 R559LGH
NV 142 R342LGH	NV 151 R551LGH	
NV 143 R343LGH	NV 152 352CLT	
NV 144 R344LGH	NV 153 R553LGH	
NV 145 545CLT	NV 154 R554LGH	
NV 146 WLT346	NV 155 R355LGH	

NV 161-187 Volvo Olympian OLY-4953 Northern Counties Palatine II DPH47/26D 1997/8

NV 161 R361LGH	NV 165 R365LGH	NV 169 R369LGH	NV 173 R373LGH
NV 162 R362LGH	NV 166 166CLT	NV 170 WLT470	NV 174 R374LGH
NV 163 R363LGH	NV 167 R367LGH	NV 171 R371LGH	NV 175 R375LGH
NV 164 R364LGH	NV 168 R368LGH	NV 172 R372LGH	NV 176 R376LGH

NV 177 VLT277	NV 181 R381LGH	NV 185 R385LGH
NV 178 R378LGH	NV 182 R382LGH	NV 186 R386LGH
NV 179 VLT179	NV 183 R383LGH	NV 187 197CLT
NV 180 R380LGH	NV 184 VLT284	

RM 9-2151 AEC Routemaster R2RH Park Royal H36/28D 1959-65 Ex London Buses, 1994

RM 9 VLT9	RM 687 WLT687	RM 994 WLT994	RM 1097 97CLT
RM 71u UFF380	RM 758 WLT758	RM 1002 OYM368A	RM 1104 104CLT
RM 202 VLT202	RM 782 WLT782	RM 1033 33CLT	RM 1119 119CLT
RM 436 WLT436	RM 787 WLT787	RM 1058 58CLT	RM 1168 168CLT
RM 478 WLT478	RM 928 WLT928	RM 1062 62CLT	RM 1174 JSJ797
RM 541 WLT541	RM 967 WLT967	RM 1082 82CLT	RM 1260 JSJ743

RM 1305 305CLT	RM 1955 ALD955B	RM 2106 CUV106C
RM 1380 380CLT	RM 1962 ALD962B	RM 2109 CUV109C
RM 1400 KGJ339A	RM 1977 ALD977B	RM 2128 CUV128C
RM 1621 KGJ187A	RM 1980 ALD980B	RM 2151 CUV151C
RM 1666 KGJ341A	RM 2022 ALM22B	
RM 1797 797DYE	RM 2051 ALM51B	

RML 883-899 AEC Routemaster R2RH Park Royal H40/32R 1961 Ex London Buses, 1994

RML 883 WLT883	RML 887 WLT887	RML 889 WLT889	RML 894 WLT894	RML 899 WLT899

RML 2262-2752 AEC Routemaster R2RH/1 Park Royal *H40/32R 1965-68 Ex London Buses, 1994 *2516 is H40/32RD

RML 2262 CUV262C	RML 2316 CUV316C	RML 2361 CUV361C	RML 2411 JJD411D
RML 2263 CUV263C	RML 2317 CUV317C	RML 2362 CUV362C	RML 2412 JJD412D
RML 2270 CUV270C	RML 2318 CUV318C	RML 2363 CUV363C	RML 2422 JJD422D
RML 2271 CUV271C	RML 2321 CUV321C	RML 2364 JJD364D	RML 2440 JJD440D
RML 2273 CUV273C	RML 2327 CUV327C	RML 2371 JJD371D	RML 2441 JJD441D
RML 2275 CUV275C	RML 2332 CUV332C	RML 2376 JJD376D	RML 2453 JJD453D
RML 2276 CUV276C	RML 2335 CUV335C	RML 2381 JJD381D	RML 2454 JJD454D
RML 2279 CUV279C	RML 2336 CUV336C	RML 2385 JJD385D	RML 2461 JJD461D
RML 2283 CUV283C	RML 2338 CUV338C	RML 2389 JJD389D	RML 2465 JJD465D
RML 2290 CUV290C	RML 2339 CUV339C	RML 2396 JJD396D	RML 2466 JJD466D
RML 2297 CUV297C	RML 2342 CUV342C	RML 2397 JJD397D	RML 2469 JJD469D
RML 2302 CUV302C	RML 2345 CUV345C	RML 2398 JJD398D	RML 2472 JJD472D
RML 2305 CUV305C	RML 2358 CUV358C	RML 2400 JJD400D	RML 2474 JJD474D
RML 2314 CUV314C	RML 2360 CUV360C	RML 2403 JJD403D	RML 2475 JJD475D

RML 2482 JJD482D	RML 2543 JJD543D	RML 2587 JJD587D
RML 2484 JJD484D	RML 2551 JJD551D	RML 2590 JJD590D
RML 2499 JJD499D	RML 2554 JJD554D	RML 2593 JJD593D
RML 2502 JJD502D	RML 2556 JJD556D	RML 2596 JJD596D
RML 2507 JJD507D	RML 2560 JJD560D	RML 2601 NML601E
RML 2513 JJD513D	RML 2564 JJD564D	RML 2604 NML604E
RML 2515 JJD515D	RML 2568 JJD568D	RML 2605 NML605E
DRM 2516 WLT516	RML 2570 JJD570D	RML 2606 NML606E
RML 2517 JJD517D	RML 2575 JJD575D	RML 2612 NML612E
RML 2520 JJD520D	RML 2576 JJD576D	RML 2613 NML613E
RML 2529 JJD529D	RML 2578 JJD578D	RML 2614 NML614E
RML 2535 JJD535D	RML 2580 JJD580D	RML 2615 NML615E
RML 2539 JJD539D	RML 2583 JJD583D	RML 2618 NML618E
RML 2540 JJD540D	RML 2584 JJD584D	RML 2626 NML626E

RML 2629	NML629E	RML 2640	NML640E	RML 2669	SMK669F	RML 2683	SMK683F	RML 2714	SMK714F	RML 2736	SMK736F
RML 2630	NML630E	RML 2644	NML644E	RML 2673	SMK673F	RML 2693	SMK693F	RML 2725	SMK725F	RML 2745	SMK745F
RML 2631	NML631E	RML 2648	NML648E	RML 2676	SMK676F	RML 2711	SMK711F	RML 2732	SMK732F	RML 2752	SMK752F
RML 2637	NML637E	RML 2654	NML654E	RML 2680	SMK680F	RML 2712	SMK712F	RML 2733	SMK733F		

SC 1t	D585OOV	Freight-Rover Sherpa 374	Carlyle Citibus	B6F	1986	Ex London Buses, 1994

SP 1-25		DAF DB250WB505	Optare Spectra	H44/27F	1992/3	Ex London Buses, 1994

SP 1	K301FYG	SP 6	K306FYG	SP 10	K310FYG	SP 14	K314FYG	SP 18	18CLT	SP 22	K322FYG
SP 3	K303FYG	SP 7	K307FYG	SP 11	K311FYG	SP 15	K315FYG	SP 19	19CLT	SP 23	K323FYG
SP 4	K304FYG	SP 8	K308FYG	SP 12	K312FYG	SP 16	K316FYG	SP 20	20CLT	SP 24	K324FYG
SP 5	K305FYG	SP 9	K309FYG	SP 13	K313FYG	SP 17	170CLT	SP 21	K321FYG	SP 25	WLT625

T 172	CUL172V	Leyland Titan TNLXB2RRsp	Park Royal	H44/26D	1979	Ex London Buses, 1994

T 329-1123   Leyland Titan TNLXB2RR   Leyland   *H44/24D   1980-1984 Ex London Buses, 1994

*T705, 709, 766, 778, 793 are H44/23D, 799-1120 are H44/26D, 803 is O44/26D, 1060 is H44/24F

T 329	KYV329X	T 764	OHV764Y	T 871	A871SUL	T 932	A932SYE	T 979	A979SYE	T 1018	A618THV	T 1071	A71THX
T 677t	OHV677Y	T 765	OHV765Y	T 887	A887SYE	T 936	A936SYE	T 980	A980SYE	T 1019	A619THV	T 1072	A72THX
T 678	OHV678Y	T 766	OHV766Y	T 888	A888SYE	T 937	A937SYE	T 981	A981SYE	T 1021	A621THV	T 1073	A73THX
T 679	OHV679Y	T 767	OHV767Y	T 889	A889SYE	T 938	A938SYE	T 982	A982SYE	T 1023	A623THV	T 1074	A74THX
T 681	OHV681Y	T 773	OHV773Y	T 892	A892SYE	T 939	A939SYE	T 983	A983SYE	T 1033	A633THV	T 1075	A75THX
T 683t	OHV683Y	T 774	OHV774Y	T 893	A893SYE	T 940	A940SYE	T 984	A984SYE	T 1037	A637THV	T 1078	A78THX
T 687	OHV687Y	T 775	OHV775Y	T 894	A894SYE	T 942	A942SYE	T 985	A985SYE	T 1040	A640THV	T 1080	B80WUV
T 693	OHV693Y	T 778	OHV778Y	T 895	A895SYE	T 943	A943SYE	T 991	A991SYE	T 1041	A641THV	T 1082	B82WUV
T 694	OHV694Y	T 779	OHV779Y	T 897	A897SYE	T 946	A946SYE	T 992	A992SYE	T 1042	A642THV	T 1085	B85WUV
T 701	OHV701Y	T 782	OHV782Y	T 898	A898SYE	T 948	A948SYE	T 993	A993SYE	T 1043	A643THV	T 1086	B86WUV
T 704	OHV704Y	T 787	OHV787Y	T 901	A901SYE	T 952	A952SYE	T 994	A994SYE	T 1044t	A644THV	T 1087	B87WUV
T 705t	OHV705Y	T 793t	OHV793Y	T 906	A906SYE	T 954	A954SYE	T 995	A995SYE	T 1046	A646THV	T 1088	B88WUV
T 709	OHV709Y	T 795	OHV795Y	T 907	A907SYE	T 955	A955SYE	T 997	A997SYE	T 1047	A647THV	T 1090	B90WUV
T 713	OHV713Y	T 796	OHV796Y	T 908	A908SYE	T 956	A956SYE	T 1000	ALM1B	T 1051	A651THV	T 1094	B94WUV
T 715	OHV715Y	T 798	OHV798Y	T 909	A909SYE	T 957	A957SYE	T 1001	A601THV	T 1053	A653THV	T 1095	B95WUV
T 716	OHV716Y	T 799	OHV799Y	T 913	A913SYE	T 958	A958SYE	T 1002	A602THV	T 1054	A654THV	T 1098	B98WUV
T 717	OHV717Y	T 803	OHV803Y	T 914	A914SYE	T 959	A959SYE	T 1004	A604THV	T 1055	A655THV	T 1102	B102WUV
T 718	OHV718Y	T 806	OHV806Y	T 915	A915SYE	T 963	A963SYE	T 1005	A605THV	T 1057	257CLT	T 1104	B104WUV
T 732	OHV732Y	T 831t	A831SUL	T 917	A917SYE	T 966u	A966SYE	T 1006	A606THV	T 1058	A58THX	T 1105	B105WUV
T 735	WLT735	T 835t	A835SUL	T 919t	A919SYE	T 967	A967SYE	T 1008	A608THV	T 1059	A59THX	T 1107	B107WUV
T 736	WLT736	T 839t	A839SUL	T 923	A923SYE	T 968	A968SYE	T 1009	A609THV	T 1060t	A60THX	T 1109	B109WUV
T 737	OHV737Y	T 844t	A844SUL	T 924	A924SYE	T 969	A969SYE	T 1010	A610THV	T 1061	A61THX	T 1111	B111WUV
T 747	OHV747Y	T 851t	A851SUL	T 927	A927SYE	T 970	A970SYE	T 1011	A611THV	T 1062	A62THX	T 1120	B120WUV
T 750	OHV750Y	T 853	A853SUL	T 928t	A928SYE	T 972	A972SYE	T 1014	A614THV	T 1063	A63THX	T 1123	B123WUV
T 752	OHV752Y	T 863	A863SUL	T 929	A929SYE	T 973	A973SYE	T 1015	A615THV	T 1064	A64THX		
T 756	OHV756Y	T 864	A864SUL	T 930	A930SYE	T 974	A974SYE	T 1016	A616THV	T 1068	A68THX		
T 757	OHV757Y	T 870	A870SUL	T 931	A931SYE	T 977	A977SYE	T 1017	A617THV	T 1070	A70THX		

T 1129	WDA4T	Leyland Titan TNLXB1RF	Park Royal	DPH43/29F	1979	Ex London Buses, 1994
VC 1	101CLT	Volvo Citybus B10M-50	Northern Counties	DPH45/35D	1989	Ex London Buses, 1994
VC 2	G102NGN	Volvo Citybus B10M-50	Northern Counties	DPH45/35D	1989	Ex London Buses, 1994
VC 3	WLT803	Volvo Citybus B10M-50	Northern Counties	DPH45/35D	1989	Ex London Buses, 1994
VC 4	WLT474	Volvo Citybus B10M-50	Northern Counties	H45/35D	1989	Ex London Buses, 1994
VC 5	G105NGN	Volvo Citybus B10M-50	Northern Counties	H45/35D	1989	Ex London Buses, 1994
VC 6	VLT60	Volvo Citybus B10M-50	Northern Counties	H45/35D	1989	Ex London Buses, 1994

VC 7-39		Volvo Citybus B10M-50	Northern Counties	H47/35D	1989-91	Ex London Buses, 1994

VC 7	G107NGN	VC 12	312CLT	VC 17	G117NGN	VC 22	G122NGN	VC 27	G127NGN	VC 32	G132PKG	VC 37	WLT837
VC 8	G108NGN	VC 13	G113NGN	VC 18	WLT818	VC 23	23CLT	VC 28	528CLT	VC 33	G133PKG	VC 38	G138PKG
VC 9	G109NGN	VC 14	614DYE	VC 19	619DYE	VC 24	G124NGN	VC 29	229CLT	VC 34	G134PKG	VC 39	839DYE
VC 10	G110NGN	VC 15	G115NGN	VC 20	WLT920	VC 25	125CLT	VC 30	G130PKG	VC 35	G135PKG		
VC 11	G647SGT	VC 16	G116NGN	VC 21	621DYE	VC 26	G126NGN	VC 31	G131PKG	VC 36	836DYE		

VWL 1	N101HGO	Volvo B6LE-53	Wright Crusader	B36F	1995	On loan from London Transport

On order for 1999:

46 x Volvo B7L/Alexander ALX 400 low floor double deckers for routes 45,63;
17 x DAF SB220LC/ East Lancs Flyte dual-door single deckers for use on shuttle services to the Millennium Dome at Greenwich.

Previous registrations:

2CLT	M402RVU	304CLT	B304WUL	C377PCD	C377PCD,	JSJ743	260CLT	OGK708Y	OJD845Y,	VLT284	R384LGH	WLT696	GUW496W
23CLT	G123NGN	312CLT	G112NGN		PCN762, VLT71	JSJ797	174CLT		545CLT	WLT346	R346LGH	WLT735	OHV735Y
46CLT	H546XGK	352CLT	R552LGH	G551SGT	JDZ2348,	K767CGK	K594MGT,	OYM368A	2CLT	WLT379	P509RYM	WLT736	OHV736Y
78CLT	BYX278V	435CLT	C435BUV		WLT548		WLT994	SGC671Y	OJD853Y,	WLT395	K595MGT	WLT789	M89MYM
83CLT	GUW483W	528CLT	G128NGN	G552SGT	JDZ2346,	KGJ187A	621DYE		VLT53	WLT432	C432BUV	WLT803	G103NGN
89CLT	C389BUV	542CLT	GYE542W		WLT346	KGJ339A	400CLT	SGK374V	BYX198V,	WLT434	C434BUV	WLT815	N415JBV
101CLT	G101NGN	545CLT	R345LGH	G554SGT	JDZ2345,	M410RVU	M410RVU,		VLT98	WLT463	GYE463W	WLT818	G118NGN
125CLT	G125NGN	614DYE	G114NGN		545CLT		WLT990	UFF380	VLT71	WLT467	GUW467W	WLT825	K325FYG
166CLT	R366LGH	619DYE	G119NGN	G560SGT	JDZ2347,	N416JBV	N421JBV	VLT9	VLT9,	WLT470	R370LGH	WLT837	G137NGN
170CLT	K317FYG	621DYE	G121NGN		WLT470	N420JBV	N422JBV		OYM374A	WLT474	G104NGN	WLT838	M408RVU
174CLT	R474LGH	698DYE	P908RYO	G570SGT	JDZ2352,	N421JBV	N424JBV	VLT29	N529LHG	WLT487	GUW487W	WLT843	GUW443W
176CLT	R476LGH	772DYE	C372BUV		352CLT	N422JBV	N416JBV	VLT46	A746THV	WLT516	JJD516D	WLT868	R268LGH
186CLT	GUW486W	836DYE	G136NGN	G647SGT	G111NGN,	N423JBV	N425JBV	VLT60	G106NGN	WLT527	N427JBV	WLT872	R472LGH
188CLT	P508RYM	839DYE	J139DGF		WLT311	N424JBV	N426JBV	VLT71	BYX171V	WLT532	H532XGK	WLT920	G120NGN
197CLT	R387LGH	ALM1B	A600THV	GUW499W	GUW499W,	N425JBV	N427JBV	VLT136	C436BUV	WLT548	R348LGH	WLT994	WLT994,
229CLT	G129NGN	C109NGH	C315BUV,		WLT599	N426JBV	N420JBV	VLT179	R379LGH	WLT598	GUW498W		VLT89
257CLT	A57THX		VLT15	H881BGN	H366XGC,	N427JBV	N423JBV	VLT180	GUW480W	WLT648	GUW448W		
260CLT	R260LGH				166CLT			VLT277	R377LGH	WLT688	N538LHG		

Special Liveries:

OMs 171, 241, 420, Ms 1432, 1440 and Ts 172 and 803 are red with white or cream relief in differing styles.
NV 1-10 carry Docklands Express between decks logos.

LONDON UNITED

A 112-130			Volvo Olympian YN3RV18Z4		Alexander Royale			DPH43/9FL 1995/6					
A 112	N112UHP	A 115	N115UHP	A 118	N118UHP	A 121	N121UHP	A 124	N124YRW	A 127	N127YRW	A 130	N130YRW
A 113	N113UHP	A 116	N116UHP	A 119	N119UHP	A 122	N122UHP	A 125	N125YRW	A 128	N128YRW		
A 114	N114UHP	A 117	N117UHP	A 120	N120UHP	A 123	N123UHP	A 126	N126YRW	A 129	N129YRW		

CD 1-8			Dennis Dart SLF SFD212		Wright Crusader 10.2m			B32F 1996	
CD 1	VDZ8001	CD 3	VDZ8003	CD 5	VDZ8005	CD 7	VDZ8007		
CD 2	VDZ8002	CD 4	VDZ8004	CD 6	VDZ8006	CD 8	VDZ8008		

DA 1-9			DAF SB220LC550		Optare Delta			*B49F 1989/90 *DA1 DP49F	
								DA1 ex Gailymatic, 1995, DA2-9 ex London Buses, 1994	
DA 1	F802NGY	DA 3	G931MYG	DA 5	G933MYG	DA 7	G935MYG	DA 9	G937MYG
DA 2	A5LBR	DA 4	G932MYG	DA 6	G934MYG	DA 8	G936MYG		

DP 1-11			Dennis Dart SLF SFD322		Plaxton Pointer 2 10.6m			B36F 1998	
DP 1	S301MKH	DP 3	S303MKH	DP 5	S305MKH	DP 7	S307MKH	DP 9	S309MKH	DP 11	S311MKH
DP 2	S302MKH	DP 4	S304MKH	DP 6	S306MKH	DP 8	S308MKH	DP 10	S310MKH		

DR 1-14			Dennis Dart 8.5SDL3003		Reeve Burgess Pointer 8.5m			B28F 1991		Ex London Buses, 1994	
DR 1	H101THE	DR 3	H103THE	DR 5	H105THE	DR 7	H107THE	DR 9	H109THE	DR 11	WLT931	DR 13	H113THE
DR 2	H102THE	DR 4	H104THE	DR 6	H106THE	DR 8	H108THE	DR 10	H110THE	DR 12	H112THE	DR 14	H114THE

DR 53-57			Dennis Dart 8.5SDL3010		Plaxton Pointer 8.5m			B28F 1991		Ex London Buses, 1994
DR 53	J653XHL	DR 54	J654XHL	DR 55	J655XHL	DR 56	J156GAT	DR 57	J157GAT	

DR 58-141			Dennis Dart 8.5SDL3010		Plaxton Pointer 8.5m			B24F 1991/2		Ex London Buses, 1994	
DR 58	J158GAT	DR 68	J368GKH	DR 78	J378GKH	DR 106	J106DUV	DR 116	J116DUV	DR 126	J126DUV	DR 136	J136DUV
DR 59	J159GAT	DR 69	J369GKH	DR 79	J379GKH	DR 107	J107DUV	DR 117	J117DUV	DR 127	J127DUV	DR 137	J137DUV
DR 60	J160GAT	DR 70	J370GKH	DR 80	J380GKH	DR 108	J108DUV	DR 118	J118DUV	DR 128	J128DUV	DR 138	J138DUV
DR 61	J161GAT	DR 71	J371GKH	DR 99	J599DUV	DR 109	J109DUV	DR 119	J119DUV	DR 129	J129DUV	DR 139	J139DUV
DR 62	J362GKH	DR 72	J372GKH	DR 100	VLT23	DR 110	J110DUV	DR 120	J120DUV	DR 130	J130DUV	DR 140	J140DUV
DR 63	J363GKH	DR 73	J373GKH	DR 101	J101DUV	DR 111	WLT946	DR 121	J121DUV	DR 131	J131DUV	DR 141	J141DUV
DR 64	J364GKH	DR 74	J374GKH	DR 102	J102DUV	DR 112	J112DUV	DR 122	J122DUV	DR 132	J132DUV		
DR 65	J365GKH	DR 75	J375GKH	DR 103	J103DUV	DR 113	J113DUV	DR 123	J123DUV	DR 133	J133DUV		
DR 66	J366GKH	DR 76	J376GKH	DR 104	J104DUV	DR 114	J114DUV	DR 124	J124DUV	DR 134	J134DUV		
DR 67	J367GKH	DR 77	J377GKH	DR 105	J105DUV	DR 115	J115DUV	DR 125	J125DUV	DR 135	J135DUV		

DRL 96-108 Dennis Dart 9SDL3024 Plaxton Pointer 9m B28F 1993 Ex London Buses, 1994

DRL 96 K96SAG	**DRL 98** K98SAG	**DRL 100** ALM2B	**DRL 102** K102SAG	**DRL 104** K104SAG	**DRL 106** K106SAG	**DRL 108** K108SAG
DRL 97 K97SAG	**DRL 99** K199SAG	**DRL 101** K101SAG	**DRL 103** K103SAG	**DRL 105** K105SAG	**DRL 107** K107SAG	

DRL 159-171 Dennis Dart 9SDL3034 Plaxton Pointer 9m *B28F 1993/4 Ex London Buses, 1994 *DRL165-169 are B34F

DRL 159 L159XRH	**DRL 161** L161XRH	**DRL 163** L163XRH	**DRL 165** L165YAT	**DRL 167** L167YAT	**DRL 169** L169YAT	**DRL 171** L171CKH
DRL 160 L160XRH	**DRL 162** L162XRH	**DRL 164** L164XRH	**DRL 166** L166YAT	**DRL 168** L168YAT	**DRL 170** L170CKH	

DT 1-47 Dennis Dart 8.5SDL3003 Duple Dartline 8.5m DP21F* 1990 Ex London Buses, 1994. *DT42 is B28F
(DT 29–47 are Carlyle Dartline)

DT 1 G501VYE	**DT 6** G506VYE	**DT 11** G511VYE	**DT 16** G516VYE	**DT 21** G521VYE	**DT 26** G526VYE	**DT 43** G43TGW
DT 2 G502VYE	**DT 7** G507VYE	**DT 12** G512VYE	**DT 17** G517VYE	**DT 22** G522VYE	**DT 27** G527VYE	**DT 44** G44TGW
DT 3 G503VYE	**DT 8** G508VYE	**DT 13** G513VYE	**DT 18** G518VYE	**DT 23** G523VYE	**DT 29** G29TGW	**DT 45** G45TGW
DT 4 G504VYE	**DT 9** G509VYE	**DT 14** G514VYE	**DT 19** G519VYE	**DT 24** G524VYE	**DT 41** G41TGW	**DT 46** G46TGW
DT 5 G505VYE	**DT 10** G510VYE	**DT 15** G515VYE	**DT 20** G520VYE	**DT 25** G525VYE	**DT 42** G42TGW	**DT 47** G47TGW

DT 48-72 Dennis Dart 8.5SDL3003 Carlyle Dartline 8.5m B28F 1990 Ex London Buses, 1994

DT 48 G48TGW	**DT 50** G50TGW	**DT 52** G52TGW	**DT 54** G54TGW	**DT 57** G57TGW	**DT 72** H72MOB
DT 49 G49TGW	**DT 51** G51TGW	**DT 53** G53TGW	**DT 56** G56TGW	**DT 71** H71MOB	

DT 73 H73MOB	Dennis Dart 8.5SDL3003	Carlyle Dartline 8.5m	B26F	1990	Ex London Buses, 1994
DT 74 H74MOB	Dennis Dart 8.5SDL3003	Carlyle Dartline 8.5m	B28F	1990	Ex London Buses, 1994
DT 75 WLT329	Dennis Dart 8.5SDL3003	Carlyle Dartline 8.5m	B26F	1990	Ex London Buses, 1994
DT 76 H76MOB	Dennis Dart 8.5SDL3003	Carlyle Dartline 8.5m	B28F	1990	Ex London Buses, 1994
DT 77 WLT339	Dennis Dart 8.5SDL3003	Carlyle Dartline 8.5m	B28F	1990	Ex London Buses, 1994
DT 78 H78MOB	Dennis Dart 8.5SDL3003	Carlyle Dartline 8.5m	B28F	1990	Ex London Buses, 1994
DT 79 H79MOB	Dennis Dart 8.5SDL3003	Carlyle Dartline 8.5m	B26F	1990	Ex London Buses, 1994

DT 80-167 Dennis Dart 8.5SDL3003 Carlyle Dartline 8.5m B28F 1990 Ex London Buses, 1994

DT 80 236CLT	**DT 85** H85MOB	**DT 147** H147MOB	**DT 152** H152MOB	**DT 159** H159NON	**DT 164** WLT804
DT 81 H81MOB	**DT 86** H86MOB	**DT 148** H148MOB	**DT 153** H153MOB	**DT 160** H160NON	**DT 165** H165NON
DT 82 H82MOB	**DT 144** H144MOB	**DT 149** H149MOB	**DT 154** H154MOB	**DT 161** H161NON	**DT 166** H166NON
DT 83 H83MOB	**DT 145** H145MOB	**DT 150** H150MOB	**DT 155** H155MOB	**DT 162** H162NON	**DT 167** H167NON
DT 84 H84MOB	**DT 146** H146MOB	**DT 151** H151MOB	**DT 158** H158NON	**DT 163** H163NON	

DT 168 500CLT Dennis Dart 8.5SDL3003 Duple Dartline 8.5m DP21F 1989 Ex London Buses, 1994

DWL 1-14 Dennis Dart 9SDL3002 Wright Handybus 9m B36F 1990 Ex London Buses, 1994

DWL 1 JDW2401	**DWL 3** JDW2403	**DWL 5** JDW2405	**DWL 7** JDW2407	**DWL 9** JDW2409	**DWL 11** JDW2411	**DWL 13** JDW2413
DWL 2 JDW2402	**DWL 4** JDW2404	**DWL 6** JDW2406	**DWL 8** JDW2408	**DWL 10** JDW2410	**DWL 12** JDW2412	**DWL 14** JDW2414

FS 29 C501HOE Ford Transit 190D Carlyle B20F 1985 Ex London Buses, 1994

L 292-305 — Leyland Olympian ONCL10/1RZ — Leyland — H47/31F — 1989 — Ex London Buses, 1994

L 292 G292UYK	**L 294** G294UYK	**L 296** G296UYK	**L 298** G298UYK	**L 300** G300UYK	**L 302** G302UYK	**L 304** G304UYK
L 293 G293UYK	**L 295** G295UYK	**L 297** G297UYK	**L 299** G299UYK	**L 301** G301UYK	**L 303** G303UYK	**L 305** G305UYK

L 306-311 — Leyland Olympian ON2R50C13Z4 — Leyland — H47/31F — 1989 — Ex London Buses, 1994

L 306 G306UYK	**L 307** G307UYK	**L 308** G308UYK	**L 309** G309UYK	**L 310** G310UYK	**L 311** G311UYK

L 312	G312UYK	Leyland Olympian ONCL10/1RZ	Leyland	DPH43/29F 1989	Ex London Buses, 1994
L 313	G313UYK	Leyland Olympian ONCL10/1RZ	Leyland	DPH43/29F 1989	Ex London Buses, 1994
L 314	G314UYK	Leyland Olympian ONCL10/1RZ	Leyland	DPH43/29F 1989	Ex London Buses, 1994

LLW1-10 — Dennis Lance SLF 11SDA3202 — Wright Pathfinder 320 — B34D — 1993/4 — Ex London Buses, 1994

LLW 1 ODZ8901	**LLW 3** ODZ8903	**LLW 5** ODZ8905	**LLW 7** ODZ8907	**LLW 9** ODZ8909
LLW 2 ODZ8902	**LLW 4** ODZ8904	**LLW 6** ODZ8906	**LLW 8** ODZ8908	**LLW 10** ODZ8910

LS 84	OJD884R	Leyland National 10351A/2R	(Urban Bus)	B38F	1977	Ex West Midlands, 1995
LS 96	OJD896R	Leyland National 10351A/2R	(Urban Bus)	B38F	1977	Ex London Buses, 1994
LS 99	OJD899R	Leyland National 10351A/2R	(Urban Bus)	B38F	1977	Ex London Buses, 1994
LS 153	THX153S	Leyland National 10351A/2R	(Urban Bus)	B38F	1977	Ex West Midlands, 1995
DLS 195	THX195S	Leyland National 10351A/2R	(DAF engine)	B36D	1978	Ex London Buses, 1994
DLS 227	THX227S	Leyland National 10351A/2R	(DAF engine)	DP36DL	1978	Ex London Buses, 1994
LS 268	YYE268T	Leyland National 10351A/2R	(Urban Bus)	B38F	1978	Ex West Midlands, 1995
LS 297	YYE297T	Leyland National 10351A/2R	(Urban Bus)	B38F	1979	Ex London Buses, 1994
LS 335	AYR335T	Leyland National 10351A/2R	(Urban Bus)	B38F	1979	Ex London Buses, 1994
LS 337	AYR337T	Leyland National 10351A/2R	(Urban Bus)	B38F	1979	Ex London Buses, 1994
LS 373	BYW373V	Leyland National 10351A/2R	(Urban Bus)	B38F	1979	Ex West Midlands, 1995
LS 385	BYW385V	Leyland National 10351A/2R	(Urban Bus)	B38F	1979	Ex London Buses, 1994
LS 395	BYW395V	Leyland National 10351A/2R	(Urban Bus)	B38F	1979	Ex West Midlands, 1995
LS 405	BYW405V	Leyland National 10351A/2R		B38F	1979	Ex London Buses, 1994
LS 411w	BYW411V	Leyland National 10351A/2R		DP35D	1979	Ex West Midlands, 1995
LS 429w	BYW429V	Leyland National 10351A/2R		B36D	1979	Ex London Buses, 1994
LS 431	BYW431V	Leyland National 10351A/2R	(Urban Bus)	B38F	1979	Ex West Midlands, 1995

LX 3-8 — Leyland Lynx LX2R11C15Z4S — B49F — 1989 — Ex London Buses, 1994

LX 3 G73UYV	**LX 4** G74UYV	**LX 5** G75UYV	**LX 6** G76UYV	**LX 7** G77UYV	**LX 8** G78UYV

M 13-52 — MCW Metrobus DR101/8 — MCW — *H43/28D — 1978/9 — Ex London Buses, 1994

*Training buses are H0/15D

M 13t WYW13T	**M 21**u WYW21T	**M 29**u WYW29T	**M 31**t WYW31T	**M 39** WYW39T	**M 44**u WYW44T	**M 52** WYW52T
M 17 WYW17T	**M 22**t WYW22T	**M 30**t WYW30T	**M 36**t WYW36T	**M 43** WYW43T	**M 46**t WYW46T	

M 59-204 MCW Metrobus DR101/9 MCW H43/28D (Training buses are H0/15D) 1979 Ex London Buses, 1994

M 59 WYW59T	M 93 WYW93T	M 110 BYX110V	M 138 BYX138V	M 159t BYX159V	M 193t BYX193V
M 68 WYW68T	M 96 BYX96V	M 122 BYX122V	M 147t BYX147V	M 162 BYX162V	M 203 BYX203V
M 86 WYW86T	M 99 BYX99V	M 131u BYX131V	M 154 BYX154V	M 183 BYX183V	M 204t BYX204V
M 89t WYW89T	M 100 BYX100V	M 134 BYX134V	M 157t BYX157V	M 187u BYX187V	

M 206-415 MCW Metrobus DR101/12 MCW H43/28D (Training buses are H0/15D) 1980 Ex London Buses, 1994

M 206t BYX206V	M 223u BYX223V	M 264t BYX264V	M 363 GYE363W	M 387 GYE387W
M 221 BYX221V	M 227u BYX227V	M 327 EYE327V	M 366 GYE366W	M 415 GYE415W

M 506-697 MCW Metrobus DR101/14 MCW H43/28D 1981 Ex London Buses, 1994

M 506t GYE506W	M 526 GYE526W	M 554 GYE554W	M 592u GYE592W	M 598 GYE598W	M 687 KYV687X	M 697 KYV697X

M 813-951 MCW Metrobus DR101/16 MCW H43/28D 1983 Ex London Buses, 1994

M 813u OJD813Y	M 832u OJD832Y	M 839 OJD839Y	M 856 OJD856Y	M 889 OJD889Y	M 932u A932SUL
M 815 OJD815Y	M 835 OJD835Y	M 841 OJD841Y	M 864 OJD864Y	M 906 A906SUL	M 951 A951SUL
M 831 OJD831Y	M 836u OJD836Y	M 844 OJD844Y	M 881 OJD881Y	M 920 A920SUL	

M 960-1001 MCW Metrobus DR101/17 MCW H43/28D 1984 Ex London Buses, 1994

M 960 A960SYF	M 963 A963SYF	M 967 A967SYF	M 980 A980SYF	M 985 A985SYF	M 994 A994SYF	M 1001 A701THV
M 962 A962SYF	M 966 A966SYF	M 969 A969SYF	M 981 A981SYF	M 990 A990SYF	M 999 A999SYF	

M 1006-1029 MCW Metrobus DR101/18 MCW H43/28D 1984 Ex London Buses, 1994

M 1006 A706THV	M 1009 A709THV	M 1013 A713THV	M 1016 A716THV	M 1021 A721THV	M 1024 A724THV	M 1027 A727THV
M 1007 A707THV	M 1010 A710THV	M 1014 A714THV	M 1019 A719THV	M 1022 A722THV	M 1025 A725THV	M 1028 A728THV
M 1008 A708THV	M 1011 A711THV	M 1015 A715THV	M 1020 A720THV	M 1023 A723THV	M 1026 A726THV	M 1029 A729THV

M 1030-1039 MCW Metrobus DR101/17 MCW H43/28D 1984 Ex London Buses, 1994

M 1030 A730THV	M 1037 A737THV	M 1039 A739THV

M 1048-1053 MCW Metrobus DR101/19 MCW H43/28D 1984 Ex London Buses, 1994

M 1048 A748THV	M 1050 A750THV	M 1053 A753THV

M 1064-1439 MCW Metrobus DR101/17 MCW H43/28D 1984-86 Ex London Buses, 1994

M 1064 B64WUL	M 1171 B171WUL	M 1191 B191WUL	M 1242 B242WUL	M 1269 B269WUL	M 1344 C344BUV	M 1360 C360BUV
M 1069 B69WUL	M 1172 B172WUL	M 1194 B194WUL	M 1243 B243WUL	M 1270 B270WUL	M 1345 C345BUV	M 1361 C361BUV
M 1073 B73WUL	M 1178 B178WUL	M 1200 B200WUL	M 1251 B251WUL	M 1271 B271WUL	M 1351 C351BUV	M 1363 C363BUV
M 1106 B106WUL	M 1184 B184WUL	M 1207 B207WUL	M 1257 B257WUL	M 1272 B272WUL	M 1352 C352BUV	M 1368 C368BUV
M 1110 B110WUL	M 1187 B187WUL	M 1212 B212WUL	M 1261 B261WUL	M 1336 C336BUV	M 1353 C353BUV	M 1374 C374BUV
M 1125 B125WUL	M 1188 B188WUL	M 1238 B238WUL	M 1262 B262WUL	M 1341 C341BUV	M 1356 C356BUV	M 1381 C381BUV
M 1166 B166WUL	M 1190 B190WUL	M 1240 B240WUL	M 1266 B266WUL	M 1343 C343BUV	M 1358 C358BUV	M 1439 C439BUV

MR 4w	D464PON	MCW Metrorider MF150/14	MCW		B23F	1986	Ex London Buses, 1994
MRL 81	F185YDA	MCW Metrorider MF158/11	MCW		B28F	1988	Ex London Buses, 1994 (carries MRL185)
MRL 82	F186YDA	MCW Metrorider MF158/11	MCW		B28F	1988	Ex London Buses, 1994 (carries MRL186)
MRL 83	F187YDA	MCW Metrorider MF158/11	MCW		B28F	1988	Ex London Buses, 1994 (carries MRL187)
MRL 87	F191YDA	MCW Metrorider MF158/11	MCW		B28F	1988	Ex London Buses, 1994 (carries MRL191)
MRL 90	F194YDA	MCW Metrorider MF158/12	MCW		DP31F	1988	Ex London Buses, 1994 (carries MRL194)
MRL 92	F196YDA	MCW Metrorider MF158/12	MCW		DP31F	1988	Ex London Buses, 1994 (carries MRL196)
MRW 2	A2LBR	MCW Metrorider MF158/11	MCW		B19FL	1988	Ex London Buses, 1994
MRW 3	A3LBR	MCW Metrorider MF158/11	MCW		B19FL	1988	Ex London Buses, 1994
MRW 4	A4LBR	MCW Metrorider MF158/11	MCW		B19FL	1988	Ex London Buses, 1994

MV 1-8   MAN 11.190   Optare Vecta   B42F   1995

MV 1	N281DWY	**MV 3**	N283DWY	**MV 5**	N285DWY	**MV 7**	N287DWY
MV 2	N282DWY	**MV 4**	N284DWY	**MV 6**	N286DWY	**MV 8**	N288DWY

RM 2033	ALM33B	AEC Routemaster R2RH	Park Royal		H36/28R	1964	Ex London Transport, 1997
RM 2078	ALM78B	AEC Routemaster R2RH	Park Royal		H36/28R	1964	Ex London Transport, 1997
RML 880	WLT880	AEC Routemaster R2RH	Park Royal		H40/32R	1961	Ex London Buses, 1994 carries number ER 880
RML 881	WLT881	AEC Routemaster R2RH	Park Royal		H40/32R	1961	Ex London Buses, 1994
RML 891	WLT891	AEC Routemaster R2RH	Park Royal		H40/32R	1961	Ex London Buses, 1994

RML 2269-2757   AEC Routemaster R2RH/1   Park Royal   H40/32R   1961   Ex London Buses, 1994

RML 2269	CUV269C	**RML 2432**	JJD432D	**RML 2489**	JJD489D	**RML 2645**	NML645E	**RML 2702**	SMK702F	**RML 2729**	SMK729S
RML 2293	CUV293C	**RML 2447**	JJD447D	**RML 2500**	JJD500D	**RML 2646**	NML646E	**RML 2704**	SMK704F	**RML 2734**	SMK734F
RML 2298	CUV298C	**RML 2455**	JJD455D	**RML 2519**	JJD519D	**RML 2650**	NML650E	**RML 2707**	SMK707F	**RML 2739**	SMK739F
RML 2349	CUV349C	**RML 2463**	JJD463D	**RML 2600**	NML600E	**RML 2662**	SMK662F	**RML 2720**	SMK720F	**RML 2744**	SMK744F
RML 2353	CUV353C	**RML 2464**	JJD464D	**RML 2621**	NML621E	**RML 2697**	SMK697F	**RML 2721**	SMK721F	**RML 2751**	SMK751F
RML 2414	JJD414D	**RML 2485**	JJD485D	**RML 2622**	NML622E	**RML 2700**	SMK700F	**RML 2722**	SMK722F	**RML 2757**	SMK757F

VA 1-10   Volvo Olympian YN2RV18Z4   Alexander RH   H45/29F   1996

VA 1	N131YRW	**VA 3**	N133YRW	**VA 5**	N135YRW	**VA 7**	N137YRW	**VA 9**	N139YRW
VA 2	N132YRW	**VA 4**	N134YRW	**VA 6**	N136YRW	**VA 8**	N138YRW	**VA 10**	N140YRW

VA 11-17   Volvo Olympian OLY-4953   Alexander RH (Belfast)   H47/25D   1997

VA 11	XDZ5911	**VA 12**	XDZ5912	**VA 13**	XDZ5913	**VA 14**	XDZ5914	**VA 15**	XDZ5915	**VA 16**	XDZ5916	**VA 17**	XDZ5917

VA 18-29   Volvo Olympian OLY-4953   Alexander RH (Belfast)   H47/25D   1997

VA 18	R918WOE	**VA 20**	R920WOE	**VA 22**	R922WOE	**VA 24**	R924WOE	**VA 26**	R926WOE	**VA 28**	R928WOE
VA 19	R919WOE	**VA 21**	R921WOE	**VA 23**	R923WOE	**VA 25**	R925WOE	**VA 27**	R927WOE	**VA 29**	R929WOE

VA 30-54		Volvo Olympian OLY-4953		Alexander RH (Belfast)				H47/25D	1998				
VA 30	R930YOV	VA 34	R934YOV	VA 38	R938YOV	VA 42	R942YOV	VA 46	R946YOV	VA 50	R950YOV	VA 54	R954YOV
VA 31	R931YOV	VA 35	R935YOV	VA 39	R939YOV	VA 43	R943YOV	VA 47	R947YOV	VA 51	R951YOV		
VA 32	R932YOV	VA 36	R936YOV	VA 40	R940YOV	VA 44	R944YOV	VA 48	R948YOV	VA 52	R952YOV		
VA 33	R933YOV	VA 37	R937YOV	VA 41	R941YOV	VA 45	R945YOV	VA 49	R949YOV	VA 53	R953YOV		

XL 1-7		Optare Excel L1000		Optare				B36F	1997		
XL 1	P151BUG	XL 2	P152BUG	XL 3	P153BUG	XL 4	P154BUG	XL 6	P156BUG	XL 7	P157BUG

On order:

Forty five Volvo B7L/Alexander ALX 400 double deckers for 1999 delivery.

Previous registrations:

236CLT	H880LOX	A3LBR	F183YDA	ALM2B	K210SAG	VLT23	J610DUV	WLT804	H264NON
500CLT	G349GCK	A4LBR	F184YDA	F802NGY	F54CWY,	WLT329	H575MOC	WLT931	H611TKU
A2LBR	F182YDA	A5LBR	F551SHX		WLT400	WLT339	H577MOC	WLT946	J611DUV

METROBUS

80	F80SMC	Leyland Lynx LX112L10ZR1R	B49F	1988	
101	K101JMV	Leyland Lynx II LX2R11V18Z4S	B51F	1992	
103	D103NDW	Leyland Lynx LX112TL11ZR1R	B51F	1987	Ex Merthyr Tydfil, 1989
104	D104NDW	Leyland Lynx LX112TL11ZR1R	B51F	1987	Ex Merthyr Tydfil, 1989
110	D110NDW	Leyland Lynx LX112TL11ZR1R	B51F	1987	Ex Merthyr Tydfil, 1989
165	F165SMT	Leyland Lynx LX112L10Z1S	B49F	1989	Ex Miller, Foxton, 1991
166	F166SMT	Leyland Lynx LX112L10Z1S	B49F	1989	Ex Miller, Foxton, 1991

501-510		Optare Excel L1070		Optare				B35F	1997	
501	P501OUG	503	P503OUG	505	P505OUG	507	P507OUG	509	P509OUG	
502	P502OUG	504	P504OUG	506	P506OUG	508	P508OUG	510	P510OUG	

701-707		Dennis Dart 8.5SDL3010		Plaxton Pointer 8.5m				B32F*	1991	*701 is DP32F	
701	J701EMX	702	J702EMX	703	J703EMX	704	J704EMX	705	J705EMX	706	J706EMX	707	J707EMX

708-716		Dennis Dart 9SDL3011		Plaxton Pointer 9m				B35F	1992
708	K708KGU	710	K710KGU	712	K712KGU	714	K714KGU	716	K716KGU
709	K709KGU	711	K711KGU	713	K713KGU	715	K715KGU		

717-720		Dennis Dart 9.8SDL3032		Plaxton Pointer 9.8m				B35F	1994
717	L717OMV	718	L718OMV	719	L719OMV	720	L720OMV		

721-726			Dennis Dart 9.8SDL3054			Plaxton Pointer 9.8m		B35F	1995		
721	M721CGO	722	M722CGO	723	M723CGO	724	M724CGO	725	N725KGF	726	N726KGF

No.	Reg	Chassis	Body	Seats	Year	Notes
727w	H840GDY	Dennis Dart 9SDL3002	Wadham Stringer Portsdown 9m	B35F	1990	Ex Eastbourne, 1997
728	H841GDY	Dennis Dart 9SDL3002	Wadham Stringer Portsdown 9m	B35F	1990	Ex Eastbourne, 1997
729	H908DTP	Dennis Dart 9SDL3002	Wadham Stringer Portsdown 9m	B35F	1991	Ex Eastbourne, 1997
730	K488XPG	Dennis Dart 9.8SDL3017	Plaxton Pointer 9.8m	B40F	1993	Ex East Surrey, 1997
731	K831SFT	Dennis Dart 9.8SDL3017	Plaxton Pointer 9.8m	B40F	1993	Ex Catch-a-bus, Hylton Castle, 1997
732	K832SFT	Dennis Dart 9.8SDL3017	Plaxton Pointer 9.8m	B40F	1993	Ex Catch-a-bus, Hylton Castle, 1997

733-739			Dennis Dart 9SDL3011			Plaxton Pointer 9m		B35F	1992	Ex Kentish Bus, 1996	
733	J223HGY	734	J224HGY	735	J225HGY	736	J226HGY	737	J227HGY	738	J228HGY	739	J229HGY

741-748			Dennis Dart SLF SFD212BR1			Plaxton Pointer 10m		B35F	1998
741	R741BMY	743	R743BMY	745	R745BMY	747	R747FGX
742	R742BMY	744	R744BMY	746	R746FGX	748	R748FGX

No.	Reg	Chassis	Body	Seats	Year	Notes
750	M150HPL	Dennis Dart 9.8SDL3035	Plaxton Pointer 9.8m	B40F	1994	Ex East Surrey, 1997
751	M151HPL	Dennis Dart 9.8SDL3040	Plaxton Pointer 9.8m	B40F	1994	Ex East Surrey, 1997
752	J752PPM	Dennis Dart 9SDL3002	Wadham Stringer Portsdown 9m	B37F	1991	Ex East Surrey, 1997
754	L354FPF	Dennis Dart 9.8SDL3035	Plaxton Pointer 9.8m	B40F	1994	Ex East Surrey, 1997
756	L726DPG	Dennis Dart 9.8SDL3035	Plaxton Pointer 9.8m	B40F	1993	Ex East Surrey, 1997
757	P895PWW	Dennis Dart SFD412BR5	Plaxton Pointer 9.8m	B39F	1997	Ex K-Line, Huddersfield, 1998
758	R58GNW	Dennis Dart SFD412BR5	Plaxton Pointer 9.8m	B40F	1997	
759	N259PJR	Dennis Dart 9.8SDL 3054	Plaxton Pointer 9.8m	B40F	1995	Ex Catch-a-bus, HyltonCastle, 1997
760	N260PJR	Dennis Dart 9.8SDL 3054	Plaxton Pointer 9.8m	B40F	1995	Ex Catch-a-bus, Hylton Castle,1997
761	N261PJR	Dennis Dart 9.8SDL 3054	Plaxton Pointer 9.8m	B40F	1995	Ex Catch-a-bus, Hylton Castle,1997
802	F802NGU	Leyland Olympian ONCL10/1RZ	Leyland	H47/31F	1990	
803	F803NGU	Leyland Olympian ONCL10/1RZ	Leyland	H47/31F	1990	

804-816			Leyland Olympian ON2R50C13Z4			Leyland		H47/31F	1990-2				
804	G804SMV	806	G806TMX	808	H808AGX	810	H810AGX	812	J812GGW	814	K814HMV	816	K816HMV
805	G805SMV	807	H807XMY	809	H809AGX	811	H811AGX	813	J813GGW	815	K815HMV		

817-829			Volvo Olympian YN2RV18Z4			Northern Counties Palatine I		H47/29F	1996		
817	P817SGP	819	P819SGP	822	P822SGP	824	P824SGP	826	P826SGP	829	P829SGP
818	P818SGP	821	P821SGP	823	P823SGP	825	P825SGP	828	P828SGP		

830-845			Volvo Olympian OLY-4953			East Lancs Pyoneer		H47/25D	1997
830	R830MFR	833	R833MFR	836	R836MFR	839	R839MFR	843	R843MFR
831	R831MFR	834	R834MFR	837	R837MFR	841	R841MFR	844	R844MFR
832	R832MFR	835	R835MFR	838	R838MFR	842	R842MFR	845	R845MFR

846-858					Volvo Olympian OLY-4953			East Lancs Pyoneer				H47/25D		1998		
846	S846DGX	848	S848DGX	850	S850DGX	852	S852DGX	854	S854DGX	856	S856DGX	858	S858DGX			
847	S847DGX	849	S849DGX	851	S851DGX	853	S853DGX	855	S855DGX	857	S857DGX					

859-866					Volvo Olympian			Northern Counties Palatine I				H47/29F		1998		
859	S859DGX	861	S861DGX	863	S863DGX	865	S865DGX									
860	S860DGX	862	S862DGX	864	S864DGX	866	S866DGX									

901-906					Optare MetroRider MR17			Optare				B26F		1996		
901	N901HWY	902	N902HWY	903	N903HWY	904	N904HWY	905	N905HWY	906	N906HWY					

907	F31CWY	Mercedes-Benz 811D	Optare StarRider	B26F	1988	Ex London Central, 1997
908	F41CWY	Mercedes-Benz 811D	Optare StarRider	B26F	1988	Ex London Central, 1997
909	F70RPL	Mercedes-Benz 811D	Optare StarRider	B33F	1989	Ex East Surrey, 1997
910	G301CPL	Mercedes-Benz 811D	Optare StarRider	B33F	1989	Ex East Surrey, 1997
911	G972WPA	Optare MetroRider MR03	Optare	B33F	1990	Ex East Surrey, 1997
912	H152UUA	Optare MetroRider MR03	Optare	B26F	1991	Ex Stagecoach Selkent, 1998
913	H161WWT	Optare MetroRider MR03	Optare	B26F	1991	Ex Stagecoach Selkent, 1998
914	H163WWT	Optare MetroRider MR03	Optare	B26F	1991	Ex Stagecoach Selkent, 1998
915	H165WWT	Optare MetroRider MR03	Optare	B26F	1991	Ex Stagecoach Selkent, 1998
916	H172WWT	Optare MetroRider MR03	Optare	B26F	1991	Ex Stagecoach Selkent, 1998
917	J326PPD	Optare MetroRider MR03	Optare	B33F	1991	Ex East Surrey, 1997
918	L735MWW	Optare MetroRider MR13	Optare	B29F	1993	Ex East Surrey, 1997
950	S950VMY	Mercedes-Benz O814 Vario	Plaxton Beaver 2	B24FL	1998	
951	S951VMY	Mercedes-Benz O814 Vario	Plaxton Beaver 2	B24FL	1998	
952	S952VMY	Mercedes-Benz O814 Vario	Plaxton Beaver 2	B24FL	1998	
953	M153LPL	Iveco TurboDaily 59.12	WSC Wessex II	B24FL	1995	Ex East Surrey, 1997

Certain other vehicles (some minibuses, Metrobuses and coaches) operate outside the area of this book.

METROLINE (Metroline London Northern and Metroline Travel)

AV 1-22 — Volvo Olympian YN2RV18Z4 — Alexander RH — H43/25D — 1996

AV 1	585CLT	AV 5	P485MBY	AV 9	P489MBY	AV 13	P493MBY	AV 17	P477MBY	AV 21	P474MBY
AV 2	P482MBY	AV 6	P486MBY	AV 10	P490MBY	AV 14	P494MBY	AV 18	P478MBY	AV 22	P475MBY
AV 3	P483MBY	AV 7	P487MBY	AV 11	P491MBY	AV 15	P495MBY	AV 19	P479MBY		
AV 4	P484MBY	AV 8	P488MBY	AV 12	P492MBY	AV 16	P476MBY	AV 20	P480MBY		

AV 23-38 — Volvo Olympian OLY-4953 — Alexander RH (Belfast) — H43/25D — 1998

AV 23	S233RLH	AV 26	S126RLE	AV 29	S129RLE	AV 32	S132RLE	AV 35	S135RLE	AV 38	S138RLE
AV 24	S124RLE	AV 27	S127RLE	AV 30	S130RLE	AV 33	S133RLE	AV 36	S136RLE		
AV 25	S125RLE	AV 28	S128RLE	AV 31	S131RLE	AV 34	S134RLE	AV 37	S137RLE		

DAF

DAF 539	H539YCX	DAF SB220LC550	Ikarus Citibus	B50F	1991	Ex R & I, 1996
DAF 848	F848YJX	DAF SB220LC550	Optare Delta	B49F	1989	Ex Merseybus, 1996
DAF 849	F849YJX	DAF SB220LC550	Optare Delta	B49F	1989	Ex R & I, 1996

DC 216-232 — Dennis Dart 9SDL3002 — Duple-Carlyle Dartline 9m — B36F — 1990 — Ex R & I, 1996

DC 216	G216LGK	DC 219	G219LGK	DC 220	G220LGK	DC 221	G121RGT	DC 224	G124RGT	DC 229	G129RGT	DC 232	RIB7002

DL 1-21 — Dennis Dart SLF SFD212BR1 — Plaxton Pointer 10m — B36F — 1997

DL 1	P201OLX	DL 4	P204OLX	DL 7	P207OLX	DL 10	P210OLX	DL 13	R113RLY	DL 16	R116RLY	DL 19	R119RLY
DL 2	P202OLX	DL 5	P205OLX	DL 8	P208OLX	DL 11	P211OLX	DL 14	R114RLY	DL 17	R117RLY	DL 20	R120RLY
DL 3	P203OLX	DL 6	P206OLX	DL 9	P209OLX	DL 12	R112RLY	DL 15	R115RLY	DL 18	R118RLY	DL 21	R121RLY

DL 75-85 — Dennis Dart SLF SFD212BR1 — Plaxton Pointer 2 10m — B35F — 1998

DL 75	R175VLA	DL 77	R177VLA	DL 79	R179VLA	DL 81	R181VLA	DL 83	R183VLA	DL 85	R185VLA
DL 76	R176VLA	DL 78	R178VLA	DL 80	R180VLA	DL 82	R182VLA	DL 84	R184VLA		

DLD 22-53 — Dennis Dart SLF SFD212BR1 — Plaxton Pointer 2 10m — B30D — 1997

DLD 22	R122RLY	DLD 27	R127RLY	DLD 32	R132RLY	DLD 37	R137RLY	DLD 42	R142RLY	DLD 47	R147RLY	DLD 52	R152RLY
DLD 23	R123RLY	DLD 28	R128RLY	DLD 33	R133RLY	DLD 38	R138RLY	DLD 43	R143RLY	DLD 48	R148RLY	DLD 53	R153RLY
DLD 24	R124RLY	DLD 29	R129RLY	DLD 34	R134RLY	DLD 39	R139RLY	DLD 44	R144RLY	DLD 49	R149RLY		
DLD 25	R125RLY	DLD 30	R130RLY	DLD 35	R135RLY	DLD 40	R140RLY	DLD 45	R145RLY	DLD 50	R150RLY		
DLD 26	R126RLY	DLD 31	R131RLY	DLD 36	R136RLY	DLD 41	R141RLY	DLD 46	R146RLY	DLD 51	R151RLY		

DLD 54-74 — Dennis Dart SLF SFD212BR1 — Plaxton Pointer 2 10m — B30D — 1998

DLD 54	R154VLA	DLD 57	R157VLA	DLD 60	R160VLA	DLD 63	R163VLA	DLD 66	R166VLA	DLD 69	R169VLA	DLD 72	R172VLA
DLD 55	R155VLA	DLD 58	R158VLA	DLD 61	R161VLA	DLD 64	R164VLA	DLD 67	R167VLA	DLD 70	R170VLA	DLD 73	R173VLA
DLD 56	R156VLA	DLD 59	R159VLA	DLD 62	R162VLA	DLD 65	R165VLA	DLD 68	R168VLA	DLD 71	R171VLA	DLD 74	R174VLA

DLD 86-100	Dennis Dart SLF SFD212BR1	Plaxton Pointer 2 10m	B25D	1998		
DLD 86 S286JLP	**DLD 89** S289JLP	**DLD 92** S292JLP	**DLD 95** S295JLP	**DLD 98** S298JLP		
DLD 87 S287JLP	**DLD 90** S290JLP	**DLD 93** S293JLP	**DLD 96** S296JLP	**DLD 99** S299JLP		
DLD 88 S288JLP	**DLD 91** S291JLP	**DLD 94** S294JLP	**DLD 97** S297JLP	**DLD 100** S301JLP		

DLS 1-7	Dennis Dart SLF SFD112BR1	Plaxton Pointer 9.2m	B32F	1997		
DLS 1 P101OLX	**DLS 2** P102OLX	**DLS 3** P103OLX	**DLS 4** P104OLX	**DLS 5** P105OLX	**DLS 6** P106OLX	**DLS 7** P107OLX

DM 242t RIB8431	Dennis Dart 9.8SDL3035	Marshall C37	B40F	1994	Ex R & I, 1996

DML 1-18	Dennis Dart SLF SFD212BR1	Marshall Capital 10.2m	B28D	1998	
DML 1 R681MEW	**DML 4** R684MEW	**DML 7** R687MEW	**DML 10** R690MEW	**DML 13** R693MEW	**DML 16** R696MEW
DML 2 R682MEW	**DML 5** R685MEW	**DML 8** R688MEW	**DML 11** R691MEW	**DML 14** R694MEW	**DML 17** R697MEW
DML 3 R683MEW	**DML 6** R686MEW	**DML 9** R689MEW	**DML 12** R692MEW	**DML 15** R695MEW	**DML 18** R698MEW

DML 33-47	Dennis Dart SLF SFD212BR1	Marshall Capital 10.2m	B28D	1998	
DML 33 R863MCE	**DML 36** R866MCE	**DML 39** R869MCE	**DML 42** R872MCE	**DML 45** R875MCE	
DML 34 R864MCE	**DML 37** R867MCE	**DML 40** R870MCE	**DML 43** R873MCE	**DML 46** R876MCE	
DML 35 R865MCE	**DML 38** R868MCE	**DML 41** R871MCE	**DML 44** R874MCE	**DML 47** R877MCE	

DML 519-532	Dennis Dart SLF SFD212BR1	Marshall Capital 10.2m	B31F	1998	(Originally numbered DML19-32)
DML 519 R619VEG	**DML 521** R621VEG	**DML 523** R623VEG	**DML 525** R625VEG	**DML 527** R627VEG	**DML 529** R629VEG	**DML 531** R631VEG
DML 520 R620VEG	**DML 522** R622VEG	**DML 524** R624VEG	**DML 526** R626VEG	**DML 528** R638VEG	**DML 530** R630VEG	**DML 532** R632VEG

DMS 1-12	Dennis Dart SLF SFD112BR1	Marshall Capital 9.4m	B32F	1998	
DMS 1 R701MEW	**DMS 3** R703MEW	**DMS 5** R705MEW	**DMS 7** R707MEW	**DMS 9** R709MEW	**DMS 11** R711MEW
DMS 2 R702MEW	**DMS 4** R704MEW	**DMS 6** R706MEW	**DMS 8** R708MEW	**DMS 10** R710MEW	**DMS 12** R699MEW

DMS 13-29	Dennis Dart SLF SFD112BR1	Marshall Capital 9.4m	*B32F	1998	*DMS 28 is B27F
DMS 13 S513KFL	**DMS 16** S516KFL	**DMS 19** S519KFL	**DMS 22** S522KFL	**DMS 25** S525KFL	**DMS 28** S528KFL
DMS 14 S514KFL	**DMS 17** S517KFL	**DMS 20** S520KFL	**DMS 23** S523KFL	**DMS 26** S526KFL	**DMS 29** S529KFL
DMS 15 S515KFL	**DMS 18** S518KFL	**DMS 21** S521KFL	**DMS 24** S524KFL	**DMS 27** S527KFL	

DNL 101-120	Dennis Dart 9SDL3034	Northern Counties Paladin 9m	B34F	1994	Ex London Buses, 1994
DNL 101 L101HHV	**DNL 104** L104HHV	**DNL 107** L107HHV	**DNL 110** L110HHV	**DNL 114** L114HHV	**DNL 117** L117HHV	**DNL 120** L120HHV
DNL 102 L102HHV	**DNL 105** L105HHV	**DNL 108** L108HHV	**DNL 112** L112HHV	**DNL 115** L115HHV	**DNL 118** L118HHV	
DNL 103 L103HHV	**DNL 106** L106HHV	**DNL 109** L109HHV	**DNL 113** L113HHV	**DNL 116** L116HHV	**DNL 119** L119HHV	

DPL 233t 33LUG	Dennis Dart 9.8SDL3017	Plaxton Pointer 9.8m	B40F	1992	Ex R & I, 1996

DP 234-239	Dennis Dart 9SDL3011	Plaxton Pointer 9m	B35F	1992	Ex R & I, 1996
DP 234 K414MGN	**DP 235** RIB5085	**DP 236** K416MGN	**DP 237** K417MGN	**DP 238** K418MGN	**DP 239** K419MGN

DP 240 M498ALP — Dennis Dart 9SDL3031 — Plaxton Pointer 9m — B35F — 1995 — Ex R & I, 1996
DP 241 M499ALP — Dennis Dart 9SDL3031 — Plaxton Pointer 9m — B35F — 1995 — Ex R & I, 1996

DP 245-248 — Dennis Dart 9.8SDL3054 — Plaxton Pointer 9.8m — B40F — 1995 — Ex R & I, 1996

| **DP 245** M503ALP | **DP 246** M504ALP | **DP 247** M505ALP | **DP 248** M506ALP |

DP 273-276 — Dennis Dart SFD212BR5 — Plaxton Pointer 9m — B35F — 1997

| **DP 273** P673MLE | **DP 274** P674MLE | **DP 275** P675MLE | **DP 276** P676MLE |

DR 15-19 — Dennis Dart 8.5SDL3003 — Reeve Burgess Pointer 8.5m — B28F — 1991 — Ex London Buses, 1994

| **DR 15** H115THE | **DR 16** H116THE | **DR 17** H117THE | **DR 18** H118THE | **DR 19** H119THE |

DR 40 H540XGK — Dennis Dart 8.5SDL3003 — Plaxton Pointer 8.5m — B28F — 1991 — Ex London Buses, 1994
DR 42 H542XGK — Dennis Dart 8.5SDL3003 — Plaxton Pointer 8.5m — B28F — 1991 — Ex London Buses, 1994

DR 81-148 — Dennis Dart 8.5SDL3010/3015 — Plaxton Pointer 8.5m — B28F — 1992 — Ex London Buses, 1994

DR 81 J381GKH	**DR 85** J385GKH	**DR 89** J389GKH	**DR 93** J393GKH	**DR 97** J397GKH	**DR 144** K244PAG	**DR 148** K248PAG
DR 82 J382GKH	**DR 86** J386GKH	**DR 90** J390GKH	**DR 94** J394GKH	**DF 98** J398GKH	**DR 145** K245PAG	
DR 83 J383GKH	**DR 87** J387GKH	**DR 91** J391GKH	**DR 95** J395GKH	**DR 142** K242PAG	**DR 146** K246PAG	
DR 84 J384GKH	**DR 88** J388GKH	**DR 92** J392GKH	**DR 96** J396GKH	**DR 143** K243PAG	**DR 147** K247PAG	

DRL 18-37 — Dennis Dart 9SDL3016 — Plaxton Pointer 9m — B34F — 1992 — 30, 35 & 36 ex R & I, 1996

DRL 18 K818NKH	**DRL 21** K821NKH	**DRL 24** K824NKH	**DRL 27** K827NKH	**DRL 30** K430OKH	**DRL 33** K433OKH	**DRL 36** K436OKH
DRL 19 K819NKH	**DRL 22** K822NKH	**DRL 25** K825NKH	**DRL 28** K828NKH	**DRL 31** K431OKH	**DRL 34** K434OKH	**DRL 37** K437OKH
DRL 20 K820NKH	**DRL 23** K823NKH	**DRL 26** K826NKH	**DRL 29** K429OKH	**DRL 32** K432OKH	**DRL 35** K435OKH	

DT 88-140 — Dennis Dart 8.5SDL3003 — Carlyle Dartline 8.5m — B28F — 1990/1 — Ex London Buses, 1994

| **DT 88** H588MOC | **DT 92** H92MOB | **DT 99** H899LOX | **DT 107** H107MOB | **DT 123** H123MOB | **DT 138** H138MOB | **DT 140** H140MOB |
| **DT 90** H890LOX | **DT 97** H97MOB | **DT 103** H103MOB | **DT 122** H122MOB | **DT 133** H133MOB | **DT 139** H139MOB | |

EDR 1-9 — Dennis Dart 9.8SDL3040 — Plaxton Pointer 9.8m — B39F — 1994

| **EDR 1** M101BLE | **EDR 3** M103BLE | **EDR 5** M105BLE | **EDR 7** M107BLE | **EDR 9** M109BLE |
| **EDR 2** M102BLE | **EDR 4** M104BLE | **EDR 6** M106BLE | **EDR 8** M108BLE | |

EDR 10-44 — Dennis Dart SFD412BR5 — Plaxton Pointer 9.8m — B39F — 1996

EDR 10 P285MLD	**EDR 15** P290MLD	**EDR 20** P295MLD	**EDR 25** P301MLD	**EDR 30** P306MLD	**EDR 35** P311MLD	**EDR 40** P316MLD
EDR 11 P286MLD	**EDR 16** P291MLD	**EDR 21** P296MLD	**EDR 26** P302MLD	**EDR 31** P307MLD	**EDR 36** P312MLD	**EDR 41** P317MLD
EDR 12 P287MLD	**EDR 17** P292MLD	**EDR 22** P297MLD	**EDR 27** P303MLD	**EDR 32** P308MLD	**EDR 37** P313MLD	**EDR 42** P318MLD
EDR 13 P288MLD	**EDR 18** P293MLD	**EDR 23** P298MLD	**EDR 28** P304MLD	**EDR 33** P309MLD	**EDR 38** P314MLD	**EDR 43** P319MLD
EDR 14 P289MLD	**EDR 19** P294MLD	**EDR 24** P299MLD	**EDR 29** P305MLD	**EDR 34** P310MLD	**EDR 39** P315MLD	**EDR 44** P320MLD

IL 208s RIB7004 — Iveco Daily 49.10 — LHE — B23F — 1990 — Ex R & I, 1996

| IR 202s | RIB5082 | Iveco Daily 49.10 | | Robin Hood City Nippy | | B23F | 1989 | Ex R & I, 1996 |

LLW 25-38 — Dennis Lance SLF 11SDA3202 — Wright Pathfinder 320 — B34D — 1993/4 — Ex London Buses, 1994

LLW 25 L25WLH	**LLW 27** L27WLH	**LLW 29** L29WLH	**LLW 31** L31WLH	**LLW 33** L39WLH	**LLW 35** L35WLH	**LLW 37** L37WLH
LLW 26 L26WLH	**LLW 28** L28WLH	**LLW 30** L21WLH	**LLW 32** L32WLH	**LLW 34** L34WLH	**LLW 36** L36WLH	**LLW 38** L38WLH

LN 1-31 — Dennis Lance 11SDA3108 — Northern Counties Paladin — B37D — 1993 — Ex London Buses, 1994

LN 1u K301YJA	**LN 5**u K305YJA	**LN 10**u K310YJA	**LN 14**u K314YJA	**LN 19**u K319YJA	**LN 24**u K324YJA	**LN 29**u K329YJA
LN 2u K302YJA	**LN 7**u K307YJA	**LN 11**u K311YJA	**LN 16**u K316YJA	**LN 20**u K320YJA	**LN 25**u K325YJA	**LN 30**u K330YJA
LN 3u K303YJA	**LN 8**u K308YJA	**LN 12**u K312YJA	**LN 17**u K317YJA	**LN 21**u K321YJA	**LN 27**u K327YJA	**LN 31**u K331YJA
LN 4u K304YJA	**LN 9**t K309YJA	**LN 13**u K313YJA	**LN 18**t K318YJA	**LN 22**u K322YJA	**LN 28**u K328YJA	

M 1-5 — MCW Metrobus DR101/3 — MCW — H43/28D — 1978 — Ex London Buses, 1994

M 1t THX101S	**M 2**t THX102S	**M 3**t THX103S	**M 4**t THX104S	**M 5**t THX105S

M 9-54 — MCW Metrobus DR101/8 — MCW — H43/28D — 1978-9 — Ex London Buses, 1994

M 9 WYW9T	**M 18** WYW18T	**M 27** WYW27T	**M 35** WYW35T	**M 42**u WYW42T	M16 & 37 ex Merseybus, 1995
M 12 WYW12T	**M 20**u WYW20T	**M 32** WYW32T	**M 37** WYW37T	**M 48** WYW48T	
M 16 WYW16T	**M 25**u WYW25T	**M 33** WYW33T	**M 41** WYW41T	**M 54** WYW54T	

M 57-199 — MCW Metrobus DR101/8 — MCW — H43/28D — 1979 — Ex London Buses, 1994
M106 & 108 ex Merseybus, 1995, 117 & 139 ex London Suburban Bus, 1995 and 135, 137, 150 & 192 are ex Atlas Bus, 1996.

M 57 WYW57T	**M 80**u WYW80T	**M 94** WYW94T	**M 111**t BYX111V	**M 126** BYX126V	**M 142** BYX142V	**M 169** BYX169V
M 58 WYW58T	**M 81**u WYW81T	**M 95** WYW95T	**M 113** BYX113V	**M 127** BYX127V	**M 150**u BYX150V	**M 178** BYX178V
M 67 WYW67T	**M 82** WYW82T	**M 97** BYX97V	**M 114** BYX114V	**M 128** BYX128V	**M 151** BYX151V	**M 180** BYX180V
M 70 WYW70T	**M 83** WYW83T	**M 98** BYX98V	**M 115** BYX115V	**M 130** BYX130V	**M 155** BYX155V	**M 181** BYX181V
M 72u WYW72T	**M 84** WYW84T	**M 102**t BYX102V	**M 117** BYX117V	**M 133** BYX133V	**M 160** BYX160V	**M 184** BYX184V
M 75 WYW75T	**M 85** WYW85T	**M 106** BYX106V	**M 118** BYX118V	**M 135** BYX135V	**M 161**u BYX161V	**M 189** BYX189V
M 77 WYW77T	**M 87** WYW87T	**M 107** BYX107V	**M 119** BYX119V	**M 137** BYX137V.	**M 163** BYX163V	**M 192** BYX192V
M 78 WYW78T	**M 90** WYW90T	**M 108**u BYX108V	**M 124** BYX124V	**M 139** BYX139V	**M 166** BYX166V	**M 194** BYX194V
M 79u WYW79T	**M 91** WYW91T	**M 109** BYX109V	**M 125**t BYX125V	**M 140** BYX140V	**M 167** BYX167V	**M 199** BYX199V

M 213-501 — MCW Metrobus DR101/12 — MCW — H43/28D — 1980 — Ex London Buses, 1994
Ms 222, 324, 352, 373 ex London General, 1995, 229 ex London Suburban Bus, 1995, 272, 276 & 407 ex Atlas Bus, 1996 and 377 & 501 ex Merseybus, 1995

M 213 BYX213V	**M 300** BYX300V	**M 328** EYE328V	**M 373** GYE373W	**M 409** GYE409W	**M 444** GYE444W	**M 461** GYE461W
M 222 BYX222V	**M 306** BYX306V	**M 335** EYE335V	**M 376** GYE376W	**M 428**t GYE428W	**M 446**t GYE446W	**M 467** GYE467W
M 229 BYX229V	**M 309** BYX309V	**M 341** EYE341V	**M 377**u GYE377W	**M 429** GYE429W	**M 448** GYE448W	**M 468**t GYE468W
M 238 BYX238V	**M 313** BYX313V	**M 342** EYE342V	**M 380** GYE380W	**M 432** GYE432W	**M 449** GYE449W	**M 473** GYE473W
M 243 BYX243V	**M 315** BYX315V	**M 344** EYE344V	**M 391**t GYE391W	**M 436** GYE436W	**M 453** GYE453W	**M 481** GYE481W
M 272 BYX272V	**M 322** EYE322V	**M 352** GYE352W	**M 394** GYE394W	**M 438** GYE438W	**M 455** GYE455W	**M 482** GYE482W
M 276u BYX276V	**M 324** EYE324V	**M 356** GYE356W	**M 403** GYE403W	**M 440** GYE440W	**M 459** GYE459W	**M 501**u GYE501W
M 294 BYX294V	**M 326** EYE326V	**M 367**t GYE367W	**M 407** GYE407W	**M 443**u GYE443W	**M 460** GYE460W	

M 512-802 MCW Metrobus DR101/14 MCW H43/28D 1981-2 Ex London Buses, 1994

M 512 GYE512W	M 564 GYE564W	M 576 GYE576W	M 616u KYO616X	M 655 KYV655X	M 693 KYV693X	M 800 KYV800X
M 524 GYE524W	M 565u GYE565W	M 578 GYE578W	M 618 KYO618X	M 656 KYV656X	M 696 KYV696X	M 801 KYV801X
M 550 GYE550W	M 570 GYE570W	M 579u GYE579W	M 620 KYO620X	M 674 KYV674X	M 739 KYV739X	M 802 KYV802X
M 560 GYE560W	M 571 GYE571W	M 594 GYE594W	M 621 KYO621X	M 677 KYV677X	M 755 KYV755X	
M 561 GYE561W	M 572t GYE572W	M 595 GYE595W	M 639 KYV639X	M 678t KYV678X	M 764 KYV764X	
M 563u GYE563W	M 574 GYE574W	M 608 KYO608X	M 640 KYV640X	M 683 KYV683X	M 797u KYV797X	

M 810-955 MCW Metrobus DR101/16 MCW H43/28D 1983 Ex London Buses, 1994

M 810 OJD810Y	M 876 OJD876Y	M 896 A896SUL	M 912 A912SUL	M 921 A921SUL	M 934 A934SUL	M 950 A950SUL
M 819t WLT342	M 878 OJD878Y	M 899 A899SUL	M 915 A915SUL	M 924 A924SUL	M 935 A935SUL	M 955 A955SUL
M 824 OJD824Y	M 879 OJD879Y	M 910 A910SUL	M 916 A916SUL	M 925 A925SUL	M 937 A937SUL	
M 829 OJD829Y	M 890 OJD890Y	M 911 A911SUL	M 917u A917SUL	M 928 A928SUL	M 945 A945SUL	

M 956-1043 MCW Metrobus DR101/17 MCW H43/28D 1984 Ex London Buses, 1994

M 956 A956SYF	M 968 A968SYF	M 987 A987SYF	M 997 A997SYF	M 1033 A733THV	M 1040 A740THV
M 957 A957SYF	M 971 A971SYF	M 989 A989SYF	M 1004 A704THV	M 1034 A734THV	M 1041 A741THV
M 961t A961SYF	M 974 A974SYF	M 993 A993SYF	M 1031u A731THV	M 1035 A735THV	M 1042 A742THV
M 964 A964SYF	M 982 A982SYF	M 995u A995SYF	M 1032 A732THV	M 1038 A738THV	M 1043 A743THV

M 1045-1052 MCW Metrobus DR101/19 MCW *H43/28D 1984 Ex London Buses, 1994
*M 1045 is DPH43/28D

M 1045t A745THV	M 1047 A747THV	M 1052 A752THV

M 1056-1431 MCW Metrobus DR101/17 MCW *H43/28D 1985 Ex London Buses, 1994
(Ms 1185, 1236, 1393 & 1396 are DPH43/28D)

M 1056 B56WUL	M 1079 B79WUL	M 1145 B145WUL	M 1168 B168WUL	M 1218 B218WUL	M 1339 C339BUV	M 1395 C395BUV
M 1057 B57WUL	M 1080t B80WUL	M 1146 B146WUL	M 1174 B174WUL	M 1234 B234WUL	M 1342 C342BUV	M 1396t C396BUV
M 1058 B58WUL	M 1081 B81WUL	M 1147 B147WUL	M 1181 B181WUL	M 1236 WLT646	M 1346 C346BUV	M 1397 C397BUV
M 1059 B59WUL	M 1082 B82WUL	M 1148 B148WUL	M 1183 B183WUL	M 1250 B250WUL	M 1348 C348BUV	M 1403 C403BUV
M 1060 B60WUL	M 1083 B83WUL	M 1149 B149WUL	M 1185 WLT893	M 1273 WLT902	M 1349 C349BUV	M 1408 C408BUV
M 1061 B61WUL	M 1111 B111WUL	M 1150 B150WUL	M 1186 B186WUL	M 1274 B274WUL	M 1350 C350BUV	M 1409 C409BUV
M 1063 B63WUL	M 1113 B113WUL	M 1151 B151WUL	M 1189 B189WUL	M 1277 B277WUL	M 1355 C355BUV	M 1414 C414BUV
M 1065 B65WUL	M 1114 B114WUL	M 1153 B153WUL	M 1192 B192WUL	M 1284 B284WUL	M 1365 C365BUV	M 1416 C416BUV
M 1066 B66WUL	M 1115 B115WUL	M 1156 B156WUL	M 1193 B193WUL	M 1287 B287WUL	M 1366 C366BUV	M 1423 C423BUV
M 1067t B67WUL	M 1117 B117WUL	M 1157 B157WUL	M 1195 B195WUL	M 1292 B292WUL	M 1369 C369BUV	M 1425 C425BUV
M 1068 B68WUL	M 1118 B118WUL	M 1158 B158WUL	M 1197 B197WUL	M 1325 C325BUV	M 1383 C383BUV	M 1426 C426BUV
M 1071 B71WUL	M 1119 B119WUL	M 1159 B159WUL	M 1198 B198WUL	M 1329 C329BUV	M 1385 C385BUV	M 1427 C427BUV
M 1072 B72WUL	M 1120 B120WUL	M 1160 B160WUL	M 1202 B202WUL	M 1330 C330BUV	M 1390 C390BUV	M 1428 C428BUV
M 1076 B76WUL	M 1141 B141WUL	M 1161 B161WUL	M 1204 B204WUL	M 1331 C331BUV	M 1392t C392BUV	M 1429 WLT826
M 1077 B77WUL	M 1142 B142WUL	M 1163 B163WUL	M 1205 B205WUL	M 1333 C333BUV	M 1393t C393BUV	M 1430 C430BUV
M 1078 B78WUL	M 1143 B143WUL	M 1167 B167WUL	M 1208 B208WUL	M 1334 C334BUV	M 1394 C394BUV	M 1431 C431BUV

MC 1	P481HEG	Marshall Minibus		Marshall		B29F	1996	

MM 254-278	MAN 11.220	Marshall C37*	B38F	1996	254-268 ex R & I, 1996 *270-278 are Marshall Capital

MM 254 N121XEG	**MM 258** N125XEG	**MM 262** N129XEG	**MM 266** N133XEG	**MM 271** P471JEG	**MM 275** P475JEG
MM 255 N122XEG	**MM 259** N126XEG	**MM 263** N130XEG	**MM 267** N134XEG	**MM 272** P472JEG	**MM 276** P476JEG
MM 256 N123XEG	**MM 260** N127XEG	**MM 264** N131XEG	**MM 268** N135XEG	**MM 273** P473JEG	**MM 277** P477JEG
MM 257 N124XEG	**MM 261** N128XEG	**MM 265** N132XEG	**MM 270** P470JEG	**MM 274** P474JEG	**MM 278** P478JEG

MMS 269	N161YEG	Mercedes-Benz 811D	Marshall C16	B26F	1996

MR 87	F87GGC	Mercedes-Benz 811D	Robin Hood	C29F	1989	Ex R & I, 1996
MR 90	F90GGC	Mercedes-Benz 811D	Robin Hood	C29F	1989	Ex R & I, 1996

MRL 213-222	Optare MetroRider MR03	Optare	B26F	1991/3	Ex London Buses, 1994

MRL 213 J213BWU	**MRL 215** J215BWU	**MRL 217** J217BWU	**MRL 219** J219BWU	**MRL 221** J221BWU	**MRL 222** K422HWY

MRL 223	P448SWX	Optare MetroRider MR13	Optare	B29F	1997
MRL 224	P449SWX	Optare MetroRider MR13	Optare	B29F	1997

MV 249-253	MAN 11.190	Optare Vecta	B42F	1995	Ex R & I, 1996

MV 249 M507ALP	**MV 250** M508ALP	**MV 251** N701FLN	**MV 252** N702FLN	**MV 253** N703FLN

MW 18-37	Mercedes-Benz 811D	Wright Nimbus	B26F	1993	Ex London Buses, 1994

MW 18 NDZ7918	**MW 21** NDZ7921	**MW 24** NDZ7924	**MW 29** NDZ7929	**MW 33** NDZ7933	**MW 36** K510FYN
MW 19 NDZ7919	**MW 22** NDZ7922	**MW 25** NDZ7925	**MW 31** NDZ7931	**MW 34** NDZ7934	**MW 37** K476FYN
MW 20 NDZ7920	**MW 23** NDZ7923	**MW 26** NDZ7926	**MW 32** NDZ7932	**MW 35** NDZ7935	

OM 243 M501ALP	Optare MetroRider MR33	Optare	B25F	1995	Ex R & I, 1996
OM 244 M502ALP	Optare MetroRider MR33	Optare	B25F	1995	Ex R & I, 1996
OM 279 P509NWU	Optare MetroRider MR13	Optare	B25F	1996	

RM 70-1979	AEC Routemaster R2RH	Park Royal	*H36/28R	1959-1965	Ex London Buses, 1994 RMs 1081 & 2097 ex London Transport, 1997 *RM 644 is O36/28RD

RM 70	VLT70	**RM 446** WLT446	**RM 646** KFF257	**RM 1348** 348CLT	**RM 1799** 799DYE	**RM 1971** ALD971B
RM 268	VLT268	**RM 644** WLT644	**RM 912w** WLT912	**RM 1700w** KGJ167A	**RM 1804w** EYY327B	**RM 1979** ALD979B

RMC 1513	513CLT	AEC Routemaster R2RH	Park Royal	O32/62	1962	Ex London Buses, 1994
RML 893	KFF276	AEC Routemaster R2RH	Park Royal	H40/32R	1961	Ex London Buses, 1994
RML 902	ALC464A	AEC Routemaster R2RH	Park Royal	H40/32R	1961	Ex London Buses, 1994
RML 903	WLT903	AEC Routemaster R2RH	Park Royal	H40/32R	1961	Ex London Buses, 1994

RML 2274-2755 AEC Routemaster R2RH/1 Park Royal H40/32R 1965-8 Ex London Buses, 1994
RML 2633 & 2659 ex London Transport, 1997

RML 2274	CUV274C	RML 2310	CUV310C	RML 2413	JJD413D	RML 2508	JJD508D	RML 2585	JJD585D	RML 2659	SMK659F	RML 2706	SMK706F
RML 2282	CUV282C	RML 2312	CUV312C	RML 2419	JJD419D	RML 2509	JJD509D	RML 2594	JJD594D	RML 2679	SMK679F	RML 2710	SMK710F
RML 2284	CUV284C	RML 2331	CUV331C	RML 2430	JJD430D	RML 2511	JJD511D	RML 2599	NML599E	RML 2681	SMK681F	RML 2713	SMK713F
RML 2285	CUV285C	RML 2348	CUV348C	RML 2431	JJD431D	RML 2532	JJD532D	RML 2603	NML603E	RML 2689	SMK689F	RML 2727	SMK727F
RML 2288	CUV288C	RML 2367	JJD367D	RML 2439	JJD439D	RML 2537	JJD537D	RML 2620	NML620E	RML 2690	SMK690F	RML 2728	SMK728F
RML 2289	CUV289C	RML 2368	JJD368D	RML 2443	JJD443D	RML 2547	JJD547D	RML 2633	NML633E	RML 2695	SMK695F	RML 2731	SMK731F
RML 2295	CUV295C	RML 2377	JJD377D	RML 2446	JJD446D	RML 2558	JJD558D	RML 2634	NML634E	RML 2698	SMK698F	RML 2737	SMK737F
RML 2296	CUV296C	RML 2384	JJD384D	RML 2471	JJD471D	RML 2561	JJD561D	RML 2649	NML649E	RML 2699	SMK699F	RML 2755	SMK755F
RML 2299	CUV299C	RML 2393	JJD393D	RML 2478	JJD478D	RML 2566	JJD566D	RML 2651	NML651E	RML 2701	SMK701F		
RML 2308	CUV308C	RML 2395	JJD395D	RML 2479	JJD479D	RML 2579	JJD579D	RML 2652	NML652E	RML 2703	SMK703F		

S 11-20 Scania N113DRB Alexander RH H47/31F 1991 Ex London Buses, 1994

S 11	J811HMC	S 13	J813HMC	S 15	J815HMC	S 17	J817HMC	S 19	J819HMC
S 12	J812HMC	S 14	J814HMC	S 16	J816HMC	S 18	J818HMC	S 20	J820HMC

T 287	KYN287X	Leyland Titan TNLXB2RR	Leyland	H44/26D	1981	Ex Atlas Bus, 1996
T 302	KYN302X	Leyland Titan TNLXB2RR	Leyland	H44/24D	1981	Ex London Buses, 1994
T 321t	KYV321X	Leyland Titan TNLXB2RR	Leyland	H44/26D	1981	Ex Atlas Bus, 1996
T 375	KYV375X	Leyland Titan TNLXB2RR	Leyland	H44/24D	1981	Ex London Buses, 1994
T 390t	KYV390X	Leyland Titan TNLXB2RR	Leyland	H44/24D	1981	Ex London Buses, 1994
T 432	KYV432X	Leyland Titan TNLXB2RR	Leyland	H44/24D	1982	Ex London Buses, 1994
T 435	KYV435X	Leyland Titan TNLXB2RR	Leyland	H44/24D	1982	Ex London Buses, 1994
T 477	KYV477X	Leyland Titan TNLXB2RR	Leyland	H44/24D	1982	Ex London Buses, 1994
T 481	KYV481X	Leyland Titan TNLXB2RR	Leyland	H44/24D	1982	Ex London Buses, 1994

V 201-217 Volvo Olympian YN2RV18Z4 Northern Counties Palatine II H47/25D 1993/4 Ex London Suburban Bus, 1995

V 201	L201SKD	V 204	L204SKD	V 207	L207SKD	V 210	L210SKD	V 214	L214TWM	V 217	L217TWM
V 202	L202SKD	V 205	L205SKD	V 208	L208SKD	V 212	L212TWM	V 215	L215TWM		
V 203	L203SKD	V 206	L206SKD	V 209	L209SKD	V 213	L213TWM	V 216	L216TWM		

On order for 1999:

65 x Dennis Trident/Plaxton President for routes 17,43,134 and 16 x Dennis Trident/Alexander ALX 400 low floor double deckers for route 16 plus 17 x Dennis Dart SLFs.
Provisional orders have also been lodged for a further 195 Dennis Tridents (bodywork unknown) as well as an additional 125 Dennis Dart SLFs for delivery over years 2000/1/2.

Previous registrations:

33LUG	J823GGF	K476FYN	NDZ7937	KGJ167A	700DYE		H403HOY	WLT646	B236WUL
585CLT	P481MBY	K510FYN	NDZ7936	RIB5082	F202HGN	RIB7004	G208LGK	WLT826	C429BUV
ALC464A	WLT902	KFF257	WLT646	RIB5085	K415MGN	RIB8431	L416PAR	WLT893	B185WUL
EYY327B	804DYE	KFF276	WLT893	RIB7002	CMN12A,	WLT342	OJD819Y	WLT902	B273WUL

SOVEREIGN

RML 2265-2756		AEC Routemaster R2RH/1		Park Royal		H40/32R	1965-8	On lease from London Buses			
RML 2265	CUV265C	RML 2404	JJD404D	RML 2538	JJD538D	RML 2582	JJD582D	RML 2663	SMK663F	RML 2686	SMK686F	RML 2756 SMK756F
RML 2322	CUV322C	RML 2487	JJD487D	RML 2563	JJD563D	RML 2598	JJD598D	RML 2668	SMK668F	RML 2694	SMK694F	
RML 2341	CUV341C	RML 2527	JJD527D	RML 2569	JJD569D	RML 2627	NML627E	RML 2674	SMK674F	RML 2719	SMK719F	

29-52		Leyland Olympian ON2R50C13Z4		Northern Counties		H47/30F	1991				
29	H139GGS	41	H141GGS	43	H143GGS	45	H145GGS	47	H147GGS	49	H149GGS	51	H151GGS
30	H140GGS	42	H142GGS	44	H144GGS	46	H146GGS	48	H148GGS	50	H150GGS	52	H152GGS

53-64		Volvo Olympian OLY-4953		Northern Counties Palatine I		H43/29F	1998	
53	S53VNM	56	S56VNM	58	S58VNM	63	S63VNM
54	S54VNM	57	S57VNM	59	S59VNM	64	S64VNM

409-424		Mercedes-Benz 811D		Reeve Burgess Beaver		B31F	1990-1	
409	H409FGS	411	H411FGS	415	H415FGS	418	H418FGS	421	H421FGS	423	H423FGS
410	H410FGS	413	H413FGS	417	H417FGS	419	H419FGS	422	H422FGS	424	H424FGS

435	K5SBC	Mercedes-Benz 811D		Plaxton Beaver		B31F	1993

455-461		Mercedes-Benz 811D		Plaxton Beaver		B31F	1995	
455	M455UUR	456	M456UUR	457	M457UUR	458	M458UUR	459	M459UUR	460	M460UUR	461	M461UUR

706	OHV706Y	Leyland Titan TNLXB2RR		Leyland		H44/28F	1983	Ex London Buses, 1993

720	NUW620Y	Leyland Titan TNLXB2RR		Leyland		H44/28F	1982	Ex London Buses, 1993
757	WYV57T	Leyland Titan TNLXB2RRsp		Park Royal		H44/28F	1979	Ex London Buses, 1994

909-931		Mercedes-Benz 709D		Reeve Burgess Beaver		B23F	1989-90	
909	G909UPP	922	H922FGS	925	H925FGS	927	H927FGS	930	H930FGS
921	H921FGS	923	H923FGS	926	H926FGS	929	H929FGS	931	H931FGS

SPEEDLINK (LT fleet only)

641-646		Volvo B6LE		Wright Crusader		B37F	1998	
641	S641VOA	642	S642VOA	643	S643VOA	644	S644VOA	645	S645VOA	646	S646VOA

On order:

Six low-floor Dennis Dart SLFs for delivery in spring 1999 to replace the above vehicles, which are currently on temporary loan from Travel West Midlands.

STAGECOACH (Stagecoach East London and Stagecoach Selkent)

DA 10	G684KNW	DAF SB220LC550	Optare Delta	DP36D	1989	Ex London Buses, 1994

DA 11-35   DAF SB220LC550   Optare Delta   DP36D   1992/3   Ex London Buses, 1994

(DA 13 & 15 are currently on loan to Stagecoach South [Hampshire Bus]).

DA 11	J711CYG	DA 15	YLJ332	DA 19	J719CYG	DA 23	J723CYG	DA 27	J727CYG	DA 31	K631HWX	DA 35	K635HWX
DA 12	J712CYG	DA 16	J716CYG	DA 20	J720CYG	DA 24	J724CYG	DA 28	J728CYG	DA 32	K632HWX		
DA 13	472YMF	DA 17	J717CYG	DA 21	J721CYG	DA 25	J725CYG	DA 29	J729CYG	DA 33	K633HWX		
DA 14	J714CYG	DA 18	J718CYG	DA 22	J722CYG	DA 26	J726CYG	DA 30	K630HWX	DA 34	K634HWX		

DAL 1-10   Dennis Dart 9.8SDL3054   Alexander Dash 9.8m   B36F   1995

DAL 1	N301AMC	DAL 3	N303AMC	DAL 5	N305AMC	DAL 7	N307AMC	DAL 9	N309AMC
DAL 2	N302AMC	DAL 4	N304AMC	DAL 6	N306AMC	DAL 8	N308AMC	DAL 10	N310AMC

DRL 109-138   Dennis Dart 9SDL3024   Plaxton Pointer 9m   B34F   1993   Ex London Buses, 1994

DRL 109	K109SRH	DRL 114	K114SRH	DRL 119	K119SRH	DRL 124	K124SRH	DRL 129	K129SRH	DRL 134	K134SRH
DRL 110	K110SRH	DRL 115	K115SRH	DRL 120	K120SRH	DRL 125	K125SRH	DRL 130	K130SRH	DRL 135	K135SRH
DRL 111	K211SRH	DRL 116	K116SRH	DRL 121	K121SRH	DRL 126	K126SRH	DRL 131	K131SRH	DRL 136	L136VRH
DRL 112	K112SRH	DRL 117	K117SRH	DRL 122	K122SRH	DRL 127	K127SRH	DRL 132	K132SRH	DRL 137	L137VRH
DRL 113	K113SRH	DRL 118	K118SRH	DRL 123	K123SRH	DRL 128	K128SRH	DRL 133	K133SRH	DRL 138	L138VRH

DRL 139-146   Dennis Dart 9SDL3034   Plaxton Pointer 9m   B34F   1993   Ex London Buses, 1994

DRL 139	L139VRH	DRL 141	L141VRH	DRL 143	L143VRH	DRL 145	L145VRH
DRL 140	L140VRH	DRL 142	L142VRH	DRL 144	L144VRH	DRL 146	L146VRH

DW 133-150   Dennis Dart 8.5SDL3015   Wright Handybus 8.5m   B29F   1993   Ex London Buses, 1994

DW 133	NDZ3133	DW 135	NDZ3135	DW 138	NDZ3138	DW 140	NDZ3140	DW 149	NDZ3149
DW 134	NDZ3134	DW 137	NDZ3137	DW 139	NDZ3139	DW 148	NDZ3148	DW 150	NDZ3150

DWL 15-26   Dennis Dart 9SDL3016   Wright Handybus 9m   B35F   1993   Ex London Buses, 1994

DWL 15	NDZ3015	DWL 17	NDZ3017	DWL 19	NDZ3019	DWL 21	NDZ3021	DWL 23	NDZ3023	DWL 25	NDZ3025
DWL 16	NDZ3016	DWL 18	NDZ3018	DWL 20	NDZ3020	DWL 22	NDZ3022	DWL 24	NDZ3024	DWL 26	NDZ3026

L 7-145 — Leyland Olympian ONLXB/1RH — Eastern Coach Works — H42/26D — 1986/7 — Ex London Buses, 1994

L 7	C807BYY	L 42	C42CHM	L 64	C64CHM	L 80	C80CHM	L 104	C104CHM	L 117	C117CHM	L 129	D129FYM
L 9	C809BYY	L 43	C43CHM	L 67	C67CHM	L 81	C81CHM	L 105	C105CHM	L 118	C118CHM	L 130	D130FYM
L 10	C810BYY	L 44	C44CHM	L 68	C68CHM	L 82	C82CHM	L 106	C106CHM	L 119	C119CHM	L 131	D131FYM
L 11	C811BYY	L 48	C48CHM	L 69	C69CHM	L 83	C83CHM	L 107	C107CHM	L 120	C120CHM	L 132	D132FYM
L 12	C812BYY	L 51	C51CHM	L 70	C70CHM	L 86	C86CHM	L 108	C108CHM	L 121	C121CHM	L 133	D133FYM
L 15	C815BYY	L 53	C53CHM	L 71	C71CHM	L 87	C87CHM	L 109	C109CHM	L 122	C122CHM	L 134	D134FYM
L 18	C818BYY	L 54	C54CHM	L 72	C72CHM	L 91	WLT491	L 110	C110CHM	L 123	D123FYM	L 136	D136FYM
L 19	C819BYY	L 55	C55CHM	L 73	C73CHM	L 92	C92CHM	L 111	C111CHM	L 124	D124FYM	L 137	D137FYM
L 23	C23CHM	L 57	C57CHM	L 74	C74CHM	L 94	C94CHM	L 112	C112CHM	L 125	D125FYM	L 141	D141FYM
L 28	C28CHM	L 60	C60CHM	L 75	C75CHM	L 97	C97CHM	L 114	C114CHM	L 126	D126FYM	L 142	D142FYM
L 29	C29CHM	L 61	C61CHM	L 76	C76CHM	L 98	C98CHM	L 115	C115CHM	L 127	D127FYM	L 144	D144FYM
L 30	C30CHM	L 62	C62CHM	L 77	C77CHM	L 103	C103CHM	L 116	C116CHM	L 128	D128FYM	L 145	D144FYM

L 260	D706YHK	Leyland Olympian ONLXB/1RH	Eastern Coach Works	DPH42/30F 1987	Ex London Buses, 1994
L 262	VLT14	Leyland Olympian ONLXB/1RH	Eastern Coach Works	DPH42/26D 1987	Ex London Buses, 1994
L 263	D367JJD	Leyland Olympian ONLXB/1RH	Eastern Coach Works	DPH42/26D 1987	Ex London Buses, 1994

LCY 1-11 — Dennis Dart SLF SFD212BR1 — Alexander ALX 200 10.25m — B29DL — 1997/8

LCY 1	P801NJN	LCY 3	P803NJN	LCY 5	P805NJN	LCY 7	P807NJN	LCY 9	R209XNO	LCY 11	S411TNO
LCY 2	P802NJN	LCY 4	P804NJN	LCY 6	P806NJN	LCY 8	R208XNO	LCY 10	S410TNO		

LV 1-12 — Dennis Lance 11SDA3108 — Plaxton Verde — B42D — 1994 — Ex London Buses, 1994

LV 1	L201YAG	LV 3	L203YAG	LV 5	L205YAG	LV 7	L207YAG	LV 9	L209YAG	LV 11	L211YAG
LV 2	L202YAG	LV 4	L204YAG	LV 6	L206YAG	LV 8	L208YAG	LV 10	L210YAG	LV 12	WLT461

MB 1-18 — Mercedes-Benz O814 Vario — Plaxton Beaver 2 — B29F — 1997

MB 1	R501YWC	MB 4	R504YWC	MB 7	R507YWC	MB 10	R510YWC	MB 13	R513YWC	MB 16	R516YWC
MB 2	R502YWC	MB 5	R505YWC	MB 8	R508YWC	MB 11	R511YWC	MB 14	R514YWC	MB 17	R517YWC
MB 3	R503YWC	MB 6	R506YWC	MB 9	R509YWC	MB 12	R512YWC	MB 15	R515YWC	MB 18	R518YWC

MT 4u	F394DHL	Mercedes-Benz 709D	Reeve Burgess Beaver	B20FL	1989	Ex London Buses, 1994

PD 1-18 — Dennis Dart SFD412BR5 — Plaxton Pointer 9.8m — B37D — 1997

PD 1	R701YWC	PD 4	R704YWC	PD 7	R707YWC	PD 10	R710YWC	PD 13	R713YWC	PD 16	R716YWC
PD 2	R702YWC	PD 5	R705YWC	PD 8	R708YWC	PD 11	R711YWC	PD 14	R714YWC	PD 17	R717YWC
PD 3	R703YWC	PD 6	R706YWC	PD 9	R709YWC	PD 12	R712YWC	PD 15	R715YWC	PD 18	R718YWC

PD 59-103 — Dennis Dart 9.8SDL3054 — Plaxton Pointer 9.8m — B37D — 1995 — Ex Stagecoach Oxford, 1998

PD 59	M59VJO	PD 67	M67VJO	PD 73	M73VJO	PD 85	M85WBW	PD 91	M91WBW	PD 95	M95WBW	PD 103	M103WBW
PD 63	M63VJO	PD 68	M68VJO	PD 81	M81WBW	PD 86	M86WBW	PD 92	M92WBW	PD 96	M96WBW		
PD 64	M64VJO	PD 69	M69VJO	PD 82	M82WBW	PD 87	M87WBW	PD 93	M93WBW	PD 101	M101WBW		
PD 65	M65VJO	PD 71	M71VJO	PD 83	M83WBW	PD 89	M89WBW	PD 94	M94WBW	PD 102	M102WBW		

PD 410-427		Dennis Dart 9.8SDL3054		Plaxton Pointer 9.8m		B40F	1996	Ex Docklands Transit, 1997		

PD 410 N410MBW	**PD 413** N413MBW	**PD 416** N416MBW	**PD 419** N419MBW	**PD 422** N422MBW	**PD 425** N425MBW
PD 411 N411MBW	**PD 414** N414MBW	**PD 417** N417MBW	**PD 420** N420MBW	**PD 423** N423MBW	**PD 426** N426MBW
PD 412 N412MBW	**PD 415** N415MBW	**PD 418** N418MBW	**PD 421** N421MBW	**PD 424** N424MBW	**PD 427** N427MBW

PD 709-722		Dennis Dart 9.8SDL3035		Plaxton Pointer 9.8m	B37D	1994	Ex Stagecoach Oxford, 1998

PD 709 L709JUD	**PD 711** L711JUD	**PD 713** L713JUD	**PD 715** L715JUD	**PD 717** L717JUD	**PD 719** L719JUD	**PD 721** L721JUD
PD 710 L710JUD	**PD 712** L712JUD	**PD 714** L714JUD	**PD 716** L716JUD	**PD 718** L718JUD	**PD 720** L720JUD	**PD 722** L722JUD

RM 613	WLT613	AEC Routemaster R2RH	Park Royal	H36/28R	1960	Ex London Buses, 1994
RM 980	USK625	AEC Routemaster R2RH	Park Royal	H36/28R	1961	Ex Bluebird Buses, 1997
RM 1289	XSL596A	AEC Routemaster R2RH	Park Royal	H36/28R	1962	Ex Bluebird Buses, 1997
RM 1527	527CLT	AEC Routemaster R2RH	Park Royal	H36/28R	1963	Ex London Buses, 1994
RM 1599	YTS820A	AEC Routemaster R2RH	Park Royal	H36/28R	1963	Ex Bluebird Buses, 1997
RMC 1456	LFF875	AEC Routemaster R2RH	Park Royal	H32/25RD	1961	Ex London Buses, 1994
RMC 1461	461CLT	AEC Routemaster R2RH	Park Royal	H32/25RD	1961	Ex London Buses, 1994
RMC 1485	485CLT	AEC Routemaster R2RH	Park Royal	H32/25RD	1961	Ex London Buses, 1994
RML 886	WLT886	AEC Routemaster R2RH	Park Royal	H40/32R	1961	Ex London Buses, 1994
RML 890	XFF814	AEC Routemaster R2RH	Park Royal	H40/32R	1961	Ex London Buses, 1994
RML 898	XFF813	AEC Routemaster R2RH	Park Royal	H40/32R	1961	Ex London Buses, 1994

RML 2272-2760	AEC Routemaster R2RH/1	Park Royal	H40/32R	1965-68	Ex London Buses, 1994

RML 2272 CUV272C	**RML 2415** JJD415D	**RML 2456** JJD456D	**RML 2497** JJD497D	**RML 2616** NML616E	**RML 2670** SMK670F	**RML 2748** SMK748F
RML 2286 CUV286C	**RML 2429** JJD429D	**RML 2462** JJD462D	**RML 2541** JJD541D	**RML 2624** NML624E	**RML 2671** SMK671F	**RML 2749** SMK749F
RML 2300 CUV300C	**RML 2435** JJD435D	**RML 2470** JJD470D	**RML 2550** JJD550D	**RML 2639** NML639E	**RML 2696** SMK696F	**RML 2760** SMK760F
RML 2303 CUV303C	**RML 2437** JJD437D	**RML 2481** JJD481D	**RML 2565** JJD565D	**RML 2641** NML641E	**RML 2705** SMK705F	
RML 2311 CUV311C	**RML 2444** JJD444D	**RML 2488** JJD488D	**RML 2581** JJD581D	**RML 2642** NML642E	**RML 2709** SMK709F	
RML 2392 JJD392D	**RML 2445** JJD445D	**RML 2493** JJD493D	**RML 2592** JJD592D	**RML 2657** NML657E	**RML 2723** SMK723F	
RML 2399 JJD399D	**RML 2450** JJD450D	**RML 2495** JJD495D	**RML 2607** NML607E	**RML 2661** SMK661F	**RML 2738** SMK738F	
RML 2402 JJD402D	**RML 2451** JJD451D	**RML 2496** JJD496D	**RML 2610** NML610E	**RML 2665** SMK665F	**RML 2743** SMK743F	

S 22-29		Scania N113DRB		Alexander RH	H47/31F	1991	Ex London Buses, 1994

S 22 J822HMC	**S 24** J824HMC	**S 26** J826HMC	**S 28** J828HMC	
S 23 J823HMC	**S 25** J825HMC	**S 27** J827HMC	**S 29** J829HMC	

S 30	J230XKY	Scania N113DRB	Northern Counties	H47/33F	1991	Ex London Buses, 1994
S 31	J231XKY	Scania N113DRB	Northern Counties	H47/33F	1991	Ex London Buses, 1994

S32-71		Scania N113DRB		Northern Counties Palatine	H44/25D	1991/2	Ex London Buses, 1994

S 32 J132HMT	**S 36** J136HMT	**S 40** J140HMT	**S 44** J144HMT	**S 48** K848LMK	**S 52** K852LMK	**S 56** K856LMK
S 33 J133HMT	**S 37** J137HMT	**S 41** J141HMT	**S 45** J145HMT	**S 49** K849LMK	**S 53** K853LMK	**S 57** K857LMK
S 34 J134HMT	**S 38** J138HMT	**S 42** J142HMT	**S 46** K846LMK	**S 50** K850LMK	**S 54** K854LMK	**S 58** K858LMK
S 35 J135HMT	**S 39** J139HMT	**S 43** J143HMT	**S 47** K847LMK	**S 51** K851LMK	**S 55** K855LMK	**S 59** K859LMK

| S 60 | K860LMK | S 62 | K862LMK | S 64 | K864LMK | S 66 | K866LMK | S 68 | K868LMK | S 70 | K870LMK |
| S 61 | K861LMK | S 63 | K863LMK | S 65 | K865LMK | S 67 | K867LMK | S 69 | K869LMK | S 71 | K871LMK |

SLD 1-29 — Dennis Dart SLF SFD212BR1 — Alexander ALX 200 10.25m — B36F — 1996/7

SLD 1	P21HMF	SLD 6	P26HMF	SLD 11	P611SEV	SLD 16	R116VPU	SLD 21	R121VPU	SLD 26	R126VPU
SLD 2	P31HMF	SLD 7	P27HMF	SLD 12	R712XAR	SLD 17	R117VPU	SLD 22	R122VPU	SLD 27	R127VPU
SLD 3	P23HMF	SLD 8	P28HMF	SLD 13	P613SEV	SLD 18	R118VPU	SLD 23	R123VPU	SLD 28	R128VPU
SLD 4	P24HMF	SLD 9	P29HMF	SLD 14	R114VPU	SLD 19	R119VPU	SLD 24	R124VPU	SLD 29	R129VPU
SLD 5	P25HMF	SLD 10	P610SEV	SLD 15	R115VPU	SLD 20	R120VPU	SLD 25	R125VPU		

SLD 30-41 — Dennis Dart SLF SFD212BR1 — Alexander ALX 200 10.25m — B30D — 1998

| SLD 30 | R930FOO | SLD 32 | R932FOO | SLD 34 | R934FOO | SLD 36 | R936FOO | SLD 38 | R938FOO | SLD 40 | R940FOO |
| SLD 31 | R931FOO | SLD 33 | R933FOO | SLD 35 | R935FOO | SLD 37 | R937FOO | SLD 39 | R939FOO | SLD 41 | R941FOO |

SLD 42-58 — Dennis Dart SLF SFD112BR1 — Alexander ALX 200 9.4m — B29F — 1998

SLD 42	R942FOO	SLD 45	R945FOO	SLD 48	R948FOO	SLD 51	R451FVX	SLD 54	R454FVX	SLD 57	R457FVX
SLD 43	R943FOO	SLD 46	R946FOO	SLD 49	R949FOO	SLD 52	R452FVX	SLD 55	R455FVX	SLD 58	R458FVX
SLD 44	R944FOO	SLD 47	R947FOO	SLD 50	R950FOO	SLD 53	R453FVX	SLD 56	R456FVX		

SLD 59-78 — Dennis Dart SLF SFD212BR1 — Alexander ALX 200 10.25m — B33F — 1998/9

SLD 59	S459BWC	SLD 62	S462BWC	SLD 65	S465BWC	SLD 68	S468BWC	SLD 71	S471BWC	SLD 74	S474BWC	SLD 77	S477BWC
SLD 60	S460BWC	SLD 63	S463BWC	SLD 66	S466BWC	SLD 69	S469BWC	SLD 72	S472BWC	SLD 75	S475BWC	SLD 78	S478BWC
SLD 61	S461BWC	SLD 64	S464BWC	SLD 67	S467BWC	SLD 70	S470BWC	SLD 73	S473BWC	SLD 76	S476BWC		

SLD 79-88 — Dennis Dart SLF SFD112 — Alexander ALX 200 9.4m — B29F — 1999 — On order

| SLD 79 | S479BWC | SLD 81 | S481BWC | SLD 83 | S483BWC | SLD 85 | S485BWC | SLD 87 | S487BWC |
| SLD 80 | S480BWC | SLD 82 | S482BWC | SLD 84 | S484BWC | SLD 86 | S486BWC | SLD 88 | S488BWC |

SLD 89-95 — Dennis Dart SLF SFD212 — Alexander ALX 200 10.25m — B..F — 1999 — On order

| SLD 89 | SLD 90 | SLD 91 | SLD 92 | SLD 93 | SLD 94 | SLD 95 |

SLD 96-106 — Dennis Dart SLF SFD112 — Alexander ALX 200 9.4m — B..F — 1999 — On order

| SLD 96 | SLD 98 | SLD 100 | SLD 102 | SLD 104 | SLD 106 |
| SLD 97 | SLD 99 | SLD 101 | SLD 103 | SLD 105 | |

SLW 15-30 — Scania N113CRL — Wright Pathfinder 320 — B37D — 1994 — Ex London Buses, 1994

SLW 15	RDZ6115	SLW 18	RDZ6118	SLW 21	RDZ6121	SLW 24	RDZ6124	SLW 27	RDZ6127	SLW 30	RDZ6130
SLW 16	RDZ6116	SLW 19	RDZ6119	SLW 22	RDZ6122	SLW 25	RDZ6125	SLW 28	RDZ6128		
SLW 17	RDZ6117	SLW 20	RDZ6120	SLW 23	RDZ6123	SLW 26	RDZ6126	SLW 29	RDZ6129		

SR 1-106 — Mercedes-Benz 811D — Optare StarRider — B26F — 1988/9 — Ex London Buses, 1994

| SR 1 | E155CGJ | SR 2 | E712LYU | SR 70 | F170FWY | SR 71 | F171FWY | SR 74 | F174FWY | SR 91 | G91KUB | SR 106 | G106KUB |

T 1-80

Leyland Titan TNTL11112RRsp   Park Royal   *H44/24D   1978   Ex London Buses, 1994
*T 63 and 80 are H44/26F

T 1	THX401S	T 9	WYV9T	T 15	WYV15T	T 21	WYV21T	T 28	WYV28T	T 35	WYV35T	T 63t	HVX770T
T 2	THX402S	T 10	WYV10T	T 16	WYV16T	T 22	WYV22T	T 30	WYV30T	T 36	WYV36T	T 66	WYV66T
T 4	WYV4T	T 11	WYV11T	T 17	WYV17T	T 23	WYV23T	T 31	WYV31T	T 37	WYV37T	T 80t	UJN344V
T 6	WYV6T	T 12	WYV12T	T 18	WYV18T	T 24	WYV24T	T 32	WYV32T	T 38	WYV38T		
T 7	WYV7T	T 13	WYV13T	T 19	WYV19T	T 25	WYV25T	T 33	WYV33T	T 39	WYV39T		
T 8	WYV8T	T 14	WYV14T	T 20	WYV20T	T 26	WYV26T	T 34	WYV34T	T 40	WYV40T		

T 86-140

Leyland Titan TNTL11112RRsp   Park Royal   H44/26D   1979-80   Ex London Buses, 1994

| T 86t | CUL86V | T 98t | CUL98V | T 114t | CUL114V | T 120t | CUL120V | T 130t | CUL130V | T 137t | CUL137V | T 140 | CUL140V |

T 142-230

Leyland Titan TNTL11112RRsp   Park Royal   H44/26D   1980   Ex London Buses, 1994

| T 142t | CUL142V | T 175 | CUL175V | T 214 | CUL214V | T 223 | CUL223V | T 230 | EYE230V |
| T 163 | CUL163V | T 193 | CUL193V | T 222 | CUL222V | T 224t | CUL224V | | |

T 260	GYE260W	Leyland Titan TNLXB2RR	Park Royal/Leyland	H44/26D	1981	Ex London Buses, 1994
T 261	GYE261W	Leyland Titan TNTL112RR	Park Royal/Leyland	H44/26D	1981	Ex London Buses, 1994
T 262	GYE262W	Leyland Titan TNLXB2RR	Park Royal/Leyland	H44/26D	1981	Ex London Buses, 1994
T 263	GYE263W	Leyland Titan TNLXB2RR	Park Royal/Leyland	H44/26D	1981	Ex London Buses, 1994

T 264-868

Leyland Titan TNLXB2RR   Leyland   *H44/24D   1981-4   Ex London Buses, 1994
*T512 is O44/24D

T 264	GYE264W	T 379	KYV379X	T 458	KYV458X	T 498	KYV498X	T 531	KYV531X	T 556	NUW556Y	T 597	NUW597Y
T 266	GYE266W	T 380	KYV380X	T 460	KYV460X	T 500	KYV500X	T 532	KYV532X	T 557	NUW557Y	T 598	NUW598Y
T 267	GYE267W	T 386	KYV386X	T 461	KYV461X	T 501	KYV501X	T 533	KYV533X	T 559	NUW559Y	T 600	NUW600Y
T 268	GYE268W	T 387	KYV387X	T 462	KYV462X	T 502	KYV502X	T 535	KYV535X	T 563	NUW563Y	T 602	NUW602Y
T 272	GYE272W	T 394	KYV394X	T 465	KYV465X	T 503	KYV503X	T 536	KYV536X	T 564	NUW564Y	T 603	NUW603Y
T 285	KYN285X	T 395	KYV395X	T 466	KYV466X	T 504	KYV504X	T 537	KYV537X	T 565	NUW565Y	T 605	NUW605Y
T 286	KYN286X	T 406	KYV406X	T 467	KYV467X	T 505	KYV505X	T 539	KYV539X	T 568	NUW568Y	T 608	NUW608Y
T 298	KYN298X	T 428	KYV428X	T 469	KYV469X	T 506	KYV506X	T 540	KYV540X	T 569	NUW569Y	T 609	NUW609Y
T 306	KYN306X	T 434	KYV434X	T 470	KYV470X	T 508	KYV508X	T 541	KYV541X	T 573	NUW573Y	T 610	NUW610Y
T 311	KYV311X	T 437	KYV437X	T 471	KYV471X	T 512t	KYV512X	T 543	KYV543X	T 576	NUW576Y	T 613	NUW613Y
T 318	KYV318X	T 439	KYV439X	T 473	KYV473X	T 513	KYV513X	T 544	KYV544X	T 578	NUW578Y	T 614	NUW614Y
T 320	KYV320X	T 441	KYV441X	T 476	KYV476X	T 514	KYV514X	T 545	KYV545X	T 579	NUW579Y	T 616	NUW616Y
T 326	KYV326X	T 444	KYV444X	T 480	KYV480X	T 515	KYV515X	T 546	KYV546X	T 580	NUW580Y	T 617	NUW617Y
T 331	KYV331X	T 445	KYV445X	T 486	KYV486X	T 517	KYV517X	T 548	KYV548X	T 581	NUW581Y	T 624	NUW624Y
T 334	KYV334X	T 446	KYV446X	T 488	KYV488X	T 521	KYV521X	T 549	KYV549X	T 583	NUW583Y	T 625	NUW625Y
T 340	KYV340X	T 447	KYV447X	T 490	KYV490X	T 522	KYV522X	T 550	NUW550Y	T 584	NUW584Y	T 627	NUW627Y
T 360	KYV360X	T 448	KYV448X	T 492	KYV492X	T 525	KYV525X	T 551	NUW551Y	T 585	NUW585Y	T 629	NUW629Y
T 366	KYV366X	T 453	KYV453X	T 495	KYV495X	T 526	KYV526X	T 552	NUW552Y	T 589	NUW589Y	T 630	NUW630Y
T 368	KYV368X	T 454	KYV454X	T 496	KYV496X	T 527	KYV527X	T 553	NUW553Y	T 590	NUW590Y	T 631	NUW631Y
T 378	KYV378X	T 456	KYV456X	T 497	KYV497X	T 529	KYV529X	T 554	NUW554Y	T 592	NUW592Y	T 632	NUW632Y

T 633	NUW633Y	T 658	NUW658Y	T 771	OHV771Y	T 812	OHV812Y	T 822	RYK822Y	T 838	A838SUL	T 856	A856SUL
T 637	NUW637Y	T 680	OHV680Y	T 772	OHV772Y	T 813	OHV813Y	T 828	A828SUL	T 841	A841SUL	T 857	A857SUL
T 640	NUW640Y	T 721	OHV721Y	T 785	OHV785Y	T 814	OHV814Y	T 829	A829SUL	T 842	A842SUL	T 868	A868SUL
T 650	NUW650Y	T 740	OHV740Y	T 797	OHV797Y	T 815	OHV815Y	T 830	A830SUL	T 845	A845SUL		
T 652	NUW652Y	T 748	OHV748Y	T 804	OHV804Y	T 816	RYK816Y	T 834	A834SUL	T 847	A847SUL		
T 653	NUW653Y	T 749	OHV749Y	T 805	OHV805Y	T 818	RYK818Y	T 836	A836SUL	T 848	A848SUL		
T 657	NUW657Y	T 770	OHV770Y	T 810	OHV810Y	T 821	RYK821Y	T 837	A837SUL	T 854	A854SUL		

T 877	A877SUL	Leyland Titan TNTL112RR	Leyland	H44/26D	1984	Ex London Buses, 1994	
T 880	A880SUL	Leyland Titan TNTL112RR	Leyland	H44/26D	1984	Ex London Buses, 1994	
T 881	A881SUL	Leyland Titan TNL112RR	Leyland	H44/26D	1984	Ex London Buses, 1994	
T 882	A882SUL	Leyland Titan TNL112RR	Leyland	H44/26D	1984	Ex London Buses, 1994	
T 883	A883SUL	Leyland Titan TNL112RR	Leyland	H44/26D	1984	Ex London Buses, 1994	
T 885	A885SUL	Leyland Titan TNL112RR	Leyland	H44/26D	1984	Ex London Buses, 1994	

T 925-1122		Leyland Titan TNLXB2RR	Leyland	H44/26D	1984	Ex London Buses, 1994

T 925	A925SYE	T 960t	A960SYE	T 988	A988SYE	T 1029	A629THV	T 1048	A648THV	T 1103	B103WUV	T 1118	B118WUV
T 926	A926SYE	T 961	A961SYE	T 1003	A603THV	T 1030	A630THV	T 1052	A652THV	T 1112	B112WUV	T 1122	B122WUV
T 949t	A949SYE	T 965t	A965SYE	T 1025	A625THV	T 1034	A634THV	T 1065	A65THX	T 1115	B115WUV		
T 951	A951SYE	T 971t	A971SYE	T 1027	A627THV	T 1035	A635THV	T 1099	B99WUV	T 1116	B116WUV		
T 953t	A953SYE	T 978	A978SYE	T 1028	A628THV	T 1036	A636THV	T 1101	B101WUV	T 1117	B117WUV		

T 1128t	HVX771T	Leyland Titan TNLXB1RF	Park Royal	DPH43/29F	1979	Ex London Buses, 1994

Note: Numerous Leyland Titans have been converted to single door configuration and have consequently changed seating layouts.

TA 1-98		Dennis Trident SFD311BR1	Alexander ALX 400	H45/22D	1999	On order

TA 1	S801BWC	TA 15		TA 29		TA 43		TA 57		TA 71		TA 85	
TA 2	S802BWC	TA 16		TA 30		TA 44		TA 58		TA 72		TA 86	
TA 3	S803BWC	TA 17		TA 31		TA 45		TA 59		TA 73		TA 87	
TA 4	S804BWC	TA 18		TA 32		TA 46		TA 60		TA 74		TA 88	
TA 5	S805BWC	TA 19		TA 33		TA 47		TA 61		TA 75		TA 89	
TA 6	S806BWC	TA 20		TA 34		TA 48		TA 62		TA 76		TA 90	
TA 7	S807BWC	TA 21		TA 35		TA 49		TA 63		TA 77		TA 91	
TA 8	S808BWC	TA 22		TA 36		TA 50		TA 64		TA 78		TA 92	
TA 9	S809BWC	TA 23		TA 37		TA 51		TA 65		TA 79		TA 93	
TA 10	S810BWC	TA 24		TA 38		TA 52		TA 66		TA 80		TA 94	
TA 11		TA 25		TA 39		TA 53		TA 67		TA 81		TA 95	
TA 12		TA 26		TA 40		TA 54		TA 68		TA 82		TA 96	
TA 13		TA 27		TA 41		TA 55		TA 69		TA 83		TA 97	
TA 14		TA 28		TA 42		TA 56		TA 70		TA 84		TA 98	

VA 44-81, 122-148 Volvo Olympian Alexander RL H51/28D 1997/8

VA 44 P644SEV	VA 54 R154VPU	VA 64 R164VPU	VA 74 R174VPU	VA 124 R124EVX	VA 134 R134EVX	VA 144 R144EVX
VA 45 P644SEV	VA 55 R155VPU	VA 65 R165VPU	VA 75 R175VPU	VA 125 R125EVX	VA 135 R135EVX	VA 145 R145EVX
VA 46 P644SEV	VA 56 R156VPU	VA 66 R166VPU	VA 76 R176VPU	VA 126 R126EVX	VA 136 R136EVX	VA 146 R146EVX
VA 47 R747XAR	VA 57 R157VPU	VA 67 R167VPU	VA 77 R177VPU	VA 127 R127EVX	VA 137 R137EVX	VA 147 R147EVX
VA 48 R148VPU	VA 58 R158VPU	VA 68 R168VPU	VA 78 R178VPU	VA 128 R128EVX	VA 138 R138EVX	VA 148 R148EVX
VA 49 R149VPU	VA 59 R159VPU	VA 69 R169VPU	VA 79 R179VPU	VA 129 R129EVX	VA 139 R139EVX	
VA 50 R150VPU	VA 60 R160VPU	VA 70 R170VPU	VA 80 R180VPU	VA 130 R130EVX	VA 140 R140EVX	
VA 51 R151VPU	VA 61 R161VPU	VA 71 R171VPU	VA 81 R181VPU	VA 131 R131EVX	VA 141 R141EVX	
VA 52 R152VPU	VA 62 R162VPU	VA 72 R172VPU	VA 122 R122EVX	VA 132 R132EVX	VA 142 R142EVX	
VA 53 R153VPU	VA 63 R163VPU	VA 73 R173VPU	VA 123 R123EVX	VA 133 R133EVX	VA 143 R143EVX	

VN 1-26 Volvo Olympian YN3RVI6V3 Northern Counties Palatine I H49/31F 1996

VN 1 P801GMU	VN 5 P805GMU	VN 9 P809GMU	VN 13 P813GMU	VN 17 P817GMU	VN 21 P821GMU	VN 25 P825GMU
VN 2 P802GMU	VN 6 P806GMU	VN 10 P810GMU	VN 14 P814GMU	VN 18 P818GMU	VN 22 P822GMU	VN 26 P826GMU
VN 3 P803GMU	VN 7 P807GMU	VN 11 P811GMU	VN 15 P815GMU	VN 19 P819GMU	VN 23 P823GMU	
VN 4 P804GMU	VN 8 P808GMU	VN 12 P812GMU	VN 16 P816GMU	VN 20 P820GMU	VN 24 P824GMU	

VN 27-43 Volvo Olympian YN3RVI6V3 Northern Counties Palatine I H49/25D 1996

VN 27 P527HMP	VN 30 P530HMP	VN 33 P533HMP	VN 36 P536HMP	VN 39 P539HMP	VN 42 P542HMP
VN 28 P528HMP	VN 31 P531HMP	VN 34 P534HMP	VN 37 P537HMP	VN 40 P540HMP	VN 43 P543HMP
VN 29 P529HMP	VN 32 P532HMP	VN 35 P535HMP	VN 38 P538HMP	VN 41 P541HMP	

VN 82-110 Volvo Olympian OLY-4953 Northern Counties Palatine I H45/23D 1997/8

VN 82 R82XNO	VN 87 R87XNO	VN 92 R92XNO	VN 97 R97XNO	VN 102 R102XNO	VN 107 R107XNO
VN 83 R83XNO	VN 88 R188XNO	VN 93 R93XNO	VN 98 R98XNO	VN 103 R103XNO	VN 108 R108XNO
VN 84 R84XNO	VN 89 R89XNO	VN 94 R94XNO	VN 99 R207XNO	VN 104 R104XNO	VN 109 R109XNO
VN 85 R85XNO	VN 90 R190XNO	VN 95 R95XNO	VN 100 R210XNO	VN 105 R105XNO	VN 110 S110SHJ
VN 86 R86XNO	VN 91 R91XNO	VN 96 R96XNO	VN 101 R101XNO	VN 106 R206XNO	

VN 111-121, 149-178 Volvo Olympian OLY-5639 Northern Counties Palatine I H49/27D 1998

VN 111 R311XNO	VN 117 R117XNO	VN 150 R150HHK	VN 156 R156HHK	VN 162 R162HHK	VN 168 R168HHK	VN 174 R174HHK
VN 112 R112XNO	VN 118 R118XNO	VN 151 R151HHK	VN 157 R157HHK	VN 163 R163HHK	VN 169 R169HHK	VN 175 R175HHK
VN 113 R113XNO	VN 119 R119XNO	VN 152 R152HHK	VN 158 R158HHK	VN 164 R164HHK	VN 170 R170HHK	VN 176 R176HHK
VN 114 R114XNO	VN 120 R120XNO	VN 153 R153HHK	VN 159 R159HHK	VN 165 R165HHK	VN 171 R171HHK	VN 177 R177HHK
VN 115 R115XNO	VN 121 R121XNO	VN 154 R154HHK	VN 160 R160HHK	VN 166 R166HHK	VN 172 R172HHK	VN 178 R178HHK
VN 116 R116XNO	VN 149 R149HHK	VN 155 R155HHK	VN 161 R161HHK	VN 167 R167HHK	VN 173 R173HHK	

VP 4	630DYE	Volvo B10M-60	Plaxton Paramount 3500 III	C49FT	1991	Ex Willetts, Yorkley, 1995
VP 5	WLT890	Volvo B10M-60	Plaxton Paramount 3500 III	C49FT	1991	Ex Wallace Arnold, 1995
VP 7	WLT898	Volvo B10M-60	Plaxton Paramount 3500 III	C49FT	1991	Ex Metrobus, 1995

301-352				Volvo Olympian YN2RC16V3		Northern Counties Palatine I			H45/23D	1995				
301	M301DGP	309	M309DGP	317	M317DGP	325	N325HGK	333	N353HGK	341	N341HGK	349	N349HGK
302	M302DGP	310	M310DGP	318	M318DGP	326	N326HGK	334	N334HGK	342	N342HGK	350	N350HGK
303	M303DGP	311	M311DGP	319	M319DGP	327	N327HGK	335	N335HGK	343	N343HGK	351	N351HGK
304	M304DGP	312	M312DGP	320	M320DGP	328	N328HGK	336	N336HGK	344	N344HGK	352	N352HGK
305	M305DGP	313	M313DGP	321	N321HGK	329	N329HGK	337	N337HGK	345	N345HGK		
306	M306DGP	314	M314DGP	322	N322HGK	330	N330HGK	338	N338HGK	346	N346HGK		
307	M307DGP	315	M315DGP	323	N323HGK	331	N331HGK	339	N339HGK	347	N347HGK		
308	M308DGP	316	M316DGP	324	N324HGK	332	N332HGK	340	N340HGK	348	N348HGK		

608	N608KGF	Dennis Dart 9.8SDL3054	Alexander Dash 9.8m	B36F	1995
611	N611LGC	Dennis Dart 9.8SDL3054	Alexander Dash 9.8m	B36F	1995
614	N614LGC	Dennis Dart 9.8SDL3054	Alexander Dash 9.8m	B36F	1995

615-640				Dennis Dart SFD412BR5		Alexander Dash 9.8m			B36F	1996		
615	P615PGP	619	P619PGP	623	P623PGP	627	P627PGP	634	P634PGP	639	P639PGP
616	P616PGP	620	P620PGP	624	P624PGP	631	P631PGP	636	P636PGP	640	P640PGP
617	P617PGP	621	P621PGP	625	P625PGP	632	P632PGP	637	P637PGP		
618	P618PGP	622	P622PGP	626	P626PGP	633	P633PGP	638	P638PGP		

Previous registrations:

472YMF	J713CYG
630DYE	H659UWR, H654UWR
D367JJD	D263FUL, VLT9
D706YHK	D260FYM, VLT20
E155CGJ	E711LYU, WLT461
HVX770T	WYV63T, WLT890
HVX771T	WDA3T, 486CLT, 630DYE
LFF875	456CLT
UJN344V	CUL80V, WLT898
USK625	WLT980
VLT14	D262FUL
WLT461	L212YAG
WLT491	C91CHM
WLT890	H660UWR, H655UWR
WLT898	H655UWR, H657UWR
XFF813	WLT898
XFF814	WLT890
XSL596A	289CLT
YLJ332	J715CYG
YTS820A	599CLT

Special Livery:

The LCY buses carry blue livery for London City Airport service.

5621RU	Mercedes-Benz 609D	Whittaker Europa	DP21F	1990	Ex Bakers, Biddulph, 1998
F71SJX	Mercedes-Benz 709D	Onyx	DP24F	1989	Ex South Lancs, St Helens, 1996
F34CWY	Mercedes-Benz 811D	Optare StarRider	B26F	1988	Ex Bridge, Paisley, 1997
F46CWY	Mercedes-Benz 811D	Optare StarRider	B26F	1988	Ex Bridge, Paisley, 1997
H120YGG	Mercedes-Benz 709D	Dormobile Routemaker	B27F	1990	Ex Goosecroft, Stirling, 1997
K949OEM	Mercedes-Benz 811D	Marshall C16	B27F	1993	Ex Merseybus, 1998
M70TGM	Mercedes-Benz 709D	Plaxton Beaver	B23F	1995	
M80TGM	Mercedes-Benz 709D	Plaxton Beaver	B23F	1995	
M90TGM	Mercedes-Benz 709D	Plaxton Beaver	B23F	1995	
N70TGM	Mercedes-Benz 709D	Plaxton Beaver	B23F	1996	
P70TGM	Mercedes-Benz 709D	Plaxton Beaver	B27F	1997	
P701LCF	Mercedes-Benz O814 Vario	Plaxton Beaver 2	B31F	1997	
P702LCF	Mercedes-Benz O814 Vario	Plaxton Beaver 2	B31F	1997	
P703LCF	Mercedes-Benz O814 Vario	Plaxton Beaver 2	B31F	1997	
P704LCF	Mercedes-Benz O814 Vario	Plaxton Beaver 2	B31F	1997	
R705MJH	Mercedes-Benz O814 Vario	Plaxton Beaver 2	B31F	1997	
R706MJH	Mercedes-Benz O814 Vario	Plaxton Beaver 2	B31F	1997	

R501-514SJM	Dennis Dart SLF SFD322BR1	Plaxton Pointer 10.6m	B39F	1997	

R501SJM	R503SJM	R505SJM	R507SJM	R509SJM	R511SJM	R513SJM
R502SJM	R504SJM	R506SJM	R508SJM	R510SJM	R512SJM	R514SJM

S515JJH	Dennis Dart SLF SFD322BR1	Plaxton Pointer 2 10.7m	B39F	1998	
S516JJH	Dennis Dart SLF SFD322BR1	Plaxton Pointer 2 10.7m	B39F	1998	
S517JJH	Dennis Dart SLF SFD322BR1	Plaxton Pointer 2 10.7m	B39F	1998	
S707JJH	Mercedes-Benz O814 Vario	Plaxton Beaver 2	B31F	1998	
S708TCF	Mercedes-Benz O814 Vario	Plaxton Beaver 2	B31F	1999	
S518TCF	Dennis Dart SLF SFD322BR1	Plaxton Pointer 2 10.7m	B39F	1999	
S519TCF	Dennis Dart SLF SFD322BR1	Plaxton Pointer 2 10.7m	B39F	1999	

Previous Registration:

5621 RU G429NET

THAMESWAY (Part of the First Group) (LT fleet only)

401-410		Mercedes-Benz 711D		Plaxton Beaver				B23F	1996				
401	P401HPU	403	P403HPU	405	P405HPU	407	P407HPU	409	P409HPU				
402	P402HPU	404	P404HPU	406	P406HPU	408	P408HPU	410	P410HPU				

805-811		Mercedes-Benz 811D		Plaxton Beaver				B31F	1989				
805	K805DJN	806	K806DJN	807	K807DJN	808	K808DJN	809	K809DJN	810	K810DJN	811	K811DJN

851-854		Dennis Dart 9SDL3053		Marshall C36 9m				B17FL	1995				
851	N851CPU	852	N852CPU	853	N853CPU	854	N854CPU						

THORPES

	D480PONw	MCW Metrorider MF150/18	MCW	DP25F	1987	Ex Metroline, 1997
	E930KYRw	MCW Metrorider MF150/46	MCW	B25F	1988	Ex Rhondda, 1995
	E134SNYw	MCW Metrorider MF150/52	MCW	B23F	1988	Ex Cardiff, 1995
	E135SNYw	MCW Metrorider MF150/52	MCW	B23F	1988	Ex Cardiff, 1995
	E137SNYw	MCW Metrorider MF150/52	MCW	B23F	1988	Ex Cardiff, 1995
	F134UMD	Mercedes-Benz 709D	Reeve Burgess Beaver	B23F	1988	Ex Speedlink, 1998
	G901UPP	Mercedes-Benz 709D	Reeve Burgess Beaver	B23F	1989	Ex Sovereign, 1998
	G894XPX	Mercedes-Benz 811D	Wadham Stringer Wessex	B25F	1989	Ex Gatwick Airport, 1998
ML 514	J514WTW	Mercedes-Benz 709D	Wadham Stringer Wessex	B19FL	1991	Ex Javelin, Wandsworth, 1997
ML 520	J520WTW	Mercedes-Benz 709D	Wadham Stringer Wessex	B20FL	1991	Ex Javelin, Wandsworth, 1997
ML 529	J529WTW	Mercedes-Benz 709D	Wadham Stringer Wessex	B23FL	1991	Ex Javelin, Wandsworth, 1997
ML 530	J530WTW	Mercedes-Benz 709D	Wadham Stringer Wessex	B15FL	1991	Ex Javelin, Wandsworth, 1997
	K2FET	Mercedes-Benz 709D	Alexander AM (Belfast)	B16FL	1993	
	K3FET	Mercedes-Benz 709D	Alexander AM (Belfast)	B16FL	1993	
	M190TEV	Mercedes-Benz 709D	Wadham Stringer Wessex II	B20FL	1994	Ex Javelin, Wandsworth, 1997
	M191TEV	Mercedes-Benz 709D	Wadham Stringer Wessex II	B20FL	1994	Ex Javelin, Wandsworth, 1997
XL 100	N100FET	Optare Excel L960	Optare	B27F	1996	
XL 200	N200FET	Optare Excel L960	Optare	B27F	1996	
XL 300	N300FET	Optare Excel L960	Optare	B27F	1996	
XL 400	N400FET	Optare Excel L960	Optare	B27F	1996	
DLF 9	R309NGM	Dennis Dart SLF212BR1	Plaxton Pointer 10m	B33F	1997	Ex Limebourne, 1998

DLF 29-40		Dennis Dart SLF SFD212		Plaxton Pointer 2 10.2m		B29D	1998		
DLF 29	S529JLM	DLF 31	S531JLM	DLF 33	S533JLM	DLF 35	S535JLM	DLF 37	S537JLM	DLF 39	S539JLM
DLF 30	S530JLM	DLF 32	S532JLM	DLF 34	S534JLM	DLF 36	S536JLM	DLF 38	S538JLM	DLF 40	S540JLM

Special liveries:
XL 100-400 carry dedicated Stationlink route branding, the DLF class dedicated route branding for route 210 and the Mercedes-Benz minibuses are dedicated LT mobility buses.

TRAVEL LONDON (Part of the National Express Group)

R401-422HWU	Optare Excel L960		Optare		B26D	1998	
R401HWU	R404HWU	R408HWU	R411HWU	R414HWU	R417HWU	R420HWU
R402HWU	R405HWU	R409HWU	R412HWU	R415HWU	R418HWU	R421HWU
R403HWU	R407HWU	R410HWU	R413HWU	R416HWU	R419HWU	R422HWU

S231-240EWU	Optare Solo M850		Optare		B25F	1999	
S231EWU	S233EWU	S235EWU	S237EWU	S239EWU		
S232EWU	S234EWU	S236EWU	S238EWU	S240EWU		